PRAISE FOR ROUGH SILK

'A Chart Buster'
~The Standard Group

'A Fine Biography'
~Sunday Nation

'A Film in Waiting'
~Dr.Zippy Okoth

ROUGH SILK

The Incredible Story of a Dad and Daughter

Deborah Auko Tendo

Published by Deborah Auko Tendo

Copyright © Deborah Auko Tendo 2023

First Published 2023

ISBN: 979-8224-84-408-1

<u>DEDICATION</u>

I dedicate this book to my children - let this story be an inspiration to the generations that will come after me. Do not forget where you came from, and the fabric of what you are made.

To George Otuoma Auko

Thanks for giving yourself so selflessly to me, everything you did, no matter how infinitesimal or grand, was not in vain. I have not allowed it to go in vain.

You are no longer part of the crowd Dad.

And to Lillian Auko, Forever and Always.

MUM'S SIDE

OTHIENO(D)
SAMWEL OSIEYO(D)
DEBORAH NYANYANDA(D)
APONG' KOR(D)
JOHN(D)
MIRIAM(D)
DR. SAMMY K'OPIYO
ANNA (D)
PHILIP(D
WASHINGTON(D)
MAMA MPENZI(A)
REAGAN OPIYO
ANGELA OPIYO SWEETIE
SAMWEL OPIYO (D)
MUSA FONI MUKWANYULE
ELIZABETH(D)
STEVE(A)
PAM(D)
DEBORAH AUKO
PHILIP AUKO

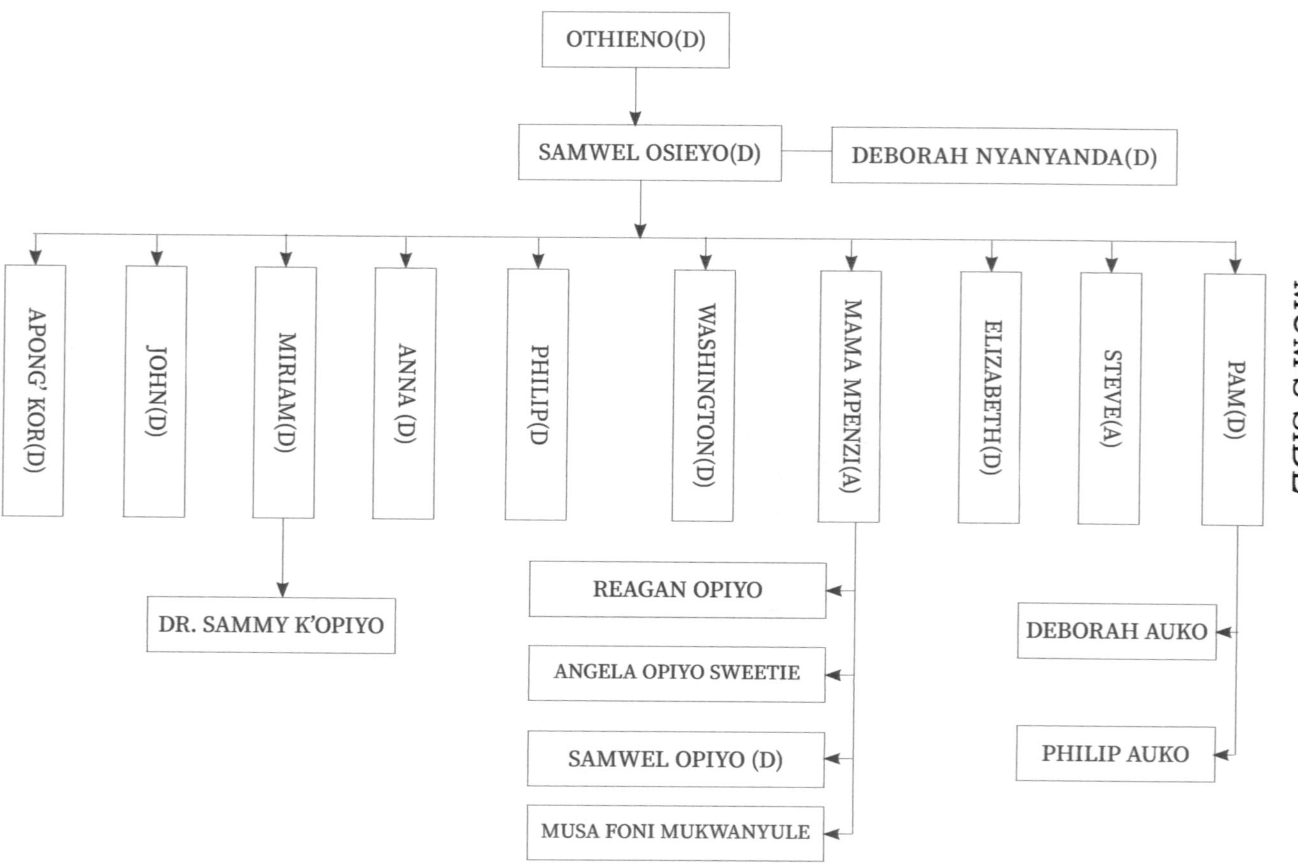

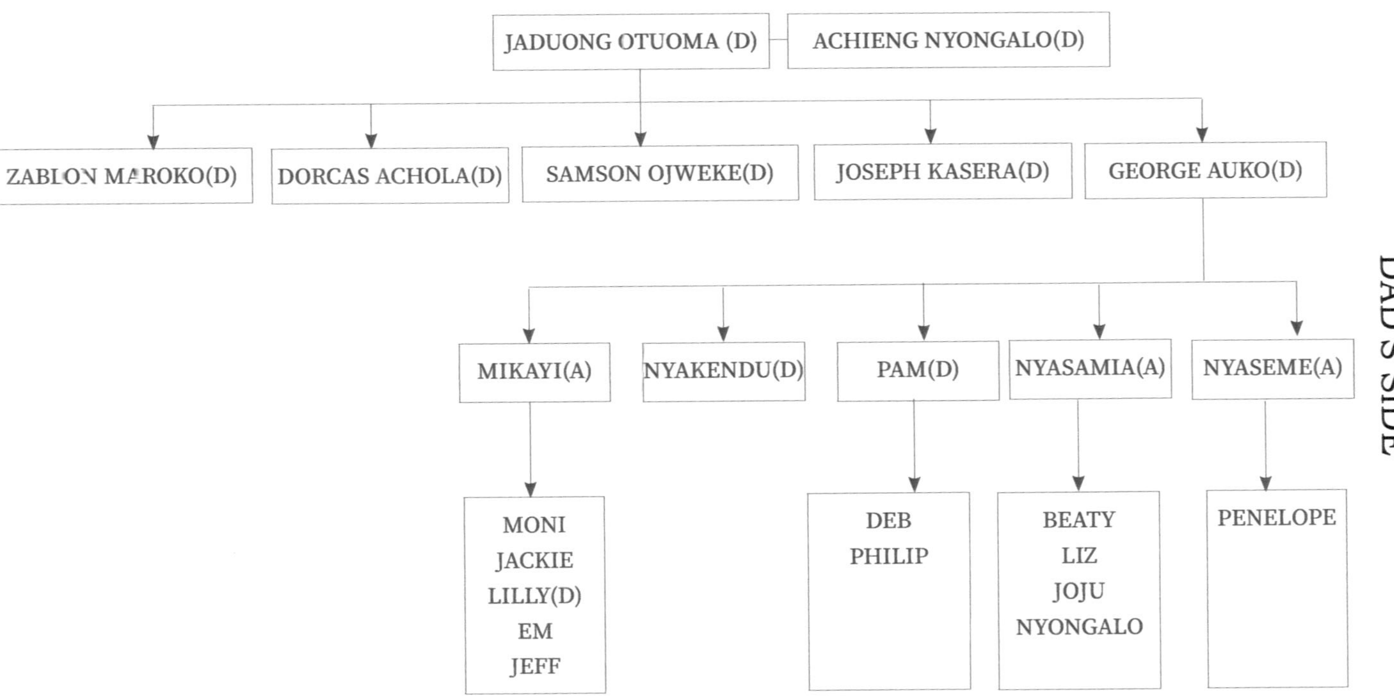

DAD'S SIDE
JADUONG OTUOMA (D)
ACHIENG NYONGALO(D)
ZABLON MAROKO(D)
DORCAS ACHOLA(D)
SAMSON OJWEKE(D)
JOSEPH KASERA(D)
GEORGE AUKO(D)
MIKAYI(A)
NYAKENDU(D)
PAM(D)
NYASAMIA(A)
NYASEME(A)
MONI
JACKIE
LILLY(D)
EM
JEFF
DEB
PHILIP
BEATY
LIZ
JOJU
NYONGALO
PENELOPE

TABLE OF CONTENTS

What is happening to you is also happening for you.

THE GENESIS

In the beginning there was an indigenous tree known as the *Otho* in the local DhoLuo vernacular. It stood by a dusty path that runs between the Migori -Sori Road in the then Migori District. The tree not only defied time but withstood the vagaries of weather existing mutually exclusively of whatever season time brought. Recently, it survived threats from a road expansion program.

No one quite knows just how old the tree is but everyone agrees that it was around to witness the exodus and its aftermath of a section of the Suba people from the southern shores of Lake Victoria, who migrated and settled into the area around Sori-Karungu in Migori County.

The *Otho* has kept reinventing itself in all seasons.

On hot sunny days, with the lakeside sun beating down like an angry fire god, the tree provided shade for weary foot travellers destined for Sori and back, weighed down as they were by the wares they carried to the market or back home. When it rained, *Otho* was where the little boys tethered their fathers' cows and goats to ensure the animals did not flee from the thunder and into the bushes, where hyenas and leopards awaited easy meals. And when the weather was fine, the tree became a living bulletin board on which flimsy posters and pretentious placards would be pinned for all to read, usually the pompous village chief summoning whoever was unlucky enough to incur his wrath for this or that of his subjects' transgression or misdemeanor.

In those days, one could get into trouble for all sorts of misadventures, real and imagined. They were small issues as we called them – flogging the 'selfish' women who dared eat dinner before their husbands arrived home from the fields. Instilling discipline into the lazy men who did not want to till their land and preferred the easy life of alcohol and easy widows. And, laying down the law to notorious village boys and their raging hormones.

Otho saw it all. Ever-present and ever-watchful. When there was nothing else to watch over, *Otho* quietly witnessed the women and girls who stopped under its refreshing shade, turning around to take in the long, calming vistas of Lake Sango, the shimmering silver sea now called Lake Victoria. As children, when travelling home, *Otho* became the landmark symbol that we had reached our destination.

My people, the Abasuba, originated from what is now Uganda. We are the Bantu group famed for the beauty and generous hearts of its girls. We stand out like sore thumbs in a sea of Sudanic Nilotes. A peaceful settled interruption in the middle of a restless, itinerant River-Lake Nilotic population. Many years and intermarriages later with River lake nilotes, the Suba community is still surviving if at all. And there are efforts to preserve whatever is left of our heritage.

The early 1950s were momentous and dramatic times for Abasuba. A decade earlier, the British had implemented a sweeping draft for their WWII effort, and a young man named Jaduong Otuoma found himself swept up in the conscription, shipped off to fight the white man's wars in faraway lands as part of the King's African Rifles. When Jaduong returned home after the war, he found his world turned upside down. His brothers had assumed him dead and taken over his land in Suba. With little prospect of regaining his inheritance, he didn't even unpack. Instead, with a newly pregnant wife, he decided to move on and ended up settling in Sori, at the borders of what is now Migori and Homa Bay Counties. Tagging along was his pregnant wife Achieng Nyongalo and 4 children in tow.

It is under this *Otho* tree that Achieng Nyongalo went into labor on 20th June 1954.

Achieng was seated at the naked roots of the *Otho*. The protective sheet of soil above the roots washed away by incessant rains streaming down to the lake. The roots created an intricate but vaguely unsettling web spreading far beyond *Otho's* shade like a many-legged spider that never actually moves. Achieng' was waiting for a passing bicycle rider to ferry her to a *Nyamrerwa* in the neighboring village, where she hoped to have her baby. But the day had its own plans. Her waters broke without warning and the pangs of labour arrived in a wall of pain so excruciating that she lost consciousness. A group of women passing by gathered around to help, recognizing that this baby was in a hurry to arrive and would not wait. And so Achieng was told to push as the men passing by stood a safe distance away.

Among my people, childbirth is the province of women. And a foolhardy man who wanders into the protective circle of midwives is sure to receive a tongue lashing and worse. The men watched beyond the bounds of the makeshift wall of hastily unpeeled wrappers. And so Achieng pushed and pushed. Soon enough, a baby's cry rent the air. The women held up a baby and it was a boy! From the safety of their vantage point, the men cheered in applause.

As the crowd celebrated the addition of another stone to Mzee Otuoma's sling, the women were getting worried. Achieng was struggling to breathe, and her bleeding was not stemming. She was getting faint, and her cries were getting weaker and weaker. They did all they could. But they needn't have bothered. As *Otho* watched on, Achieng breathed her last, leaving her newborn son in her stead. The boy she died giving life to, the baby whose umbilical cord was cut from an already dead mother, would be named George Auko Otuoma, my father.

Her blood followed the bare roots pattern. Still warm as a mother's love.

MY DAD

My father, George Auko Otuoma, was a beautiful man and even more so to his daughter. Every little girl who has been bathed and drenched in a litany of fatherly affirmation will tell you that their father was the most handsome man they ever saw.

But Dad really was.

It was an idyllic childhood for me, and my fondest memories are from before I started going to school. I must have been four or five years old. While most kids that age ran around playing, I loved sitting out in front of our house on the verandah and would just watch the day drift by.

We lived in one of the larger post-colonial housing developments in Nairobi. A sprawling but tidy neighbourhood to the north of the city. It was called Umoja; Swahili for unity. It was built by the local government in the 1970s to provide housing for the rapidly expanding Nairobi middle class.

Umoja's original houses were designed like what Kenyans imagined British middle-class houses looked like; there was a small yard in front of the house which also had a verandah that allowed all homeowners to see each other's front doors. The typical Umoja house was two-bedroomed and was targeted at the young and relatively well-off families that were springing up among the educated elite of Nairobi in the post-independence decade. The houses were fairly similar in design. And there were no fences between them – until some richer families began buying televisions and so erected fences around their properties to keep out uninvited or unwanted guests curious to see and watch the TV, which was something of a novelty and status symbol in the Kenya of the 1970s and 1980s.

Nairobi is famous for its cold. But an unremarked feature of the mile-high city is just how dry it is. The Green City in the Sun straddles two radically different climatic zones. The west and south of Nairobi are extensions of the cool well-watered Central Highlands that gave Nairobi its name, *Enkare Nyairobi*, a Maasai phrase meaning the place of cool waters.

In Nairobi's western-most suburbs and outlying areas like Limuru, in the southern regions like Kiambu and the Ngong Hills, a winter's morning will see temperatures falling as low as 8° Celsius or even lower. It's little wonder that during Kenya's colonial period, these parts of the city were reserved for the British colonists who looked to recreate a little corner of England on the Equator. To this day, these regions remain the most sublime suburbs of the city.

The East and North of Nairobi make up the western-most reaches of the dry Ukambani plateau, marked by hot temperatures most of the year, with suffocating dust that frequently gets sucked up into small dust storms when the dry Kusi and Kaskazi monsoon winds are in season – which is most of the year save for the short September to November period.

Umoja's location north of Nairobi's city centre puts it squarely within the hot, dry zone. The dusty houses in the estate bore witness to the unrelenting dust that blew ceaselessly around the year.

Our Umoja house was marked by a browning lawn scorched dry by the merciless African sun, with a lone banana plant or cluster of sugar cane struggling to eke out an existence in the forlorn shadow of the house. At night, when the streetlights came on and everything grew horns in the gloom, the shadows of the sugar cane and banana plants peeped into windows as the wind blew their leaves this way and that.

It's a stifling hot January day and I am seated on the verandah, unseen ribbons rising from the burning tarmac ahead. Dad is armed with a pail, a basin and a heap of dirty clothes he is rinsing and hanging on the cloth liner. He is wearing a brown pleated skirt and a blouse and mid washing, he dances to the inimitable sounds of Congolese Rumba music blaring from the radio he always carried around with him.

Must be a Soukous number by Aurlus Mabele. The Congolese crooner famed for originating many Soukouss dancing styles. As he washed and rinsed the clothes, the rhythms of the guitar would prove futile to resist. Dad would dump the clothes he was wringing back to the pail, splashing foam and water all over. He would recoil with pleasure as the music came to a crescendo. Resistance was hopeless. And he would let himself go. As the song peaked, he would grab fistfuls of air, swaying like a man possessed – while I, his audience, shrieked with delight.

Sometimes Dad would make a sudden dance move to where I was seated only to retreat as the tempo soared, his waist a whirl. The skirt whizzing about to reveal legs made muscular by the Nairobi commute, which regularly involved walking long distances, His audience – myself and my little brother Philip, would be up in enraptured glee. Cheering and singing along. The laundry that should have taken half an hour would invariably last twice as long – or longer, depending on how many seductive Rumbas the radio host played.

For a long time in Africa, domestic duties have been the role of women who were expected to handle laundry and cleaning but my father unashamedly enjoyed performing these tasks on our front yard much to the chagrin of many passers—by.

Almost every morning, he would be seen emerging from the house carrying an oversized mattress dripping of urine to dry. I wet my bed till quite late and I doubt if we had a Macintosh or the polythene covers because we never used it. Dad would wake up at 11pm or midnight and ask me to go relieve myself just to avoid dealing with a wet mattress the following morning. He would be lucky at times but often, he would wake me up just as I had left my playmates to hide behind a thicket and pee in my comforting dreams.

Whenever he overslept and forgot to wake me up, he had to deal with two episodes of 'hiding behind the thickets'. I remember the frustration on his face every time he discovered the dreaded urine stain but he did not once scold me. Instead, he would use scaring Luo folklore fibs meant to deter children from bed wetting. A famous one had a snake that would be tied to your waist and would bite you whenever you wet the bed.

In time, his labor of love 'wake up' pattern got embedded in me and I would instinctively wake up just before I crouched at this famous 'thicket'.

I would call out to him in the dark to accompany me to the washroom. I eventually stopped wetting my bed.

The mattress episodes were interesting. I would wake up in the morning having urinated all the way to my hair. Dad would take my mattress out and hang it to dry in the yard. I would sit on the sofa butt naked with my head hanging in the air waiting to be washed. Vaseline sessions would follow. Then black tea and the thick white Elliot branded bread so loved by Kenya's middle class. He would then drop us off at a kind neighbour's house loaded with food he had packed in a lunch box before setting off to the Central Business District to earn a living. That is how my father would start his day.

As little children, we played outside until he came back. The first thing he would do was to pick the now dry mattress, take it to the house, inspect us and ask how our day was, look at us keenly like a judge about to deliver a verdict then announce that he was about to cook the best meal we ever had.

He cooked while listening to news on the radio.

I recall situations when he would hang out the mattress to dry then it rained before he got back. Philip and I would seek shelter back at the neighbours, leaving the mattress to soak in the July rain. This meant we had to share his bed and I would wet his bed as well! If they did not suffer this predicament, they suffered the stench my dry mattress emitted even on hot days, warm air rose in the bedroom in intermittent layers.

It was quite a relief for both of us when I stopped wetting the bed because my Dad remains the neatest person I have ever seen.

Dad was fastidiously, almost antiseptically clean. He absolutely hated filth. His daily morning routine was testament to his pathological dislike for dirt. His would begin with a glass of salted water, a traditional *nyamit amita* wooden toothbrush and a modern toothbrush. The wooden toothbrush would be put to use first with the salt water before the more modern toothbrush got its turn. He had a little mirror where he would show his teeth and breathe on to inspect his work. Then a nail trim would follow, if necessary, before bath time. We did not take showers those days because even then, Nairobi's infamous dry taps were a daily inconvenience. So a bucket bath would then follow. He would get into the bathroom with three types of scrub materials. A scrubbing stone, a woolen piece of cloth and a husky wild fruit called the *suthru* in DhoLuo.

Dad would take so long in the bathroom that when he finally emerged, he looked pale. He would train me on how to shower.

"Start by scrubbing under your feet methodically with the stone. Ok now soap the *suthru*. Scrub yourself. Okay. Now rinse yourself. Okay now use the softer flannel. You have missed a spot here. Yes...scrub that part too. Squat under the tap and properly clean yourself. Clean your buttocks. Scrub yourself... you peed all night now you have to clean up even your hair... okay now rinse yourself...rinse yourself well I don't want the cows I will receive from your marriage to reduce because you cannot even shower."

This is a process he followed religiously all his life. Infinite small hygiene tasks performed to exacting proportions.

My father preferred to iron his clothes and brush his shoes by himself all his life - much to the relief of everyone. I hated to deal with the heavy charcoal metallic iron box he loved. He never owned an electric iron box. "It doesn't do a good job!" He would declare. He could never shake off the feeling that someone had left a spot and that was even after hawk eyed desperate supervision by himself.

Before taking a normal meal where you wash your hands with soap and water, he would doubt the purity of the water or the cleanliness of the flannel used to dry his hands. I remember instances where he would request for his nail cutter right as he was washing his hands before a meal and yet in Africa, one cannot eat before the man of the house starts eating, so we would all be there working up an appetite as he meticulously took his time trimming his nails. Woe unto us if he stumbled upon a stubborn cuticle.

My father loved reading newspapers and would buy three different ones whenever he could afford. The first thing he would do was write his name and sign on the top page. He would keenly look at the pictures before concentrating on politics, sports then finally obituaries. After reading an interesting article, he would mark it with a tick precisely at the corner of the page and nod approvingly as if his editorial skills mattered.

We were excited about newspapers for different reasons. I would pull out the cartoon pages before anything else. Later in life, I joined him on the politics and sports sections. He often rebuked me for pulling out pages and not returning the sheets aligned to the rest of the newspaper. He would adjust the pages while fuming at my perceived 'mutilation' of his papers. Eventually when he realized he could not wish me away, he just returned the pages himself.

When reading, his face would frown and he would throw epithets whenever he came across an article about a politician he disliked. Conversely, if he found a story about his favourite politician, his face would light up like a Christmas tree. There are times he read the newspaper silently but when he was deeply invested in a story, you could watch him and see his lips moving. This was when the news had to do with Raila Amolo Odinga; the regional Luo kingpin and the doyen of progressive politics.

My people, the Abasuba, are surrounded by the Luo. We fight to maintain and retain our identity in the middle of an overwhelming tide of Luo culture all around us. Raila Odinga, My Dad's hero, is a Luo. His father, Jaramogi Oginga Odinga, was one of the four or five founding fathers of independent Kenya. Men whose legacies and sons continue to tower over Kenya's public affairs and its business sectors.

Kenya's first president, Jomo Kenyatta, was an insurrectionist who got locked up by the British because of his incessant demands for independence in collaboration with the famous militant grouping Mau Mau famed for fighting in Kenya's independence over land rights.

During his imprisonment together with five others; Kungu Karumba, Achieng Oneko, Paul Ngei, Fred Kubai and Bildad Kaggia, the British looked around for a figurehead to hand nominal rulership to. They eventually settled on Jaramogi Oginga Odinga, then a budding businessman, politician and activist. They offered him the role of Prime Minister if he would denounce Kenyatta and accept continued allegiance to the British throne and to London.

In a show of defiance, Jaramogi rejected the appointment insisting he was not forming a Government unless Kenyatta was released from prison. That's how Jomo Kenyatta ended up becoming Kenya's first Prime Minister and later President. His first Vice President was Oginga Odinga. However, relations between Kenyatta and Jaramogi quickly soured, and the latter was forced to resign the vice presidency. An enmity developed between the Kikuyu, Kenyatta's people, and Luos.

The seed had been planted for Kenya's noxious ethnic politics, which continues to this very day. When Kenyatta died of a heart attack in August 1978, the presidency moved on to the quiet – and poorly-rated former teacher, Daniel arap Moi. Moi was a quiet but determined man who did not know much of governance – unlike Kenyatta – and did not understand how to play the politics of patronage subtly. He openly favoured his own ethnic kinsmen in governmental and corporate appointments. The resultant tribalism and nepotism wrecked Kenya's economy, at that time, one of the leading developing economies of the world. The increase in poverty and inequality that followed was fodder for government dissatisfaction. An ageing Jaramogi and his family became the centre of resistance against the Moi regime. Among Jaramogi's children, it was upon Raila that leadership fell, almost naturally. Before long, he was the focal point in Kenya's opposition politics.

In 1982, Raila and his inner circle allegedly attempted a coup against the Moi regime. The coup failed, but it cemented Raila's credentials as the leading anti-Moi voice in Kenya. Moi's response was brutal. A number of the coup plotters were tried and then hanged while Raila and others whose connection to the coup could not be fully established were locked up in detention without trial.

Popularly known as Agwambo or Baba, the cult following among his peers, the Luos and post independence reformists was awakened and the voice of dissent coalesced around him. Raila slowly became the poster boy for political activism.

Raila Amolo Odinga had my father's heart. He resided right at the very core of it. He would switch off the cooking stove midway if Raila's voice happened to be over the radio at the expense of apparently annoying hissing sounds of pan-frying onions. We, the children, had to tiptoe just in case we knocked off something to avoid distracting Dad when Raila was on the radio. Meanwhile, a newspaper cut out photo of Raila hang precariously on our bare living room wall.

As a child, I would see in neighbours' houses writings like 'Christ is the Head of this House' or 'Go placidly amidst the storm.'

For us it was, 'Go placidly with Raila.'

Dad loved reading the obituaries because, in Africa, death is revered. There was no social media, very few television sets, and no cellphones. The only reliable means of communicating death were radios and newspapers. Obituaries proved a reliable way to break sad news with details of meeting venues, burial dates and where the service would be held. His face would fall on the ground and he had to gather himself back quickly whenever he saw someone he knew in the death pages.

"Oh my God...Mami!" He would show me a photo of the deceased and would not say any word thereafter.

I would help him peer closely through the picture usually of a man or woman with the words 'Untimely death of...' I could see that he genuinely felt sad when he met the picture of a dear friend or acquaintance. Dad did not interact well with death, I recall days later he would still be mulling over whoever he saw in the obituaries.

The other news Dad was seriously interested in was football and he closely followed his favourite teams; Manchester United and Gor Mahia FC. The Mighty Gor is a community club that was formed by first generation Luo leaders in 1968 and still draws majority of its fan base from the community. It is famously known as K 'Ogalo and once was the most successful club in East Africa.

If you are born Luo, you most probably support Gor Mahia whose main rival is AFC Leopards. The latter has a fan base drawn from the Abaluhya community whose geographical origin is also in the Western part of Kenya.

These two clubs have shared a sporting rivalry that stems all the way from the 1960s to date. AFC Leopards was founded as Abaluhya FC in 1964.

There is only one derby in Kenya and it is called the Mashemeji Derby, pitting the two popular clubs. An undercurrent of this famous Kenyan derby is that there is a very high rate of intermarriage between the Luo and Luhya communities – and so the derby is referred to as the Mashemeji Derby, 'Mashemeji' being the Kenyan Swahili word for 'in-laws.'

Dad would shed tears whenever his favourite team Gor Mahia lost the derby.

The siege mentality of the Luo people, cultivated by marginalisation during the Kenyatta and Moi regimes, created a cultural and social unity at a time when Kenya was a de jure one-party dictatorship.

Only the ruling KANU political party was allowed to exist. As a result, political and social sentiment found outlets of expression in cultural outfits like football clubs – and for the Luo, this was Gor Mahia.

This in a way made the club very successful in many local and international outings. So successful that Gor Mahia recorded the first major success in 1987 when they lifted their first continental trophy against a wily Tunisian side Esperance FC.

They bagged winners cup fondly named Mandela Cup after South Africa's first African president. Gor Mahia's heroics are considered to have been founded by pedigree legendary heroes like Allan Thigo, William Chege Ouma, Nicodemous Arudhi, Fred Siranga, Bobby Ogolla, James Ogolla Kadir, Jerry Imbo, Nahashon Oluoch Lule, Sammy Owino, Joe Okeyo, John Chore, Ben Oballa, Dennis Olando, Dan Odhiambo, Andrew Obunga, James Sianga, Steve Yongo, Peter Ouma, Dan Odhiambo, Tim Ayieko, Ben Oloo, William Obwaka, Hesbon Omolo, Abdalla Shebe, Abbas Magongo, David Ochieng, Tairus Omondi, Nick Okoth, Virgo Otieno and many others.

As a child, I spent most weekend afternoons listening to soccer matches on radio around my father. We shared pre and post match reviews, build up, anticipation, disappointments or wins. You could tell from the commentator's voice that it was a good ball or not. You hang onto his every word. You move with him. You move closer to the radio. The striker hits the ball, Dad kicks out, his toe meeting one of the table's legs, he retreats in pain limping on one leg as I follow him around to see how bad his toe is.

Whenever Gor won, he would send for a Fanta which we often shared while dancing around the black radio that seemed louder than its size. At times he would also dance facing Raila's photo dedicating the goal to his political hero. He would toss Philip or me into the air and we would giggle wildly mid air coming back down, never imagining he might miss and we would fall. He would definitely catch us because he was our father.

It was an old radio, black, the National Panasonic model, favoured for its solid audio quality and its hefty weight. It wasn't very well put-together, and usually operated on batteries as it was carried around the house by Dad. Cockroaches had long taken residence in its warm battery compartment, and every so often a roach would crawl out of the radio, look around, and then scurry back into the safety of the radio. My brother and I would joke about the radio audio being the voices of cockroaches inside the radio.

We enjoyed that radio every so often. It would malfunction and would start producing wheezing static sounds. Dad would then 'adjust' it by way of a severe slap or two and the radio would suddenly come back to life!

The radio wasn't just for sports. Kenya had just the one radio station those days. The Voice of Kenya (VOK), now called the Kenya Broadcasting Corporation (KBC). VOK operated three services: the English Service, the Swahili Service, and the Vernacular Service, which would broadcast in each of Kenya's 42 languages, each with its own slot on a particular day of the week.

Dad listened to the Swahili Service, whose offerings were threefold: the hourly news bulletin, the obituaries read twice a day, and 'salaams' programmes in which people across the country sent greetings to each other by buying VOK postcards to be read out on air accompanied by Rumba music.

A television was a luxury beyond many Kenyans in the early 80s and radios served just fine.

Away from Raila Odinga and Gor Mahia, the radio connected us to the beauty of African rhythms and Rumba music. Dad loved Rumba music from the DRC Congo that would be served in either Soukouss or Odemba Rumba. The former was very fast and the latter slow and cool.

Congo has for long been Africa's musical centre. Historians have traced the pioneering Blues and Rumba music of the Americas to enslaved Africans from the Congo region, who carried the music of their people with them across the Atlantic and into slavery. Africa's contemporary music is also Congolese in origin, and the Bantu five-note rhythm can be heard all across the continent - from the shebeens of Cape Town to the illegal taverns of Cairo.

As the 1980s progressed, the music of Congo was undergoing a brief but explosive revolution. The slow old numbers, the crooning Rumbas of Franco and Tabu Ley were still in vogue – but there was a brash new sound in town. It was called Soukous and was marked by an up-tempo beat about twice as fast as the traditional Rumba. Soukous is music designed to be danced by the young with no focus on social messaging – its emphasis is on having a good time. When Soukous played, Dad would jump up and dance like he had composed the song. But when the old Rumba numbers played, he would descend into a soulful mood, sometimes holding my hands and dancing with me as he sang along. We didn't understand the words, as the songs were almost all in Lingala - a Bantu language of Congo that is not widely understood in Kenya. That didn't stop us – "Music is like love. You don't need to understand it. You just need to feel it!" Dad would say.

The days spent listening to Rumba with Dad bequeathed me a keen ear for Rumba music, as well as an enduring interest in dancing.

When dancing to Soukous, he would suddenly hop forward then retreat, wringing his waist. For Odemba, he would remain seated gazing into the air, whistling, trying to sing words he did not understand and at times he stood and danced with me, holding my hand as my nose pressed on his knees.

From the DRC, my father's favourite artist was the legendary Luambo Luanzo Makiadi popularly known as Franco.

The Congolese artist was born in Sona Bata in Congo DRC. He dropped out of school after few years to help his mother who was an eclectic hawker with no focus product in the local market, selling fish or shoes depending on whatever moved faster. Young Luambo would fiddle with a wooden guitar to attract clients towards his mother's wares. He had developed an interest in the guitar.

You see, where he lived with his mother who was a widow was a well established guitarist by the name Emengo Dewayon who let little Luambo play his guitar every once in a while.

The neighbour realised the boy actually had a gift in memory and in technique and decided to train him fervently.

He also began carrying the boy to his musical concerts.

While playing music in DRC, Franco also reached Kenya through a small radio in Umoja Estate where he would sting father and daughter with the wizadry of his guitar. I had no choice but to develop a keen interest in Rumba as it was all we could do for recreation. I sharpened my liking and good ear for the guitar and vocals. I quickly learnt how to follow the repetitiveness of words in all the lyrics he would play.

In his hey days, my Dad was built with clearly defined muscles as the Greek Statues that decorate cities in Europe, or renaissance paintings I see in museums. He also had the most amazing genuine smile that always ended up in dimples. It did not help that he was on the lighter skin spectrum.

You see, colourism is not a monopoly of the west, or even Asia. It's alive and well in Africa too – the incessant drumming into an African's mind that black is inferior and white is superior still hangs on.

For Luos, one of the most predominant feature is deep dark skin. Its also among the Luo that colourism is at its apex even presently. Too many songs about light skinned women and very few about their darker counterparts. The likening of light skinned men or women to 'Mzungu' or 'Murabu', 'clean like Mzungu, neat like Mzungu' **Mzungu** here means a white man, **Murabu,** an Arab.

So entrenched was colorism, that it was not uncommon to find Luos who inter marry with lighter shaded communities or races to lighten their subsequent generations.

It was also among the Luo women folk that bleaching was rife.

Dad was a very light skinned Luo man and therefore stood out effortlessly.

THE ROOTS

Since my paternal grandmother Achieng Nyongalo died during childbirth, Dad was raised by his stepmothers. My grandfather, Jaduong' Otuoma eventually married five wives who took care of all the children in the traditional home that included my father and his siblings. My grandmother, Achieng Nyongalo was the first wife and in her demise, she left behind five children, four boys and a girl.

Dad went to Luanda Primary School, a walking distance from the village he was raised in. On completion, he was admitted to Homa Bay High School further away in Homabay town. He was a brilliant footballer and immediately made the first eleven in the school team. As a striker, he made waves and all the village girls were falling at his feet. We are told by older relatives that he was such a maginificent and popular footballer that parents travelled to Jaduong' Otuoma's homestead to betroth their daughters. Such was the pressure that by the tender age of seventeen, he secured his first wife; Nyar Denja, Who became the *Mikayi*. She was fondly called Nyar Denja because her father was the record breaking polygamist, Akuku Danger.

Nyar Denja the *Mikayi*, was extremely tall, dark skinned or what we call in DhoLuo *dichol*, with long legs and very long natural jet black hair that rested on her neck like a lion's mane. Even in old age, she still has the hair although greyed. Akuku Danger was the world famous Luo from Aora Chuodho with an unconfirmed Guiness World Record for marrying upto one hundred wives who bore him more than five hundred children. A school had to be built on his land for his offspring. Although

Nya Denja was not my biological mother, we were all categorized as Danger's grandchildren. My father would attend school and go back to his wife over the holidays. She grew up humble. A devout SDA, and was married really young by my father. She moved down south towards the lake into Sori.

Then in the 70s, it was not as elaborate as it is now. A few cows to be paid as dowry and a woman would move into the man's father's compound. The man would build her a grass thatched house and point her towards where the garden plus some livestock were. She would farm and life together would begin.

During my father's teenhood, right after high school, most young men left the village for college in the city, got jobs, then sent money back home to their wife and kids. It was their obligation to send money for upkeep to their wives and children back home.

Right after high school, armed with some education and not fated to be a fisherman like most of his peers, Dad stood at the *Otho* tree with a metallic box, city bound.

The sturdy tree had now acquired a new status as a bus stop serving villagers between Migori town and Sori.

A rickety ford stopped by the *Otho*. One of its tyres unbalanced by a formidable root above the soil. He boarded and it belched forth to Sori Bay on its way to Nairobi City, Kenya's capital.

For his good grades, he got employed at the Department of Immigration where he was making a decent amount of money every month and would go back home every December to visit his family.

On one such visit back home, a different set of parents who had been negotiating for Dad to take their daughter's hand arrived with a demure, subservient girl.

The girl from Kendu Bay- Nyakendu became his second wife.

Nyakendu was every inch the consummate African woman. Heavily built with strong arms and legs and a very healthy bosom. Decorated with a gap between her teeth traditionally considered a hallmark of beauty. Much later as she grew older, I noticed she had a beard which she did not bother to shave.

Dad already had two girls from the *Mikayi*. It was a concern and he had to add a second wife to try bear him a son.

Nyakendu was introduced to the family to help with the prospect of a son. Her hut was built just next to our *Mikayi's* hut but in our grandfather's homestead.

Among the Luo, it is mandatory for a son to build a small structure called *Simba* in his father's compound. It's in this *Simba* that sons learn how to be men. To live alone. To be independent and also to seduce girls.

A lot of African girls of the rural areas have been victims of the *Simba* detours when they are supposed to be heading straight home after fetching water, grinding flour, picking firewood or vegetables or whatever other errand they are supposed to run.

There is a facade that girls raised in the cities loose their virginity very young. That could not be further from the truth. The fact that in the villages there is an established source of private accommodation very far from the prying eyes of adults, nobody will raise an eyebrow when a young man with a newly constructed *Simba* steals an often underage female to sow his very impatient oats.

Eventually when a boy identifies a girl and asks for her hand, she first stays in the *Simba* before his parents are required to visit the girl's people to declare their intention with their daughter. Other formalities like dowry and gifts would follow on agreed dates.

However, before my father's generation and Christianity, there was an elaborate structure as to how a traditional Luo marriage was initiated. First, the girl would be identified and the man's family would visit her family to negotiate her bride price. Once the bride price was agreed on, and *'Ayie'* meaning 'I agree' had happened, the bride price would be paid in cow heads. It is after *Ayie* that the wedding ceremony would take place.

The wedding event would start with *Meko-* to catch. In practise, the groom and his friends or relatives would 'kidnap' the girl while she was going about her business of fetching firewood or water from the river. The capture would be met with unsuccessful thwarts by the girl's relatives to test the groom's strength and how much he cared for their daughter. The daughter would also try to wriggle her way out of capture to show her attachment to her family although she had already approved the marriage and was aware her bride price had been paid.

The girl would then be delivered to the *Simba* where deflowering happened within the earshot of four witnesses to ascertain that the girl was a virgin measurable by her anguish and blood on the mat.

Once virginity was confirmed, the largest bull would be slaughtered by the bride's parents and given to the groom's parents and the party would start till dawn. That marked the end of the wedding ceremony.

Indeed, in most African setups, there was nothing wrong with polygamy and nobody would frown at men who had more than one wife. To them, polygamy helped ensure no women were left unmarried and hence not taken care of because the essence of polygamy was for a man to take care of his women and children. Women were not considered bread winners and had to be taken care of.

In Africa, children give people the sense of immortality so polygamy was also seen as a way of ensuring the community subsists by maximising on child birth.

While a man with one wife would have only one child in say two years, a polygamist would get five children in one year without burdening one woman.

In monogamous marriages, a woman who had twelve children would have lived her entire marital life as a breeder. Whereas in a polygamous arrangement, five wives would probably each have four children resulting into twenty within a very short time.

The man would have a hut called Duol where all the wives would take whatever food they had cooked and all male children would eat with their father. The man would sometimes decide if he was going to eat with his sons or with a particular wife. It was also the man's duty to see that all his wives were sexually satisfied by ensuring equal visits to their huts.

Times have however changed and with adopted Christian values, most of these habits have died. Polygamy has also been seen as sexually oppressive to women who have to share and compete for a man's attention. Women are now educated and can fend for themselves and do not need to be in the institution of marriage for survival.

The result is obviously more single women, fewer nursery schools and extremely empowered women both financially and sexually. The population outburst experienced in Africa towards the end of the twentieth century is shrinking just as in the west. Life is more expensive and any man wishing for polygamy may not afford it. They end up marrying one woman or stay without known spouses just like their female counterparts.

At the time my father was marrying Mikayi and Nyakendu, women in rural areas were not empowered and their main focus in life was to get married, procreate and spend their lives tending to family.

If a woman's husband was educated, lived and worked in the city, like my father was, a woman became the envy of the village because most men existed on subsistence farming or casting fishing nets all night in the lake for paltry sums. This is the setting George Auko was raised in. He only ventured into the city to get a job but at that time he was hardly twenty three with two wives and kids in tow.

The city of Nairobi introduced him to glitz and glam in the post-independence era. There was plenty of employment opportunities and loads of money in people's pockets.

My father, a village boy, got assimilated very fast and got sucked in as soon as he set foot in the razzmatazz of Nairobi. He learnt fast how to fuse and blend in the entertainment world where beer flowed as freely as the continent that burst with hope on free governance.

What he did not have to learn was how to be a charmer because that came naturally to him. My father was wired to look good and impress anyone at first encounter. He topped his likeable demeanour with good vibes around both men and women. He was really good company and interesting to have around especially when cracking his popular jokes.

MY MOTHER

My mother was the happiest person I recall. Then I later realised she was the happiest unhappiest person in any room.

As a child, I remember the grace with which she carried herself. Her tiny twig waist, long neck, high cheek bones, big eyes and dimples. Like Nyakendu, she also had the much coveted diastema between her front teeth, a symbol of unrivalled beauty among the Luo and largely in Africa. She had the poise of a gazelle with small, delicate-looking even shoulders that seemed like they could break. She had beautiful legs which are still talked about by her friends whenever I am introduced as her daughter. Old men still remark, "Oh your mother had very beautiful African legs." She had a husky voice which I inherited, and was described by most of her peers as the friendliest and most helpful person they ever met.

She was a great conversationalist, was the queen of impressions, and would light up the darkest rooms filling them with laughter how we fill empty rooms with furniture.

Her personality stuck on people. Stuck on walls. On cutlery and on people's hearts like a stain of love. She paid other people's school fees and salvaged friends in distress.

My mother came from a family of ten siblings who hailed from the dominant Kager clan in Ugenya, Siaya County. My grandmother, her mother, came from the Boro clan also in Siaya. My grandfather's position had relative privilege with proximity to the white highlands.

My mother was born Pamela Akelo but baptized Pamela Jennifer Odede Mtanda. She was named 'Akello' which means child born after twins. Part of her father's responsibility included taking care of a ranch in Songhor where the white man kept horses. Pamela had the privilege of sometimes wearing clothes bought from England's Lenners Mail Order Stores. Lenners later changed their name to Littlewoods that used to sponsor the FA Cup football tournament in England.

As Luos name on events as well, the name Pamela was made popular after the wedding of powerful minister Tom Mboya and his supremely endowed and educated wife Pamela Odede of Uyoma.

My maternal uncles were grown men when their father retired early on medical grounds and died of diabetes on 28th February 1965. They had been taken to good schools and most became professional accountants. My mother was lactating then.

John Nyawallo Kosieyo, my mother's second eldest brother was a renowned trade unionist and co-founder of the Central Organization of Trade Unions (COTU). Uncle John was among the first few Kenyans to qualify as a chartered accountant and he worked in Jomo Kenyatta's office before starting his private practice. At first, he lived in Westlands before moving to Parklands. He was an astute businessman and became the proprietor of the first secretarial college and accountancy school that served East Africa. He was a co founder of The Kenyan School of Accountancy. He later gave it away in 1980's.

My mum lived with her brother, Uncle John, in both Westlands and Parklands but she moved out when he got married. Her brother Philip Osieyo took her and the brother she followed, Stephen Osieyo who was still a student, as their immediate guardian. Philip, the third son in the Osieyo family, was also an accomplished accountant.

Philip lived in the then BuruBuru Estate. Rumour has it that Buru, as it was popularly called, was a housing project meant for Uganda but with turmoil by dictator Idi Amin, the

Commonwealth Development Corporation relocated it to Kenya. Naturally, the outright capitalistic Kenyans gobbled it up plus many other Uganda destined projects.

BuruBuru in the 70s was an upper middle class estate, home of the well to do upcoming Nairobians. It was actually termed the last hall of residence for fresh University of Nairobi graduates. As a result, all manner of professionals would be found there. That is where my mother lived in uncle Philip's house. They were joined by other relatives and siblings in the three bedroomed maisonette with an own compound.

My mother was not very keen on going to school, and somehow nobody wanted to push her anyway. In any case, she was the family trophy and with professionally successful brothers, she was guaranteed a comfortable life, or she would be married off to a wealthy man because her family was well connected and that would be that.

It's interesting that while all my maternal uncles were educated and pursued their careers, my maternal aunties were the complete opposite. They either got married early but to accomplished men, or preferred to just live off their brothers. Miriam Alice was amongst the first Kenyans to train as a cateress but abandoned her career to marry a high ranking police inspector instead. Risper Anna Awuor was a trained NCR key punch operator stationed in Mwanza, Tanzania. During her time, she was the only NCR operator and her services sought after in the whole of East Africa. She one day just quit her job because it was conflicting with the career of her East African Railways and Harbours signal operator husband.

My auntie, Mama Mpenzi, was a trained stenographer but quit her career when she got married to a high ranking manager at Shell BP. Elizabeth Rhoda, Stephen's twin, was never engaged in formal employment opting to instead marry an army officer.

When my mother was around fifteen years old, her brother Stephen insisted that she had to go to school. Having never gone to any school before, she was enrolled to Indian owned Khalsa Secondary School in Nairobi to keep her busy.

At Uncle Philip's house in Buru Buru where he was raising my mother, he had a penchant for inviting his friends home for nyama choma, alcohol and booming music. They indulged in dancing to hits from vinyl records of Franco, Rochereau and Sam Fan Thomas. The house was a beehive of fun and activity. An entertainer's loft. Uncle Philip was probably the most agreeable guy I had ever seen. His home was open for everyone; from his siblings and their friends to sisters whose marriages weren't going well - and most were not going well. He also welcomed any cousins who had marital problems to back packers looking for a place to squat.

Food was plenty and uncle Philip's kitchen ran like a commercial venture. They woke up when the sun rose partying, and they went to bed when the sun set, partying - inexhaustible amounts of food being churned from the kitchen like a conveyor belt. Uncle Philip was swimming in money those days. Uncle Philip and my father George Auko met in a bar on a Rumba night and they hit it off like a gas station on fire.

Uncle Philip introduced my father to the urbane Nairobi city life in the late 70s, men in afro hairstyle dressed in bell-bottom high waist trousers accompanied by women in red lipstick, thickly lined lips and mini dresses. Bar talk had it the two would spend up to Kshs. 25, 000 a night. They could go as far as to sponsor full Congolese bands to travel from DRC to perform in Kenya.

So, on one of the house parties that my father was invited to, he met my mother Pamela, last born sister to his friend Philip who had just completed High School and was pursuing secretarial courses.

By sheer coincidence, my father was actually a classmate to my uncle Stephen in Homabay High School. To date, Stephen marvels at the fact that my father was a very talented footballer in school, a legend who helped them win the Kenya National Secondary School football championship. It is this proximity to the Osieyo family that strengthened the closeness between my father and mother. Both Uncle Philip and Stephen were speechless when mum declared she intended to marry George Auko.

He was mesmerised by her grace and beauty and she thought he was the *whitest* Luo she had ever seen.

Having been a schoolmate, Steve was privy to information that George Auko was already married and actually had two wives back home in Sori. When he brought up the issue, George Auko vehemently denied terming them false allegations. As a matter of caution, Steve insisted that someone had to travel to Sori to confirm his fears. When that happened, no woman was found in the home.

Desperate at the prospects of losing his first ever choice in a woman, George Auko had sent an advance party home whose task was to find a way of sending the two wives and now four children back to their respective ancestral homes if only temporarily.

A grand Catholic wedding was organised at Our Lady of Visitation Catholic Church, Jogoo Road. The Nairobi City life was lightened up when the who is who were invited courtesy of Uncle Philip. George Auko and his new bride, Pamela Akello, moved into their house in Umoja estate looking forward to a glamorous bright future ahead.

They would wake up, Dad would go to work at the Immigration Department and mum would head to Riley Security Services where she was now serving as the Managing Director's personal secretary.

Suddenly, he stopped going to work.

Apparently he had been transferred to Mombasa in a move necessitated by a bribery allegation at work. When the letter was handed to him, he tore it up and defiantly told the Human Resource fellow he would not go to Mombasa. During the disciplinary meeting convened to decide his fate, he got agitated and punched the HR boss in the face earning himself a summary dismissal.

Meanwhile, his social life Nairobi continued undeterred. He was no longer earning but was keeping up his flamboyant lifestyle, going out with friends for drinking sprees. He also now had me and a pregnant wife to take care of.

I was a little girl when one day I saw mum writhing in pain in her bedroom. Dad went to the bedroom to check on her and with a little bag, they left. He returned later in the night and told me mum had gone to purchase a baby.

She came back two days later with the most white little baby who had the curliest of hair. He looked like a doll and I fell in love with my little brother Philip instantly - I went out and told all the other kids that mum had purchased a white kid and kids gathered at our window trying to peep in to see him.

About a week later, Dad's first wife the Mikayi, whose existence he had previously vehemently denied, appeared at our door unannounced like a lost delivery man. One of Dad's relatives had showed her exactly where we lived.

Word had reached the village that Dad had been married in a church wedding and had even got a baby boy in the family. The Mikayi had come to see the new boy child of the family and to also make her presence known and felt. She also wanted to meet her new co-wife - the third in a polygamous set up.

In patriarchal Africa, not having a son was a big deal, especially if like Dad you already had four girls. With me in the fold, he actually had five girls and no boy. I could see how proud mum was that she had delivered the much coveted boy child to the family, a very big chip on her little shoulders.

Mikayi could not stay the night because Dad admonished her for ambushing him. She took the same evening bus back to the village. He insisted there was actually no marriage between him and Mikayi.

My mother, reeling from the shock of this new revelation and the wound of child birth still being nursed, looked every inch the gazelle caught in the headlights.

Since Dad was jobless and wasn't even looking for a job yet was still going out with friends, the financial wire started stretching. Fault lines started showing in their marriage that had not even lasted three years.

My first interaction with violence happened when one day mum came home from work and Dad ransacked her bag for money. I realised he was doing this to get money for partying with his friends. They ended up physically fighting and mum who was of very slight build ended up freeing herself from his vice grip, ran and locked herself in the toilet.

Dad stepped up the gas on alcohol, and eventually would not come back home for the night. Then it became two nights. Then three nights.

Philip and I would be seated around mum in the kitchen as she prepared food in the deathly silent house. We had elaborate furniture the two had been gifted during their wedding; a six seater sofa set, a centre piece and I remember a black wooden wall unit. We also had a black radio which she hardly played. In the wall unit was their dummy blue and white souvenir wedding cake on display. It looked delicious and I always wondered why we did not eat it. On top of it were the bride and groom dolls. They seemed very happy, which was an antithesis of the cake owners.

My mum loved cooking pork and also made a fantastic meal of mushrooms. Most nights when Dad was away partying, she cut a lonely figure trapped in deep thought.

In the day, she would take us along to visit her elder sister in Umoja market. She would lift Philip up to her back and tag me by hand across the estate to her sister's salon where she would share her troubles.

My auntie, who in this book I shall fondly call Mama Mpenzi because that's what I have called her all my life, was a big woman. Tall and thick. At the time, she was already separated from her oil professional husband and was a single mother of three.

After listening to their last born marital woes, she would look outside menacingly, kiss her teeth and predict Dad's ill fate the day she'd meet him.

Because indeed, immediately Dad's marriage to mum took a dip, whenever Mama Mpenzi met Dad, she would take off her shoes, fold her blouse and engage Dad in a full blown street brawl. She was a strong woman but I believe Dad would spare her as he still was very good friends with their brother uncle Philip who by now was bankrolling all the expensive night activities.

Mama Mpenzi would meet Dad in a bar, and Dad would take flight.

If he was going to alight at the bus stop which we shared with the market and through the window saw Mama Mpenzi also waiting for the same bus, he would have to ride to the next stage then take a long walk back.

Mama Mpenzi was the family rebel who, as early as the 70s, was smoking cigarettes publicly. To excite more anger, she would smoke two cigarettes from both sides of her lips in bars. When her wealthy husband brought home a second wife to tame her wild ways, she contemptuously moved out. She was a talented hair dresser who was making a living on her craft. She had decided not to be a housewife in a big mansion but to live a simple life off her sweat and do whatever she wanted. She had no time for pesky husbands interested in controlling her life. Mama Mpenzi was the kind of woman you do not let in a hen house. You will find blood and feathers all over the place.

At some point, she got married to a Congolese guitarist much to the angst of her siblings, but to my mother she was a rock. On that fateful day the Mikayi arrived at mum's, Mama Mpenzi was out in the yard, calling Dad to filth and daring the Mikayi to leave or else.... And as quietly as she came, left for the village.

Mum never fully recovered from the change of fortunes and reality life check. Here she was in her early 20s, married in a church wedding to a man with two wives and four kids. Stuck with a man with no means of income, who sleeps out and beats her.

I was five and on this particular day, Dad had been away for close to a week. Come Sunday, mum folded us as usual and set off for Umoja market to see her big sister Mama Mpenzi. We found her working on a client's head expertly rowing the corn but also suffering a massive hangover as she had been out drinking all night. She was doing the most, ordered food to be brought to us before mum could start speaking.

"He hasn't been home a whole week," my mum broke the silence. "Well, ask your brother Philip. They were together last night in the club. I saw them," replied Mama Mpenzi.

With tear tracks stiff on her face, she gathered us and we set off on foot to Buru Buru like a gypsy caravan. She held my hand by her side and my little brother Philip on her back. We crossed Outer-ring road that separates Umoja One from Buru Buru, past the railway tracks before passing through Mutindwa market all the way to Buru Buru Phase 2.

Uncle Philip's Ford Mustang was parked outside and the gate's latch was open. She had grown here and she knew her way around it. She unlatched it and we got in. The main door was closed but not locked and mum just pushed it open. On a makeshift mattress by the floor were men and women sound asleep although it was around eleven in the morning; some naked, others half dressed probably blacked out after a night out debauchery. Among those dead asleep was dad completely oblivious.

Mum's body slumped, releasing Philip from her back who crampled to the floor like a stage curtain whose rails broke. She backed away from the scene, walking backwards then suddenly turned and ran out of the gate that we had left ajar. That was the last time we interacted with our mother in a family set up. Little Philip started crying from the sudden drop and yank off the comfort of his mother's back.

One of the sleeping women woke up and looked straight at us. Her face was smudged in makeup and dark eye pencil in a drag queen fashion. She thought she was dreaming because she started waking up the rest without moving her wide eyes from us. Every adult woke up and as soon as they saw us, they grabbed the sheets above their naked bodies like Adam in Eden.

Dad woke up. He looked confused then asked in a whisper; "Deb...where is your mother...what are you doing here?"

Their marriage fell apart like a necklace whose string had been cut apart.

Henceforth, we started life without our mother around us. Dad decided to raise us by himself while also trying out new jobs to provide for us. My mother and Uncle Philip never saw eye to eye again. Dad tried all he could to get her back. In a bid to save the furniture, he even travelled upcountry to appease mum's mother with more cows. His relationship with Uncle Philip became frosty because word had gone around the family that uncle Philip was responsible for the breakup.

I recall nights when I could hear Dad crying in the dark especially when my brother Philip kept asking for his mother. I always assured him she would be back sooner than later. I would help Philip sit outside in the yard waiting out for our mother to come back. I remember our mum loved wearing her yellow dress and whenever Philip saw any woman in a yellow dress, he would shoot from his tiny feet running only to realise it was not our missing mum .

Meanwhile, the cake that outlasted the marriage sat cooly in the wall unit. The perfect couple dolls at the tip of it smiling. I realised they were still here because they did not have to talk to each other. They did not even have to look at each other.

NOW YOU SEE ME. NOW YOU DON'T

Mum left without anything and all her earthly possession including her clothes were still in our Umoja house. How she left her wardrobe, her sandals, her lipstick was how it remained so that on her return, she would seamlessly carry on.

But that was not the case because what followed is what I wish to call 'the stealing game.'

I would be out playing with friends and suddenly Mama Mpenzi would appear from nowhere and beckon me over. Philip was never far behind and soon we would be in a bus to an unknown place where we would be hidden. Mum's friends would come and take Philip with them to mum, while I remained with Mama Mpenzi.

Days or weeks later, I would be playing with friends and would hear Dad's voice from some corner "Mami..Mami........ come." He was never bold enough to just walk straight up to me like Mama Mpenzi did. He would stand resolutely next to an electricity pole or some thicket nearby. Soon,I would be in a bus across the country to be hidden elsewhere.

This went on for quite some time, denying me the chance to attend nursery or pre-unit school due to the constant exodus with both parents exercising their rather crude powers of custody. Wherever I was hidden out during the day I remember being lonely because my agemates had gone to school and I had to play with children much younger than me. But when my peers came back home around noon I was curious as to know what they were learning.

One day, Mama Mpenzi came home midday from the salon to find me playing by myself and asked where my friends were. I told her they were all in school and it suddenly occurred to her that I had attained school going age. Rather than take me to a nursery or pre-unit school next day, she took the bus with me into St. Annes Girls Primary School Jogoo Road to start Primary School straight away.This was her choice because her daughter who was older than me was in the same school.

Mama Mpenzi's daughter who we still call Sweetie to date as she was a very cute child had been instructed to keep a watch of me during break and lunch hours. She was also instructed to accompany me and ensure I took my bus before she went back to her afternoon classes.

Our headmistress, Mrs Macharia could not believe I had never stepped inside a school. She also felt it was impossible for me to start school straight at Standard One when my age said I should be at nursery. What she did not know was my ability to sing nursery rhymes courtesy of interacting with my school going peers once they got back in the afternoons. I could also count from one to fifty besides reciting the entire alphabet.

Standing there a few feet tall among these adults, Mama Mpenzi's pleas were not convincing the headmistress. It did not make matters easier that she had been out the previous night and was suffering her usual hangover. At some point, she walked out to light a cigarette, often turning to address the headmistress amidst billows of smoke, any chances I had went from thin to non existent.

While the headmistress was still looking for the nice words to reject us, I suddenly moved next to her, looked at her in the eye, got into character and started singing fitfully and inteminably.

"Hallo Teacher! How do you do? I am so glad to be back in school!" "Hallo Teacher! How do you do? I am so glad to be back in school!" "Hallo Teacher! How do you do? I am so glad to be back in school!"

I got admitted to school.

The reason Mama Mpenzi was the one to take me to school happened during the last stealing episode. She had now taken permanent and complete custody of me and sent word to Dad not to dare come for me or he would regret.

Mama Mpenzi narrated the story of how I got admission to every single client who visited her salon and every single supplier to the last person in the market. She said it with a sense of bravado, pride and laughter until she would tear. I loved her great big confidence.

In the meantime, mum was with Philip wherever she was.

My life with Mama Mpenzi was very simple. Her Congolese guitarist boyfriend, Sitho, who everyone disapproved of, stroked the wires of the guitar and smoked from his dark lips through out the day. I would come from school and find him practicing tunes that made me miss my father. He would pluck the guitar with his dark fingers that did not look like his obviously bleached skin. He would allow me to try on a few tunes. He tried to teach me a bit of Lingala as he could not speak Swahili.

Mama Mpenzi would leave in the morning to her salon and back in the evening with meat and make the most amazing dishes.

They would settle to an evening of smoking cigarettes with Sitho playing tunes of *Ebale ya Zaire*. They would smoke in that tiny studio apartment that they would have to peer to see each other in the fog of smoke. When it became unbearable, she would open the door letting in a swarm of mosquitoes.

On weekends, Sitho would leave early because he was a regular performer with a legendary Congolese band who decided to try their luck in Kenya due to the saturation back home.

There was also aunty's friend, a very beautiful Tanzanian Chagga lady who was a tailor. She would design lookalike dresses which they would wear. Aunty on her part designed their hair in the same styles. They would put on red lipstick, eye pencil and badly done eye shadow, smoke weed, give me food and head off into the vagaries of the Nairobi night life.

I would stay alone in the house at night, cigarette and bhang aroma lingering in the air. Most often, I wondered how my little brother Philip was doing and why I was here and not where mum and him were. It was a permanent puzzle to my little mind. There was a little radio that would sometimes keep me company before I dozzed off.

Every once in a while the radio would talk about Raila Odinga and I would follow keenly. Apparently, he was now out of detention and with others, were now agitating for multi party democracy in Kenya. At times, I would try smoking the half cigarettes Mama Mpenzi left stuck on the sand in the ash tray.

One time I tried the cigarette while lying in bed and slept forgetting to rid of it. Mama Mpenzi came back home while I was asleep. In her drunken stupor, she always lifted my blanket to give me a kiss before hopping into her bed with shoes on.

She saw the cigarette but did not wake me up. But the next day I paid heavily. It was the first and last time Mama Mpenzi ever whipped me.

One lunch time I left school accompanied by my cousin to the bus station to wait for bus number 59 that plied the Eastlands route. She had to go back to school and catch up with afternoon classes.

Once inside the bus while holding the seat rails, someone held my hand gently. It was Dad and I started laughing while hugging him. We alighted at the next stage and took a different bus. Mama Mpenzi had underestimated my father who was like a dog with a bone when it came to me.

The hide and seek game was alive and well.

NYASAMIA

That night I found myself in Eastleigh estate. To my amazement and excitement, my little brother Philip was there. There were three other kids I didn't know.

There was also a most kind and loving looking woman I remember to have probably met after one of those 'Dad stealing me' days but did not pay much attention to. She was preparing a dish of githeri when she called me by name.

"I have heard very nice things about you, welcome home," she remarked in her welcome. I gathered she was called Nyasamia and was indeed Dad's now fourth wife. I was immediately introduced to my new step sisters and even a second brother. The environment was organised and conducive. It looked like the children books I read and how they portrayed an ideal family. It was warm and cosy. A picture perfect environment. I enjoyed hot and well cooked meals, served four times everyday. We had breakfast, lunch, evening tea and dinner. Both Dad and Nyasamia left in the morning and came back in the evening. Nyasamia had connected him to her network and he was now in imports and exports.

Dad looked happy and somewhat healthier. I think he had even stopped drinking and would be found helping around the house on weekends. I had known him as a very hands-on-man so was not surprised; he only broke this routine when Gor was playing.

Dad would leave early and join his friends where they would head to an open air eatery that goes by the name Burma, famed for budget friendly, very fresh Barbecue in Nairobi, only pet peeve is you had to battle swarms of flies as you enjoyed your meal.

They would eat to their fill and stroll straight into City Stadium across the road. City stadium is strategically placed at the tail of end of a road called Jogoo which ushers you into the expansive Eastlands region of Nairobi.

Eastlands is the home of Middle lower to lower class civil servants and was then massively populated by the Luos in Nairobi hence most Gor matches were played at City Stadium due to proximity to its fans.

The matches would go either way but most times when one team scored and the other team felt it was an unfair score (which was the feeling all the time), a stone would find its way onto the pitch, or a man by the name Odero Spoiler would make his way into the stadium to accost the referee and the war would begin.

The police would join with teargas and soon it'd be everyone for himself. The running battles between the police and fans would spill over to Jogoo Road and beyond leaving in its wake shoe soles and other personal effects strewn all over the roads. In those days a match would hardly run its full course unless played without fans.

Most times Dad would arrive from these matches and request for water to wash his face after encountering first grade tear gas. He never came from the stadium hurt though. I suspect he was among the stone throwers. Most friends who went to watch soccer together had no idea how the rest arrived home until the next day. The stadium was not a place for women and girls.

I gingerly asked Philip how he came to live with Nyasamia. He was not very clear with his explanation although I later learnt Dad stole him from one of mum's friends after mum left him there for some days. Mum's friend may have sold her out.

On Sundays we would dress up and go to the nearby St. Theresa's Catholic Church. Strange enough, my Dad never switched my school and I continued going to St Annes Jogoo

Road. Each day, I always waited for Mama Mpenzi's voice from the bushes to steal me but none came. I guess she gave up the chase. There are moments in life when avoidance, if not retreat, is the better part of valor. My classwork improved tremendously because I concentrated better and for the first time I topped my class after stagnating at position 6 in my first and second years.

There was nothing but love between myself and step siblings. Even if Nyasamia felt the burden of two extra kids, she never once showed it. I felt very safe and grounded around her. Granted, if one is not mainstream family one may try to compensate by being overly helpful; going beyond to secure your place, justify the welcome and add value.

Everything among us as children was shared equally and infact I recall when I arrived I had no proper clothes. Nyasamia took her daughter's clothes and shared them out with me.

Boarding schools were becoming increasingly popular in Kenya and the top most schools were conducting interviews. I needed to go to a boarding school to avoid being always on the lookout for mum Dad or Mama Mpenzi appearing out of the blues. I was constantly looking over my shoulder as a child. We would be playing in the field and I would miss a ball because I was checking the fence and peers would always follow my eyes to see what was at the fence.

I was also tired of making new friends or explaining to old friends where I had been. The uncertainty was nerve wrecking that at some point I stopped making new friends altogether.

Admission to boarding school would be based purely on performance after sitting three interview exams; Maths, English and Science. I recall preparing for this exam by even topping my class at the end of the term that was preceding my moving to the boarding school. I told my classmates that I would not be coming back to school the following year as I was sure I was going to join boarding school. I was a member of the drama club and even helped steer the school all the way to the Nationals with a Junior Category poem titled 'Malaria'. It was an own composition by my then English teacher Mrs Nyamu who I loved and admired.

I was sort of a small celebrity if you will, who was now bidding them goodbye.

Dad took both my step sister and I for the interview. Most boarding schools were upcountry for the tranquility and order away from city life and most were Catholic sponsored. The journey to St. Anne's Girls Boarding School in Mumias took a whole day.

We spent the night at a family friend's in Mumias, woke up early the next day for the interview - as far as I recollect, it was a very easy exam.

We travelled back to Nairobi and waited for the results with bated breath but it was Dad to bring the results and he had not been home almost a week.

That month, Raila Odinga, his hero had sprung back like a weed and was in a new movement in Kenya by the name Saba Saba. Every 7th of the month, the Saba Saba activists would be out on the streets protesting the single party rule and agitating for multi party democracy giving speeches as angry as the sun was hot. Dad would wake up with a furious sense of mission hitting the streets to engage the police in running battles, getting back in the evening to listen to the radio on how well they had performed.

On some days, he came back home in ripped clothes. On some, he came back with fresh bruises or with red eyes after absorbing teargas all day. They were resilient in their cause and picketed without cease, were prepared to resist with armour plated resolve the single party rule in Kenya.

When the movement bore its own print and brought the city to a halt, President Moi got impatient and ordered mass arrests of the picketers who were all thrown in remand including my Dad.

Things worsened when human rights activists joined the protest agitating for the release of picketers. Their voices were amplified by the West who now threatened sanctions on an already plundered and limping state of the nation.

The West insisted that President Moi must promote free speech and desist from unleashing violence on his people. Moi was forced to yield to multiparty democracy demands or face donor cuts by the IMF and European Union.

President Moi caved in and in 1991, Kenya became a Multi Party state. Jaramogi formed a party called FORD which naturally became my father's political party and to seal his loyalty, he registered as a life member.

One by one the picketers were released from remand. Dad was released in the night, arrived and stayed out in the darkness insisting that nobody should go near him because he was full of lice, bedbugs and fleas. He stripped naked outside as Nyasamia took a basin full of water to him. More and more basins of water were taken outside in the dark as he cleaned himself. The Kenyan prisons had not yet undergone reforms and a night in a cell seemed like a lifetime in a rat infested urbanite city sewer.

The court system was slow, teeming with cases and files with a back breaking log. Offenders would be held in remand upto a month waiting a first hearing. If your relatives had the money to bribe either the court or remand officers, you had a chance to get out. Otherwise you would have to languish and wait in the crazy court systems where files so often grew legs.

A remand is a holding place as you wait for your first hearing and possibly bail. You were not supposed to spend more than 24 hours in remand unless its the weekend according to the constitution then. Due to its temporal nature, not much resources are vested in there. There is no water for a shower. The food was mostly beans. At times no toilets and remandees would have to go right there where they were seated in tins or just urinate on the wall.

Cases of sodomy or even rape were not uncommon. Remandees caught strange skin diseases and even TB in cells and never recovered. That's where Dad spent a week, the very same OCD guy I had introduced to you earlier.

When he got into the house, he had what looked like insect bites all over his light skinned body - lice and all sorts of vermin had fed on him during his time in. They had also shaved his head bald. His scalp was whiter than his skin in a Tibetan monk likeness.

Wives feared to visit remandees because secretly the elaborate spy network President Moi had so much invested in, as with many dictators who are insecure about their misrule, could trace back where one lived. Wives just waited out hoping their husbands would show up.

They had been beaten and tortured the whole time they were in for disturbing the peace or undermining the Government.

Later in the week, he announced that the school we had interviewed in had responded. Only one letter had come, and it was not mine. This was easily one of those times in my life when I was truly devastated. How did I not make the cut? It did not make any sense to me. I recall looking at my Dad, and him avoiding eye contact.

I had to be happy for my sister as she prepared to go to our dream school; the shopping, clothes and all the possibilities of adventure, new friends, some sort of independence from the nest that was now only but a dream for me.

I endured another year of day school, had to go back with an egg on my face while my teachers wondered how I did not make the cut yet I had topped my class in the previous year. Some kids made fun of me saying I had failed. It was a difficult year.

One day during break time, from the bushes appeared Mama Mpenzi, my mum and Sitho in tow.

I was so excited to see mum . I briskly looked at the kids playing or seated in little groupings sharing out their snacks. I moved stealthily to the bush, and jumped fence to join them.

She did not hug me, but was surprised at how tall I had grown.

I thought I was being stolen again and was ready to go. But mum told me about her certificates that Dad was holding onto, that she was angling for a job and she needed them, requested that I steal them and bring them to her the next day.

She looked at me more intently and then half whispered to her sister with her palm on her mouth, "My goodness. She looks so much like her Dad," and Mama Mpenzi amused said, "I know its amazing how genes work!"

I was happy to hear that because as I told you, my Dad was the most beautiful man on earth.

The job to smuggle mum's certificate was my first duty ever for her. I took it with the seriousness of Mission Apollo 2. I was going to be able to prove to mum that I was a big girl now and that I could get things done.

I left school and was home by 1500hrs. Obviously both Nyasamia and Dad were not home yet and it was not a difficult task.

My step sisters were doing their homework, and the little ones were playing outside.

I had lived with Dad and knew he kept his documents very meticulously in an orange file. I only needed to locate the file and since it was a one bedroomed house and the bed had four side drawers, that's where I started. It did not take long before I located the file and unclipped every last certificate that had my mother's name from High School to Graffins Secretarial College to a Diploma in Administration and other short courses that she had been taking. I took them all and stuffed them in my school bag in the middle of a text book.

I did not sleep at night; I was thinking about life with mum.

Of course I could not carry Philip with me to school. He had hardly started school. But I told him to be on the watch the next day as we would come for him.

Nyasamia was amazing, granted. But I was looking at the possibility of my own mother. I hadn't seen her in years. My own mother despite that she had left, was better any day than the best stepmother in the world.

Here I was, being offered a real chance at living with her. Getting a kiss and hug while leaving for school. Coming back to her warm embrace. Calling her Mummy. Maybe we could read a book at night together. Maybe I could try on her lipstick. Maybe she would cook as we sat around her and would tell us stories. I was going to show her just how great I was at reciting poems. And all these compositions of mine that were being displayed in class for my classmates to emulate; she would have to read them - I was going to make her so proud. You just wait.

The next day, the trio arrived promptly at break time and I joined them without hesitation. I only carried the book that had the certificates since carrying a whole bag would have raised eyebrows.

I proudly handed her my conquests which she pored at very carefully and said, "Yes!"

I really felt affirmed and useful.

We left school together as she had promised, to Mama Mpenzi's.

I was really happy to see my mum . It was like I had received my heart back. I loved that woman so fiercely. I had so much warmth in my heart and belly just seeing her and being in her presence - I admired how beautiful she was. How charming she was and how she kept churning stories which would leave the room in stitches, she was quite the orator, entertainer and impressionist. I hung onto her every word. All afternoon she engaged people in inexhaustible stories, each more thrilling than the last.

She seemed different. She seemed happy. She had bloomed. She had grown bigger; no longer slim. No longer had a long neck. It was shorter but with rings all over it. She had on a curly kit and wore red lipstick.

Amidst much distraction in the room, I tried to pitch in the shortest time possible that I had topped my class for two terms straight. I also explained that I was representing my school at the Provincial level in poetry. I told her that I was so good in my English and we would have to go pick my bag from school so she could read my compositions.

She asked how my brother was doing. I explained how fast he runs and that he was quite talkative and that I had told him to wait out for us next day.

We were having this revolutionary conversation then to my shock and mortifying consternation, she abruptly asked everyone in the room, "Which bands are playing tonight? Where? We need to prepare before front seats are taken."

I recall Mama Mpenzi asking "What about her? I don't think she has eaten even. We got her off school at break time." She was referring to me.

"That's why we need to move. We are taking her back to her Dad. Hope we drop her in time for their dinner. In fact Eastleigh is near Mateso."

My heart crashed on the ground like a glass and shattered. Then I assembled myself real quick and picked up the cue without missing a beat and contributed to the conversation suggesting that we needed to go as Nyasamia served dinner strictly by 8:30 p.m.

They were hilarious women. Mama Mpenzi kept saying, "Are we just going to drop her here like thieves? Let's get in guys," to which my other Auntie Apiyo objected.

"But we have you here. You are a fighter too Apiyo. Why don't we just knock and get in and beat both him and his new wife guys?" Said Mum to her cousin Apiyo while laughing.

Mum, who from what I recalled as a little girl avoided conflict, picked a small stone, hid behind Mama Mpenzi and said, "I will be here to defend you as you deal with them. George is the one you must castrate at least."

They all laughed but I did not. I had moved past them, their conversation and whatever else that was. I was thinking about the fact that I had not done my homework because my books were still in school.

They let me walk into the gate by myself and got back into their cab.

I knocked the door and Dad was not home at this point; he legit knew Mama Mpenzi had struck again and this is the kind of drama and distraction he did not need when he was getting a new lease of life. But still he had gone all the way to school to try and trace my footsteps.

The odd conversation was when I tried to explain to Nyasamia where I had been.

"So why did they bring you back?"

She was peering out the curtain worriedly as the women in my mum's family had a reputation in Nairobi to fight like the vikings.

"And where are they? There is also Philip here who will want to see her?"

My Dad rarely beat me up. But the next morning after much questioning, I faced a beating and had to go to school with swollen eyes. He had arrived in the night with my little bag which I left in school.

At the end of that year, Dad informed me that he was taking me to yet again another interview, in a different boarding school, which I prepared even more adequately for.

THE BOYS' CLUB

By early 1980s, the post-independence second generation men and women were beaming and booming. The creation of Kenya as a new republic came with its good tidings. People had good jobs, some little but disposable funds and if one went to school properly, was guaranteed a comfortable life.

You could feel the excitement throbbing from under your feet. In my community, many people were educated but did not venture much into commercial activities or added value to their land. Quite a good number or the semi-illiterate pursued blue collar jobs and ended up being very skilled in craftsmanship like tailoring, carpentry, mechanics, electrical technicians, masons, panel beaters, plumbers, welders and painters. They became very industrious and skillful along these lines.

Many got self-employed while some were engaged by the state corporations in positions that kept them in the city but did not really help them thrive. Historically, they had earlier observed the white colonialists and knew from the word go that education was important. They survived on bare minimum but insisted on educating their children to acquire the best academic skills.

Tom Mboya was an example of those who went out of their way to source for scholarships that would train African children in Western universities for them to take over from the departing colonial masters. The initiative benefitted many Luos from underprivileged backgrounds; from doctors, engineers, lawyers and researchers. Many pursued professions that paid and the community saw lots of disposable income circulating.

This programme produced Obama Senior and eventually Barrack Obama.

They lived in posh areas of Nairobi and took advantage of the finer things in life, as fun loving people. They exemplified opulence in its highest echelons and there were no dull moments in the entertainment scene. It is on this background that the famous Congolese Rumba maestro, Luambo Franco, had to tour Kenya. The Luo justified it and there was definitely going to be a return on investment by the organisers. Kisumu had to be among the cities in this itinerary.

From the early '70s well into the entire '80s, Franco and his band TPOK grew into a real music colossus from the little boy who played in the markets, save for the mid-70s when Vercky's and his Orchestra Lipua Lipua or Orchestra Veve disrupted Franco's ascending trajectory. There was no stopping the Rumba master. Hits like Tangawizi, Princess Kikou, Pesa Position, Ndaya, Mamou and Mario traversed the continent and rumbled in Luo patronised spots. Franco's haunting contralto conveying depth of emotion that drew out the crowds.

When Franco toured Kenya in 1988, Dad was in the entourage of the Luos that travelled to Kisumu to attend his concert. The city was on musical fire and the whole country knew Franco was in his 'homeground'.

I will not say here that Kisumu, the Luo capital was charged. Kisumu is usually charged at room temperature. Physical temperatures are usually hot in Kisumu due to its proximity to the lake.

Kisumu's history is tied around the Kenya-Uganda railway, the colonial monster that reached the city in 1906. The colonialists had endeavoured to enter the hinterlands and get access to the raw materials produced by the newly settled white farmers. Kisumu was strategically situated at the tip of Lake Victoria. The Railway brought Indians who were used to provide cheap labour and eventually settled as shopkeepers to provide basic commercial needs to Africans.

In 1972, when Idi Amin expelled Indians from Uganda, many of them moved to Kenya as a holding point on their way to the United Kingdom. Indians form a very close knit society of very enterprising people in Business, Engineering and Manufacturing. Many Indians in the UK like Rishi Sunak, the Prime Minister, have their roots in Kenya. There is still a very large fourth generation Indian community in Kisumu who know the city as home and can speak DhoLuo language with no qualms.

Fish is the staple; you cannot go to Kisumu and not eat fish - nobody will believe you.

But Kisumu is also an emotional city. Earlier on, it is in Kisumu that the people stoned the founding father Mzee Jomo Kenyatta after the ouster of Jaramogi Oginga Odinga from Government and casted the animosity dye.

We, the Luos, are deliriously happy or deliriously unhappy. We are very easy to impress and also very easy to annoy, a bipolar community if there is such a thing

For Franco, the Luos were deliriously happy. Luos made it a pilgrimage; they flew in, walked, drove in and had vigils of merry making even on the night before the concert. On the concert day, the stadium was packed to the rafters, way above its capacity. Fans lined up as far as the eye could see waiting to go in.

In the mayhem and because it was taking long to have the massive crowds settled in, Franco got on stage. Loud speakers had been perched all over the venue. The massive crowds that were outside were still queuing to get in when Franco hit the first note to test his Gibson guitar. The fans outside heard and a wave of frenzy swept over them like a typhoon.

The roar they produced was not recognisably human but the rolling crash of ocean waves that recede and then batter the shore. The push from outside was massive that the walls of the stadium collapsed falling inside to reveal the packed stadium and injured scores.

It's a concert my Dad attended and would never forget – he had a scar on his left foot from the stampede which he proudly would show around as his badge of Franco honor.

With the advent of Congolese Rumba, Luo Rumba was also born and our own artists came up with their version which is the Benga, an offshoot of Congolese Rumba, mixed up with traditional Luo percussion.

Musicians like Daniel Owino Misiani, Collela Mazee, George Ramogi, George Ojijo, Paul Orwa and later Okach Biggy emerged. When one was not listening to Congolese Rumba, it was definitely one of the local stars. Okach Biggy was particularly home grown and had amassed a cult-like following among Luo revellers.

DO Misiani was my father's boyhood star and on his wedding day, he danced to the 1973 hit 'simaya Chunye Oketo,' a chart buster.

On the day when I was headed to my second interview to a boarding school, we hitched a lift in one of Dad's friend's car - a cream Peugeot 504.

I will always remember because the whole trip, they kept marveling at how serious the car was.

In this 504 were four men with only one mission in Kisumu - they were travelling to dance to Okach all weekend long. And were well prepared as they were playing Okach's music all the way; songs like *Nyowila* where Okach is lamenting over his girlfriend who seems to be having overt affairs with his friends with whom they party together. He questions why Nyowila is seen loitering in Kendu Bay. He decries the fact that it is now his friends sleeping with Nyowila. Drunkards are all over with her and concludes that he will visit the mother to narrate all Nyowila is putting him through.

Hits like *Helena wang'e dongo, Nyathi Nyakach,* and *Dorina.*

Looking back, I am so amused; all these Luo artists did was sing about women - women who were beautiful. Women who walked into their lives, ripped their chests open, took their hearts and left, or the anatomy of women.

Dad and his team would sing along Okach's words and inject character in them.

Grown men travelling into Kisumu on Friday, dance to Okach and journey back to Nairobi on Sunday.

So there we were, four men and a child. All through the journey they kept transitioning between TP OK Jazz and Luo Benga. Midway they would argue about Raila Odinga. One of them, Odiek Songa was a Moi stalwart, a very rare occurrence because Luos absolutely loathed President Moi but the ones that agreed to work with him made a lot of money. So naturally, he was the owner of the Peugeot 504. He kept reminding his passengers that he walked into Marshalls and paid for the car in cash when the mileage was zero.

Odiek Songa would throw unprintables at Raila and they would argue to the point Dad would demand that we alight at that very point, and the car would stop. Dad would get out of the car and would scream, "*Omera an okasechi!JaLuo Oksechi! Kokidwar miya lift to we!*" Meanwhile their back to me as they relieved themselves in some bush.

They would take the argument by the side of the road as I watched from inside the car. Dad would call out to me, 'Mami get out of the car. This is not worth it! Magi nonsense!' To which Odiek would laugh and calm off and tell me, "*Babau nosar gi Raila*. Mami stay put we are finishing this journey."

They would eventually agree and keep the journey on. There would be tension and a momentary quiet with my Dad fuming and Odiek Songa's slit dancing eyes bemused.

On the stereo, Franco's song Serment Kikam would fill the car.

'Napesi yo motema cherie kikame...'

And all of them would reunite with...

'mama aaaaaa aaaa'

And they were good friends again.

One of the gang members was a dwarf and hunch back but also a notorious polygamist who for everything he lacked in height, he compensated in the gift of gab and expletives. In fact, he christened himself *Otieno Owadgi Omande Nyamson Area* cautioning anyone who cared to listen about his sexual prowess.

He would actually feel Franco's songs to the point of tears. He would be quiet still and would shake his head in awe. He would then invite each and everyone to his funeral.

"Omera ubi uika to kik ayud ka ng 'ato otero Nyatanga kayudo tachieni ma giri no okchung," while licking his index finger and pointing it up to the sky in a vicious swear.

It was beautiful witnessing this bromance, boys in overgrown body suits.

They spoke about their women. All of them were polygamous and all of them were in various stages of a heart break. At some point my mum came up. The Kisumu frequent flyers confirmed she was the hottest thing since bread and butter in the city, was in a clique of independent women of means and was also quite the beer guzzler.

I watched a shadow pass by Dad's face.

I arrived for my interview with a gang of unruly men in their 40s. They kept telling me I was the brightest and that I should annihilate the exam and promised to buy me French fries at the Kakamega Golf Club where Odiek Songa was a member. And he did buy me French fries and two hot sausages when I was done with the exams which consisted Math, English and Science again.

Nyamson Area's only concern was whether the headmistress was single and needed a husband because he still had room for one more wife. When Dad said it was a Catholic school and the headmistress was a nun, he swore he once made love to a nun sending everyone in a fit.

But hey, this was Owadgi Omande. He could say anything.

NUNS WITH LOVE

I joined boarding school the next year. I was relieved to be shut out into this monastery of a Catholic boarding school with all its chappels, nuns, and girls like myself, where everything worked like a clock and on schedule, no surprises.

When the Vatican came to Africa to spread the word, they managed to secure the most sought after lands, in the most scenic landscapes for the churches, schools and hospitals they were building. In Africa, it's not easy to find an institution by the Catholic that does not sit on prime land.

Mukumu school was awash with oak trees, plush grass, beautiful gardens, ancient architecture and the convent was in a massive campus looking compound, always a bell chiming, always a melancholic choir of singing nuns in the air.

The chapels wore frescoed ceilings and stain glass windows, cool renaissance interiors with sharp beams of light criss crossing the hallways like swords in lilac and blue.

In the Kenyan education system then, a term would last about three months then you recess for a month.

A term in Dad's life is a long time.

When we closed school, I realised Dad would now come home later than usual. Maybe 4 or 5 in the morning and drunk. When he was taking me to school, he was only an acquaintance but now he had drawn himself inside this circle of Okatch chasers and was right at the nucleus of it.

I know that because I saw them pick him up from home every weekend, Okatch bound in the many bars that sprouted in Nairobi including the famed Jon Saga, Mateso, Safe life and Bombax.

The same look I saw on my mom's face as a child, I started seeing it with Nyasamia. A face of despair, uncertainty, loneliness and mental strife.

In fact, Dad would love opening and closing dates as my school was a paltry 30 minutes away from Kisumu, the nerve centre of Sodom. He would misuse the opportunities of taking me to or picking me from school, to party with his friends in Kisumu.

One time when I was twelve years old, Dad and his team picked me up from school.

We drove into Kisumu and they dropped me at a nurse's house. It was a pretty small duplex, the kind given to staff in an institutional complex.

She was on the heavy side, very bleached and with very fat legs - my Dad had a thing for women with fat legs.

The lady was polite, subservient - these people who look like they are smiling even when they are not. She cooked for me, and later Dad came picked her up and they all went merry making.

I was half asleep when they got back, she had set me up on the couch a few feet from the bed. But I heard them in the darkness because I am a very light sleeper.

The next morning, we set off back to Nairobi.

When we arrived home, Nyasamia was looking at me very keenly. She was not going to be the wife who finds out last, her eyes stabbed and stalked me and there was no escaping her - I tried very hard to avoid eye contact.

She cornered me the next day.

I did not wait for the long rope of truth to be pulled from me, I volunteered it willingly because of how good she had been to Dad, Philip and I.

I told her about the nurse.

She was extraordinarily quiet that whole holiday. I recall it was the Christmas break.

On this Christmas she shopped for us, and took us to Uhuru park at the centre of the city.

We could not afford to ride the ponies or the carousel or anything like that but we were happy to watch other kids do it. We watched kids and their parents row boats too. She had cooked and packed and lay a picnic on the ground and we ate to our fill, and we played and rolled on the grass till evening.

Dad was with us too. I kept exaggerating my laugh and the fun I was having so he could see that we were happy and that we needed to be here, basically telling him, 'Don't mess this up!'

It remains the best Christmass of my childhood.

Nyasamia is hands down the best mother in the world.

I opened school, and closed in three months – when I arrived home, I found that in one of those nights when Dad disappeared with his groupies, Nyasamia had packed her stuff and her kids and left.

A truck had come and reversed with the entry on the door, and they loaded all furniture in it, because, well, they were hers. Dad had moved in at hers, and was only a plug and play.

She however left my brother Philip in the lone house, left him with food and locked him in so he doesn't leave the house, wander and get lost.

All day Philip had been seated by the window watching other kids play and when it got dark, he started to cry, neighbours broke the door and took him.

I don't know if this is true for everyone, if it is mere superstition or common sense.

There are people who leave and everything leaves. The joy, happiness, colour finds any available ediflce and dissipates,

All that is left is a yawning chasm and memories of yesterday. Darkness descends upon your lives because, apparently, they are the sun.

This same house that was once exuberant, healthy, productive, promising became an off representation of its former self. Worse, the main contacts Dad was using to make money actually came from Nyasamia and now all that was gone too and we were now facing a financial slump.

Dad became a Pariah among former family friends.

She also left with my step siblings - I had formed a deep bond with my step sister, we could never wait to close school and would spend the entire holiday discussing what went down while in school, I also loved my little step brother George, who unlike Philip, was quite the extrovert like myself. I also had a little sister Nyongalo, who I always helped baby sit and even name. We even had a cousin who always played the role of a big sister and is easily the neatest person I ever saw. I was quite messy and cumbersome but she put me in proper perspective in terms of being neat and I owe it to her.

All these emotional investments, gone. A very familiar feeling.

So all we had were four stools with one at the centre to act as a table, a stove in the kitchen, and two mattresses, one where Dad lay with Philip and one where I slept in, on the kitchen floor.

Dad busied himself punching nails on the walls and hanging his clothes on since the wardrobe was gone and his clothes had been left in a pile on the floor.

But we also had a radio, and a radio meant we had everything. Around this time, Franco and TPOK Jazz were at their peak career wise with 100 albums under their belt, becoming one of the most successful musical groups in the continent. He now had two bands, one in DRC and another in Brussels Belgium producing hit after hit with unforgettable artists like Madilu System, Josky Kiambukuta, Lutumba Simaro, Ndombe Opetum. Mpudi Decca, Empopo Loway, Isaac Musekiwa, Ntesa Dalienst,

Aime Kiwakana, Djo Mpoy, Papa Noel, Wuta Mayi, Malage de Lugendo and others. Franco was killing life out of his guitar which when he plucked you had no choice but obey.

Left as a unit, Dad and I would drift into the world of Salima, Illouse, Asumani, and the greatest propaganda song Franco made for Chief kleptomaniac Mobutu 'Candidat Na Biso.'

Franco was more the guitarist than the vocalist and so whenever he came in songs like 'Non' I was a child but it really lifted me up, or 'Kikou.'

Music normalised our suffering, we would often sing together.

Music lifted us and it made us feel better, it lessened our burden, made our hearts light.

It sometimes inflicted us with pain. I do not know about his but I would often think about my mother, now that I had a real taste of how a mother could impact me.

We did not understand a word but Music is art, it's for us the consumers to interpret.

Here we were listening to songs in Congolese, in French, in Lingala and shedding tears from happiness or from sadness.

Later on in life I learnt one of Dad's favourite songs Azda that he would swear was about a long lost lover by the name Azda who needed to return, was actually about Azda who was a car dealer and Franco was promoting his VW business.

All the emotions Dad had invested had been going to waste.

Words limit the art in Music. Music is so much more than language can afford.

You also appreciate the instruments more if you have no idea what they are saying, while if you can understand you will center the words.

I believe the oppressed make good music, make good art.

Troubled people are creative; they channel their pain more intentionally and more coherently.

Congo DRC is right at the center of Africa and could as well be the richest country in the world. The country astride the Equator has endured untold suffering since the era of King Leopold of Belgium. It is rich in rubber, gold, diamonds, copper and many other minerals. It saw the plunder by dictator Mobutu Sese Seko, civil wars and serious interference from Western powers interested in exploiting their resources.

South Africa also comes to mind, followed by African Americans. Generally, where there is pain, there is good music. There is nothing like being an outcast to galvanise one's inner amazon.

Dad's favourite song was Franco's Temps Mort.

Dad had to drop his little groupie because who would he leave kids with all weekend long?

Now we were living just the three of us, on our own terms.

I was now old enough to do house chores like clean the house, wash clothes and Dad would help in cooking. Franco would serenade him that we would not even eat on time, we would listen to music and realise it was almost 3pm and we had not had anything to eat.

I had watched Dad cook from when I was a very young girl.

The kitchen was for women it was said, but Dad saw it differently, the need to eat was human and not gender specific.

He was particularly good at simple dishes like omelette, fried eggs, and Kenya's staple which is ugali.

Ugali is simply corn flour added in water to make a porridge like dish, then more flour is added to make it harder and less viscous.

He loved his ugali tough, and would let it burn a bit for the aroma – If dad could not smell the aroma coming from the kitchen he would accuse whoever was cooking of a half cooked ugali and would complain bitterly.

I got my first lesson of cooking ugali from Dad.

I was there watching him cook the vegetables and he said "Today you learn how to cook ugali."

"For who?"

"For your husband"

"I thought you said you never want me to ever get married?"

"You and your smart mouth, you will learn to cook Ugali to save your life"

Philip was watching on the floor amused.

And so my father taught me how to cook ugali.

A perfect ugali should not stick on the fingers. If anything, the Luhya tribe make a fist and hurl a mound of ugali on the wall. If it falls its perfect. If not, it's a tragedy.

Dad's OCD would inspire him to mould the ugali on the plate to a perfect circle with no bumps. I on the other hand, had the shaggiest of ugalis which when I presented he would froth and remind me that I had better work hard in school because no man would accept that sort of ugali.

Dad made the meanest ugali, even when I grew up, a mother, I would still coax him, convince him to hit the kitchen and cook for me, on condition that I would fry everything else.

His ugali came in hot, still smoking and would be tough and with the smell of burnt corn, it came a perfect round with no bumps. You would eat Dad's ugali and proceed operating your phone without smudging it, because your hands always emerged clean.

He would proudly present it as one presents a wedding cake, set his arms akimbo and marvel at how skilled he was.

I would reward him with praises of him being a Michelin star ugali cook. He was.

We were living a humble, simple and happy life. Dad was buying furniture here and there, stocking the kitchen, even got himself a bed and graduated from sleeping on the floor.

Philip also started going to school. St. Theresa's Boys Primary in Eastleigh was the same school that Nyasamia's son, George, just a year younger than Philip was going to. They would be in the same class with the same surname, but at the end of the day would take separate routes.

NYASEME

I kept going back to boarding and coming back home to find improvements here and there.

And one time I left for school and bid Dad and little Philip bye.

But because three months is a long time in Dad's life, When we closed school, I found that he had married a new wife. Shall we call her Nyaseme?

Yeah, let's call her Nyaseme - This was fifth wife in the pecking order.

She was feisty, extremely beautiful with great legs but a sharp contrast from Nyasamia. She had been born and raised in the city and knew her way around the fold. Strong willed and held her own ground which she was unwilling to cede.

Nyaseme moved in with a daughter who was also Dad's and a son from a previous relationship that did not work out.

When you do the math, it was hilarious, her last born daughter was a year younger than Nyasamia's last born and yet Nyasamia had lived with us till her last born was about 3 years old.

Nyasamia's son was a year younger than Philip yet Mum and Dad stayed together about three years after the birth of Philip.

It was a match not made in heaven.

Dad struggled to govern her like he used to Nyasamia.

Dad also lost a certain contract he was servicing, after losing all the contacts Nyasamia had connected him to. So here we had two adults, no jobs and four kids.

Nyaseme loved her bottle and was not willing to let it go. She also had her own parallel life outside her marriage which she was not about to give up for anyone.

These personality clashes eventually snowballed to the most tumultuous times of our lives.

They fought like cats thrown in a fire – I watched in amusement as tables turned. Nyaseme would be out drinking while Dad would be in the house up late in the nights waiting for her, seething and steaming probably plotting her demise at the end of a guillotin. She would never come back earlier than 4am.

Philip, her son, her daughter and myself would sleep in the kitchen while they occupied the one bedroom.

She was the kind of lady who would make an entrance.

She would start shouting from the gate about how nobody would tell her what to do.

I am generally a very light sleeper and I would wake up almost immediately. The fact that she was out would also make her kids restless and they too would kind of be half asleep until she showed up.

The moment she stepped in, they would argue and soon, terrifying sounds of wares smashing, breaking glass, breaking wood, odd thuds, heavy breathing and cries would take over our house.

The kids would all curl up next to me as we listened in.

They would fight in the still of the night until they would both go silent and I would sit up in the darkness holding my breath for any sign of life between them.

I was terrified at the thought of Dad dying. Who would take Philip and I? Where would we go?

By this time we had completely cut off from mum's side. My yearning stopped after the returnee incident, and I guess Mama Mpenzi decided to mind her own business too.

She was also fighting her own custody battles when the father of her children took them and consigned them to boarding schools all over Siaya.

Neighbours would gather in small groups at our door and absorb the horror of it all in its banal pageantry. They would urge the two to let us out of the house.

There was one particular horrible night. They fought till Nyaseme fainted. We were sleeping on the kitchen floor.

Our mattress suddenly got moist on the edges and while I thought my little sister was wetting the bed, because like me when I was little she did that a lot, it was blood streaming into the kitchen floor from the adjacent living room and seeping into the matress.

The intensity of the fights did not deter Nyaseme. She was so defiant that she was now being dropped home late in the night by Dad's own previous groupie friends - I think Dad had fallen out with some of them.

Dad's social life had taken a blow. He had children to tend to, was broke and embarassed even to be seen in social places as Luo men of his time would question why his house was not in order.

Nyaseme and Dad would splatter each other with acidic drops of verbal vitriol.

"Why is it taking you long to return this kid to her people where she belongs like we agreed? There is hardly enough food for all of us!" Referring to me.

And because there was no road too low for her to take, while Dad was away she extended her insults to me.

"Your mother is a prostitute in Kisumu and you will turn out just like her."

I turned and walked away, her words hit the back of my head and fell to the floor.

As a child you are affected by this level of hostility without being able to intellectualise or articulate it, you think you are the problem.

I remember there were a lot of cracked things in the house, broken stools, a cracked portait of Raila Odinga, a cracked radio which were all caught up during the crossfire of battle. The notable cracks resembled the irredeemable fault lines in their marriage.

I always went back to school, worried for my little brother, I was at least sheltered momentarily by the high walls of the convent but he had to live this life every day of his life.

Three months is a long time in Dad's life. I came back from school and found the two warlords had reached an interminable end and had parted ways, Dad took her last born daughter who now joined Philip and I.

Their violence reached its absolute nadir, that one day the police had to come and arrest Dad.

My little brother Philip told me all about it.

Now Dad was unemployed, was not in good books with most of his friends who would loan him here and there, and had an additional child from Nyaseme.

The Mikayi was introduced in our lives again, as she had to travel from upcountry to get us food.

The Mikayi and Nyakendu were used to the abandonment back upcountry, had forged their lives as wives of an absentee husband,almost like widows, tending to their gardens, trading, rearing chicken and livestock.

I doubt Nyakendu even cared anymore. She carried on her life without complaining. She was yet to have a child,3 wives and 7 kids later by dad after her own marriage.

Mikayi had to still lap after Dad,as she was depending on Dad to pay school fees for her children back in the village.

The Mikayi had to travel with food from upcountry that she was tilling with her own hands, because it reached a point we were starving and had to be eating at neighbour's houses.

It was a tactic I had perfected as a child.

I had to be friendly with all kids, stay in their good books, agree with everything they say and stay humble even when being bullied. I would approach their homes around midday pretending to watch TV but sit quietly with my little brother Philip. We had to contribute to ongoing conversation and add laughter to even not so funny jokes.

I had to offer to help with any household duties even if it was babysitting and feeding a little child. I was particularly good at helping kids with homework which could drag on to lunch hours. I knew I would not be chased away.

My predatory skills would seem unplanned but I actually had my own roster not to stick to one house every day. I kept on rotating houses.

My little brother Philip with eager trusting eyes always following my cues, always knew when we are performing and when were ourselves, when he should jump up and help with something or just sit and be quiet or laugh loudly at Tom and Jerry.

I recall one time we were invited to a birthday, we left home having eaten. Okay, we had black tea and ugali from the previous day.

This birthday was for one of the popular kids in the estate, it had all sorts of snacks, foods, biscuits, candy.

And anytime Philip was given anything to eat, he did not eat. Instead he wrapped the food in a sweater I had carried for him since the clouds were billowing and I suspected it may rain. The liquids he put by his side, guarding them so the increasingly fidgety kids would not pour it.

I did not notice this because as usual I was doing the most; earning our place, washing dishes, mopping, cleaning up as the party progressed.

And eventually his little sweater was so full of biscuits, sweets, cake and one of the kids pointed it out drawing all the attention to him and suddenly all kids in the party started laughing at him, and yet he was a very shy boy.

He started to cry and I had to sit with him and show him it was okay to eat, I unfolded his sweater and started to eat his stuff then he joined me.

The Madam of that house, who understood how scarcity mentality works, packed a lot of food for us to take home.

Most of these households thought we were such good kids, and maybe we were but as far as I was concerned then, we were performing, we were surviving.

There is a particular household that had a little infant who would not eat unless I was present to perform, and so you would find them coming to look for me and I would head there with my brother.

Dad never encouraged this predatory behaviour, but also did not actively disapprove.

I recall Dad actually walking to the CBD in sandals. We already had an Angella Basset moment long before *Waiting to Exhale* as Nyaseme had set aflame all his clothes and shoes in one of their dark days.

If any of his last friends called him out for a meal, he would pack some of it and bring to us.

Many nights when he said he was going out to drink with friends, I would expect him to come back high, but he would come back sober with food from the bar and would wake Philip and I to eat.

Kenyans have a culture of eating while drinking apparently to waylay the hangover. We call it 'laying the foundation' At times the food he brought home was leftover, I could tell because if it was meat, you would see a piece of ugali here or there.

Some weekends he would send me over to a friend who lived nearby to borrow newspapers which he now could not afford.

My heart was always happy because we had newspapers covering a whole week and I would pore over them one by one.

I recall big on the papers was the story of Dr. Robert Ouko, the then Foreign Minister who had been found murdered, his body burnt and discarded at Got Alila - He was a Luo.

The nation was shocked but the Luo nation was stunned.

Ouko was a favourite of the west and was being pitted to take over from the then President Moi.

His death sparked protests in the urban areas and especially in Kisumu.

A commission of inquiry was quickly formed and hearings on his death were now on.

As most could not afford televisions, the hearing was being printed on the papers.

I would read testimonies from the witnesses with keen interest because it mattered so much to Dad. I did not understand most of it and I kept asking Dad what it meant.

It looked like justice was being served; unfortunately we could not get Ouko back, I did not understand what sort of justice that was.

Dad's friend would supply us with newspapers. His name was Abong'o Jakoyugi.

A very happy and jolly guy.

He had maintained his job where they first worked with Dad and was earning well.

He would ask how Dad was fairing. He would then summon his house help to arrange all the papers for the week and while that was being done, he would ask if I had breakfast. I would nod in the affirmative.

I wouldn't have minded the bread, jam, butter and assortment of condiments that were laid on the table though, because I had only had black tea and ugali, but it was not a matter of life and death.

"Do not wear your problems like a badge." Dad always said.

Abong'o's home had marble floors as smooth as frozen lakes, covered partly in a red carpet, he had a leather six seater sofa and a wall unit with not only a system but a Television and DVD. The home even had a designated place for eating with a dining table and chairs arranged methodically.

It was a beautiful home.

I would wait outside because after walking so many miles to collect the papers, my legs were dusty and I would have dirtied the carpet.

Dad had a method of getting things on credit – When we were well off, my brother Philip would go to the shop and buy stuff and if I offered to go he would say no.

When we needed credit, he would go to the shop himself and make promises and get stuff.

But when things were really thick, it's me he sent.

I would go to the shop and start with a smile and ask how the shopkeeper was doing. Knowing him to like politics as most Kenyans do, I would ask him about his favorite politician to which he would really get into the mood and expound on the current situation, I would pretend to agree with everything he said then quickly slot in my request for bread and milk on credit. That would remind him about an unpaid debt but still serve me with a stern warning.

It was so hilarious that store owners would see me and start picking up the story from where we left and in the middle of that give me flour or sugar or whatever.

Dad was a diehard Raila fan, and he passed that passion to me as a child, but all the store owners were from the Kikuyu tribe who unfortunately, due to divisive and tribal politics by leaders on both sides, had a long standing polarised relationship with Luos. I would definitely tell them even Luos were warming up to their leader. A fact that excited them out of their wits.

Dad would never vote for anyone who is not Raila if he had a gun to his head.

I think when it rains it pours. Right in the middle of this vortex I fell so ill.

Nyaseme did the most; she not only moved out with her stuff, but also with some of our stuff like the mosquito net.

There are people whose blood mosquitoes love. I am people.

In one of those holidays, I started feeling my joints aching and just general weakness and I told Dad. It was the last thing he wanted to hear. He could not afford a sick kid.

Previously if you were not covered by insurance, which we were definitely not, you would have to get some money or go figure.

Free or subsidized public medical care came with Kenya's third president, the late Mwai Kibaki. Before Kibaki, the medical situation would be so bad that mothers who delivered kids in hospital and could not afford the fee, which could go as low as a paltry 30 dollars, would spend months, some even years detained in hospital.

Maternity wards were where you met full grown kids running around, playing. In the worst case scenario, the same mothers would get pregnant yet again inside maternity wards as they got sexually abused for survival.

I struggled in the night with fever and by morning I was dealing with a full blown Malaria.

Malaria is a common tropical disease that affects children in Africa after a bite by the female anopheles mosquito,the situation is better now with lots of aid coming in from NGOs and research colleges mostly from the US.

Shivers, fever, headache are the main symptoms.

Dad left with the only radio we owned and came back with medicine. He left the radio with the chemist and was just self-diagnosing because the hospitals would either ask for consultation fees or have me admitted and that would be a disaster, we would join the list of the detainees.

He administered the Quinine that tasted so bad first day with some pain killers and recorded my symptoms and progress on a book.

Day 1

Gave her 2 tablets - Mami is shivering and crying and not eating.

Gave her 2 tablets – Mami is shivering and crying and not eating.

Gave her 2 tablets – Mami is still sweating and shivering but took krest.

Day 2

Gave her 2 tablets – Mami is sweating and crying and refused breakfast.

Gave her 2 tablets – Mami is hot and shivering and is vomiting.

Gave her 2 tablets - Mami is very hot and still vomiting and not eating.

Day 3

Gave her 2 tablets – Mami is not very hot and is not crying but refused breakfast.

Gave her 2 tablets – Still not very hot,not crying but not eating.

Gave her 2 tablets – Mami asking for krest or a mango gave her.

Day 4

Gave her 2 tablet - Mami's eyes are coming she is smiling but still not eating.

Gave her 2 tablets – Mami took krest.

Gave her 2 tablets - Mami went outside to get some air and is scratching all over with an Osogoro (Maize husk).

It was right after this illness that Dad became the king of self-medication.

He would never ever buy medicine without recording on a book the name of the medicine and the reaction and time it took for the reaction. So in future if he or any of us was ill, he would just refer back to his book and look for a familiar pattern, go straight to the chemist get the drugs and administer.

In Africa, most drugs including antibiotics are over the counter, nobody really cares what you are going to use the drug for and this has been sustained by the high cost of medical care which a large majority cannot afford.

This is a habit a lot of us took on from dad, even in adult hood – we would feel a certain way, we would go straight to the chemist and get whatever we felt was suitable. It's how we grew. I only accessed medical Insurance the day I got a formal job. All my life I survived on self medication.

I got well, but at the cost of the radio that made our lives bearable.

Now there would be no Gor, No Franco, No Raila until the sun shone on us again. The radio never ever got back, silence deafened us and made our problems as big as they really were.

I resorted to reading books, magazines and newspapers when back from boarding school. Back in the day, we had mobile libraries plying estates of Nairobi. Kenya National Library Services would send its mobile library on a van that would be parked under a tree opening us up to a world of books. Every Saturday and Sunday afternoon, I would clean up, apply Vaseline which if was in short supply, apply cooking fat and sit outside waiting patiently for the van. Most of the books stocked were donations from different foundations or individuals in Anglophone speaking countries like the USA, UK or Canada.

Donors of used books may not be aware of the impact they have on the third world or on little children. Here I am, a direct beneficiary and I say thank you very much.

I read Children's books, poetry, novels to do with the famous five, mystery solving books and as I grew older, I encountered William Shakespeare and fell in love with him.

I sat every afternoon and read his plays from Romeo and Juliet to MacBeth to The Merchant of Venice to Hamlet, to Othello, to King Lear.

I loved books. I loved to witness other people's lives.

Books are good, but for a poor kid, books are everything - they widen his screen, they feed her imagination, expand her world view. Books are an escape - you could be holed up in a little metal shack but solving a case with Sherlock Holmes on 221 Baker Street. You could be surrounded by an earthen wall covered in a grass thatch but could be at the West side or Broadway on a set.

And this is what kids need, the ability to dream.

I would get lost in this world of print and the smell of aged paper that told stories of distant travels.

I would open some pages and find little notes, some had markings. I would wonder about the people that had previously read the book; why did they give up this book? Did they know that one day a little girl would be seated reading the same book?

I always felt the urge to write 'Thank you' at the end of a good story like my Dad signed his newspapers.

I would be buried in these pages and would not leave the movable library until they absolutely needed to go.

When I went to boarding school, I missed this mobile library and it was the one thing I always looked forward going back home to, this is because our school library was only full of text books, no fiction, no biographies, just curriculum books.

The mobile library administrator back home, a volunteer from the NYU, realised my love for Shakespeare and started allowing me to carry a book home, and I would go on reading most of the night.

We formed such a lasting and formidable friendship that when she was done with her volunteer work, she kept on writing me personal letters and shipping in more books by Shakespeare. She would narrate how she missed Africa apart from finding out how I was doing. My father kept on asking me what sort of books I read that would keep me engrossed forever. Curiosity would sometimes overcome him making him peer over my shoulders only to be met by Shakespeare's sonnets. What would follow was "Who are these people? Who is Beth?"

I would try to explain Macbeth in the simplest way possible but he maintained his skepticism.

"I hope it's a good book for children, I better not find you reading adult stuff."

He was too late. Mukumu is a whole commune with kids ranging from grade school all the way to High school and every girls section also has a corresponding boys section and since we shared church with the older students, I had been baptized with books by Jackie Collins, Sidney Sheldon, the infamous Meja Mwangi and his little book 'Unfit for human consumption.'

I think someone even smuggled in a hustler magazine which we all pored through and this was way before even the age of 12.

There is an old age saying that goes 'If you want to hide something from an African, put it in a book.'

This was only true with our fore fathers, or people like my Dad- because their parents did not expose them to books that were not curriculum based.

Parents hardly bought books for kids that were not required in school.

Parents hardly read books, they mostly read newspapers. I never once saw my Dad read a book in his life, not once.

And children do what parents do - and so for a long time indeed, African children only got access to books that were examinable.

Literature is introduced in the last two years of High School, and is not a main but a component of the English subject. It was not given due emphasis but instead received token appreciation in the grand scheme of things.

Literature acted as the entry point to non-academic reading material for the poorest African children. For a long time, examinable literature text books were from the west.

Those who went to school in my father's time were examined on books like 'A Tale of Two Cities' or Jane Austen's 'Pride and Prejudice.' Since they could not relate to the alien context, they absolutely hated Literature in English.

Gradually, educational reforms in Kenya saw African authored books given a chance. That is why Chinua Achebe became a legend across the continent. Most students were examined for his literary genius 'Things Fall Apart.'

Sadly, that is where it ended because students read to pass examinations and not for leisure or personal growth. If you ask most followers of Chinua Achebe which other books by the same author they have read, they will definitely fumble. They only know what they call 'the story of Okonkwo.' So where our parents failed, the mobile library took space - most kids would crowd on the cartoons or magazine sections and did not really have the patience to read a whole book.

Still that's information and powerful.

The current African is different. Not only are we reading books outside exams, we are buying our kids books that are non-examinable.

Not only are we trying to read, we are writing books. You can no longer just name African writers born and bred and living in Africa with the palm of your hands.

Whenever I travel it's not uncommon to see an African reading a book in flight. On Vacation it's not uncommon to see an African reading a book while sunbathing.

In Kenyan bookstores you will find more and more African writers, on the shelves telling stories that are familiar to us, stories that look like us.

We are watching podcasts, webinars, documentaries, discovery - we are curious.

We are having more and more Africans win literary awards and that in itself is progress for motherland.

For the longest time, the stories of our heroes whether it is Mandela, or Biko, or Sankara, Wole Soyinka or even the Congo have been written by non-Africans. As we change the tide, It would be great to read about Africa from Africans.

Dad valued education and he valued books and the one thing he never hesitated for me to do, was to read.

Dad was a very positive man, even in his dark pit, he could afford to make promises.

This one time, I was doing my homework on the floor, he looked long and hard at me and I caught him at it. I knew it was not about him helping with homework, Dad never ever helped anyone with homework.

I do not have a single memory of my dad sitting to do my homework with me. In my generation we did not have the teacher/ parent/child involvement when it comes to school work, teachers did what teachers did, parents did what parents did, kids did what they did which was homework – I gave up on asking him questions to do especially with science as he would also ask me what I thought.

So on this day he spontaneously declared that if I topped exams he would buy me a Wimpy.

Anytime we were in the Central Business District(CBD) and this was rare, we would pass by these fancy restaurants. They had floor to roof pane glass walls, and if you looked in from outside, they had pictures of nice looking food. Food we had never eaten; they showed burgers, hot dogs, some of the cleanest fries I had ever seen, potatoes with no blemish. The fries we always got were from a back street location called Luthuli, they were dirt cheap but served really generous portions, there was nowhere to sit and you would eat standing. There is an explanation to the generous portion - you would have to filter off half the portion if you are choosy on clean or blemished fries, but they served, we always left fulfilled.

But in Wimpy were families that seemed well put together, fathers with pot bellies and dangling car keys on their hands, mothers who seemed well taken care of and kids who looked happy, confident and assured.

Dad would explain methodically that a hot dog was not dog meat and that a burger should be eaten one layer after the other.

These families operated in these restaurants like it was the norm, they looked bored even. They also had nice clothes on, most probably from clothing stores and not thrifts where we shopped and carried all the lice and ticks home, they were the same kids we saw on the merry go rounds swinging every Christmass as we cheered on.

I longed to eat at Wimpy.

So this time when I had passed exams I reminded him of the promise. I only did so for the record, but I knew it wasn't going to happen.

That weekend he told me to wear my best dress,we set off in the CBD and we walked straight into the Wimpy. And for the first time I was looking outside through the glass.

Dad was asking for instructions and I realised it was his first time too, and they explained to him how you press, pay then wait for your food to pop up.

We waited and our number came up and Dad went to fetch my burger and fries. He only bought one. I asked him where his was and he said he was still full from last night's meal.

So I carried on eating my burger while he tasted a bit of this, a bit of that and at the end of the day he ate half my meal!

We set back home.

I narrated my Wimpy experience to everyone who cared to listen as Dad munched on a piece of boiled maize and tea in amusement.

One evening, we were just settling in when auctioneers came hunting for Dad's scalp.

Dad had not been paying rent for over six months and the landlord had it. If anything his first tenant Nyasamia, with whom the lease had been drawn had left 2 years earlier.

The dam gave way.

You have to be actively watching to realise just how auctioneers can be ruthless, they took whatever was there ,and it was really nothing of financial value; our stove, our cutlery, my matress, Dad's bed, our stools. They took our clothes including my school uniform.

To this day, I do not like the sound of furniture being moved. Both Philip and I can live in the same house for ages until we absolutely have to move. The sounds of stuff being bundled out, sounds of wood, metal, crockery, glass breaking and the mayhem that ensued since they hired casuals to help with the moving remained seared in our memories.

They took my Shakespearian books.

They took books I had borrowed from the mobile library.

And they threw us out.

Reduced in volume but not in spirit Dad walked with us from door to door to his friends who told him they could not accommodate us.

Our little sister had to go to her relatives in Huruma estate as she was too young for that life.

We settled in a shack next to a compost pit, the ugliness of the slum life embracing us, bowed buildings, shattered windows, planks held together by rope, moisture rising from festering gutters, uneven roads that puffed up dust clouds every time a car upset them

I had to go back to boarding as I was on the first term of three of my final year of Primary preparing for High School.

When first term ended, I really needed to go back and find out how the two were doing. I did not leave them in a good place, in fact it was a slum.

Somehow to a child, the present parent is so important no matter how bad the situation is.

Kids in boarding schools hardly sleep the night before closing day, from the excitement and anticipation of going back home to eat their mum's home cooked meals, reuniting with siblings and friends from the estates, to the coziness of home. I did not have those to look forward to though, but I was looking forward to seeing my Dad and little brother.

Kids wake up so early and start waiting for their parents to pick them, and some parents arrive as early as 4am in the morning.

Dawn came and more parents came, around 11am is the climax most parents who live near the school and do not have to travel far arrive at this point, they took their kids.

By lunch hour parents of far flung areas who had to travel six hours arrive they took their kids.

We can now count each other in the school and the school matron who has had a long term and is hoping to finally go on holiday is exhausted, she admonishes you back to the dining begrudgingly.

"Where are your parents? Nobody budgeted for your food today." 4pm arrives and it's now a crisis. 5, the very late parent who got a mishap arrives. 6, you are alone in the school. 7, you are now summoned to the convent where you spend the rest of the holiday.

A month later, kids open school and you hope they will not realise you were in school the whole time.

I soon realised it was better for me to rejoin Drama despite that it was my final year and I needed to concentrate in school, because the nationals were held in the capital, and I would not have to go back and if fare was the problem at least the CBD was a walking distance from wherever Dad lived.

Maybe I was a talented poet, or dancer or actor or maybe I was performing to get home.

The cast was performing to earn certificates, I was performing to go home.

It was always obvious that I would sail past the provincials to the nationals.

So on the day those of us qualified to the nationals were taking the trip to the capital, the bus would first drive through Kisumu, at times even make a stop - and Kisumu was the city where mum worked. The bus would then proceed to Nairobi and as we entered the city that was all too familiar to me, I only needed to finish with performances and see how I would get home. I always tried to write a letter to Dad through his friend's address informing him I would be performing and that he only needed to pick me up from the KICC and no money was required.

My peers, who had less roles than mine, would be performing and their parents would come backstage to give them a pat and encourage them, they would be in the crowds. I once saw the whole family of one extra who did not have a role unless any of us fell ill, come backstage and pray for her.

I kept looking to see if Dad was in the mass of crowds.

I won a national award, actually quite a few but nobody showed up.

I was always a hero being feted by strangers.

But even more hilarious, once in the previous year I had travelled back to school upcountry from Nairobi because nobody came to pick me after the competition and the school could not just leave me in the streets of the capital.

I mildly understood these mishaps by Dad. I remember earlier in Class 7, I stayed home for two months into a term without going to school for lack of both bus fare and school fees. Since there was an exam to be done to issue index numbers,

I sat it quite late and got index 27 yet I was a top student. This number was very important in my time especially for composition ranking. We were made to believe some examiners were biased just by looking at the index number. They would read one's composition more keenly if your index number was among the top.

Dad was wading through a murky financial swampland, with nowhere to live at some point and he probably figured I was better off living with nuns.

I had a huge debt in fee balance but the sisters of Mary, God bless their soul, did not really bring that up.

Dad was in the CBD trying out anything and everything to at least take care of Philip even gave him to one of my maternal cousins who was a bachelor for a while.

Usually when kids in Africa are seating exams, parents send them success cards. Success cards come in normal sized card with words of encouragement. They mean a lot to candidates in terms of boosting their morale to perform but they are also a flex of love from friends, parents and one's crew.

We had all sorts of success cards, from the tiny ones that costed 5 shillings to slightly bigger ones that costed around 50 shillings and to the ultimate that were not only big but had tunes when you opened them.

I received so many success cards ,easily the most, from fellow pupils. I was popular enough as I had spent my time in school as the time keeper, won the school so many awards in poetry and was best actress three years running, was also in the school dance that took awards year in year out nationally. I was also a top performer in class and would at times make a living from the rich kids doing their homework, and I did have quite a lot of friends - I think I learnt the art of co-existing quite early in life.

I got cards from my peers, from pupils below my class but I was waiting for two particular cards.

Any letters or cards were usually announced in the parade after assembly and it's obvious we could see the big cards and really admire whoever's name would be mentioned.

There were pupils who could receive up to 20 cards in a day, and I was one of them but all were from fellow pupils.

To this day, I do not know if they pitied me or if I was popular, I never really got to know.

Days went by, cards kept coming until the very last day and I was now really worried because I had not received a single card from the person I most hoped it would come from.

On the very last day among the big cards, my name was mentioned.

I took the card casually, trying to hide its importance. I also did not open it up immediately like how other kids would yank their cards open and show us who gifted them that bigly. I wanted that moment for myself, a treasure to be unwrapped at a quiet moment but also partly, I wasn't sure who it came from, it could be my English teacher, Mr Ram, who I adored so much, or the Sisters of Mary who I was family to, or my own mother. This may just have been it, this she must have remembered.

It was not like Dad to send a card, he was going through so much financial distress. I just wanted to seat the exam, join him and finish with this chapter of my life – Mum on the other hand was less than 100 kms away and she had the means and I knew she would send a card, she really was that kind of person.

I settled down in the dormitory, on my bed alone and tore open the card carefully.

There it was, at the end.

'Your loving Dad' and in it he had inserted a 100-shilling note.

Dad did not add any words to the card like most people do, you know.

I thought he would have said how he was doing, had we got a place to live? How is my brother? Were they okay?

I took the note, walked to the canteen and bought myself a loaf of bread and a cold Fanta and walked back to my bed.

I got so many cards but this card meant so much to me. I was balancing tears as I feasted on this loaf of bread and downed it with a cold Fanta. I could feel tears on my gum mixing up with the soda as I swallowed hard.

I can't quite place this emotion whether I was happy that Dad sent a card or that I was sad that mum did not or that I had lowered my expectations of Dad.

The sight of me eating bread and Fanta surprised the pupil whose bed was next to mine and she asked if the school had offered candidates bread and Fanta.

I hung the card my Dad sent me at the board of my metallic bed wide open for everyone to see it.

It sang and shrilled itself out.

I was ready to face this exam

THE CALLING LETTER

I left the sisters of Mary, Mukumu Girls Boarding Primary School having lots of experience with a well balanced view of religion and religiosity, people who dedicate their whole lives to their faith, the ultimate lesson of giving back and I must say the hippy side of Catholics; whether smoking or imbibing on wine when most other religions are more hypocritical on this front.

I lived with the nuns quite a bit and I learnt the community, sisterhood and their coded language, something that would shape my life in the future. The convent was aware I would definitely make the school's top five national examinations but probably not sure I would make the cut for a national school because they were very few anyway. They were only about eighteen with only seven being girls' schools that had limited slots for every district. One district would have up to half a million candidates and this created a very competitive situation where only the creme de la creme made it. One could be top in a school but rank 100 in the district, locking oneself out of any national school.

Being a top institution in Kenya, Mukumu always churned out about 3 students in a year to national schools. Long before we sat for our exams, I was offered a place in the sister school. The Sacred Heart Mukumu Girls High School, a provincial boarding School which admitted brilliant students who did not qualify for national schools.

I already had a role in the high school play in readiness for the next year given I was quite the star in the neighbouring primary school. I was even offered full scholarship if I were to accept to pursue the option of being a nun if it was my calling.

That December after completing Primary School, I joined my family at the shack near the compost pit.

I was having a terrible episode of pains in my tummy.

And it had lasted for a few days now, Dad was wondering what could be the problem as paracetamol did not seem to help.

I went to the loo and I saw the red strip. I was on my period.

I was as surprised as I was relieved since I was among the very last people among my peers to see her period.

I left the toilet and announced, amused, "Dad I just started my periods."

"What, Really? How do you know?" I went back to the washroom, wiped a strip and brought it back to him.

"Here…Look!"

"Gosh, go flush that away!" He said while shielding his eyes and I laughed that I sat on the floor. He looked at me thoughtfully and said "We will need to get you some sanitary pads."

We owed the store guy money and he thought we were coming to pay, only to realise we were borrowing some more. He frowned exasperated. But when Dad mentioned we needed Stay Free, his fat wife who was counting money behind him like she had just woken up from the nightmare of poverty looked at us, and then sternly at the shopkeeper, and the shopkeeper hurriedly fished a packet from a box. We did not get Always which has been the brand of choice in most of Africa for a long while. We got a different brand that was cheaper but an upgrade from cotton wool.

He was standing there, having the packet wrapped on a newspaper while women were looking at Dad and I stood behind him amused. On reaching home, dad summoned me to get a pant.

"Not this one with a hole mami?"

"I have three, I am wearing one, the other is outside to dry."

"Ok, my goodness… ok, ok let's do this." He said, defeated.

Then he explained, like how you would the Nuclear codes to a POTUS, how to use a sanitary towel.

I of course understood how it was done, we had been taught in school, and I had seen some of my peers do it as I was in a boarding school.

But I let him shine in that moment because he prided himself in impacting me with any form of knowledge.

He was elaborate on how many times I should shower in a day, and how many times I should change the sanitary towel which got me giggling.

And then he got to the topic of sex education.

Very carefully he explained that if I dared play with boys, I would have a child.

Being a reader, I probably knew more about theoretical sex than he would ever know, but I was stringing him along to make his life more difficult.

"So by playing you mean if I play soccer I get pregnant?"

"No, soccer is fine, but if you allow the boys to touch you, you will be pregnant"

"So now I should not touch either you or Philip considering you are boys?"

"No, I am your father and Philip is your brother."

"So how exactly does this work Dad? If a boy touches my palm in church do I get pregnant, that moment when the priest says we shake hands, I will get pregnant?"

Dad struggled and fumbled though sex education and I was in stitches internally. Very rich, for a serial polygamist.

In modern Africa, the sex topic has been left for kids to figure out from books, TV, radio, songs peers or magazines. Go figure.

Traditional Africa had systems and structures that were used to usher youth and ultimately adulthood.

Boys would be gathered, taken to an exclusive location and spend a fortnight there. They would receive advise and lessons from elders and uncles.

This included how to be responsible, how to be a man, seduction, sex, fatherhood, dispute resolution, provision, accountability, respect to self, to elders and to peers.

It was so intense that some sort of initiation would take place.

It could be circumcision or if my tribe the Luo, men would have four of their lower teeth knocked off.

Girls would go through the same rite of passage. On the side of girls though, the lessons were geared mostly to support marriage: bodily cleanliness, cleaning your home, cleaning your kids, how to cater to your man in bed, sexual prowess, submission, pregnancy, cooking.

And for a long time these systems held.

With modernisation, rural to urban migration, the empowerment of women, the breaking down of communal living, these systems and structures are past gone. Africans now live in urban areas, mostly in seclusion from their kin, different areas, different estates depending on their earnings that it's difficult to track one another. The initial notion that women lived their lives to end up in marriage no longer holds even in Africa. Marriage is now a choice of human interaction and fulfillment.

Women empowerment and feminism have taken root and marriage is no longer a survival tool. The fear that you would outgrow your age at home as a woman as you could not own a home, a house, could not live alone - are all draconian and outgrown.

And so we have with us a generation of kids who depend entirely on their parents for sex education or initiation and their parents do not have the manual because it was not handed over and prefer not to delve into the uncomfortable topic –it's left to teachers in school and books, churches and whatever material the children will find.

Most African societies have not provided a structure even for men to vent, to fellowship and deal with mental health.

On the other hand, and rightfully so, girls are being empowered to go to school, to go for jobs, to be entrepreneurs and have structures for venting, fellowship and mentorship and now we have a generation of disillusioned men and very strong women in most societies of Africa.

We are also seeing more and more women led or matriarchal families and societies in Africa. Families where the girls are the financial backbone while the boys follow.

Menstrual periods joined the myriad of challenges I had to survive. Sanitary pads were not a guarantee. And this is replicated in many parts of Africa.

It first starts with the issue of cramps, and there is no medicine for that. Ponstan Forte and Buscopan plus are available but not affordable and so you have to endure the pain for five days monthly – depending on the diet, the pain would be unbearable to the point I really could not go to class.

There are traditional herbs given apparently to deal with the problem but they also did not work for me.

In boarding schools, if you run out of pads, you would resort to tissue, or cotton wool, or your school socks. I did use socks many times as I recall, and the problem was that it did not have retaining power.

A few drips, it got wet and soiled my uniform.

Cotton wool had better retaining power but was infection prone and not affordable.

Tissue was really bottom shelf because, it was costly, had no retention power and would also give you an infection.

Socks worked for me because I could wash them in the night when it was dark and nobody could see my indignity.

Later, all these issues that associated with periods affected my learning, whether it was the anticipation, the pain, lack of sanitary towels and the shame of washing socks, or just managing the flow as classes ensue, being conscious of your clothes when you rise, or during outdoor events like PE.

There is more trauma, if for instance, a girl with my circumstance is in a mixed school of boys and girls.

If you soiled your uniform or desk and the boys saw it, it would take days for you to recover from the shame and stigma.

In some rural areas, girls just don't go to school 5 days of every month to alleviate the problem, and we have not yet tackled lack of water.

The problems poor girls in Africa face with their periods is a another serious challenge, also not beyond the bounds of human ingenuity to solve.

Across Africa, the one favor governments will do for little girls is to make available, free of charge sanitary towels, give free education but also take care of the sanitary towels – girls are not fully free if their bodies are trapped by periods.

There have been many initiatives to try alleviate this problem, whether it's free sanitary pads donations which are not sustainable because Periods are a 30 year or so problem that cannot go away by someone donating 3 packets, picking their photo opportunity and leaving.

There are organisations now pushing the period caps, and sanitary pads that are washable (a better version of the sock).

But ultimately governments will need to come up with a lasting and sustainable way to deal with periods and the challenge girls face.

COURAGE. HONOR. INDUSTRY

When the National Exam results are announced in Kenya, High Schools select kids and send them an invitation letter.

I did not receive one letter, I received two.

The letters were type written my name, and we both looked at them like foreign objects then looked at each other before opening them in our shack.

I had been called to not one, but two National Schools. The first ever feat in my family.

My Dad was over the moon; he kept staring at me like a stranger, then shaking his head while whistling.

Philip, sensing something good had happened to us, kept asking if we had gotten some money and if we were going to buy ice cream.

We were excited when we opened the two letters. One was from the Alliance Girls High School and the other was from Moi Girls High School Eldoret.

My excitement vanished momentarily. Because looking at the fee structures, we would not even afford a term at Moi, Alliance was actually worse. High School fees were yet to be subsidised.

Peering through the fee structure had me laughing. It was coming to easily four times what we were already struggling with, and that's not including the shopping of uppity stuff like tennis racket, badminton set, swimming cap... I had never been in a swimming pool all my life.

There was Alliance which I dared not even think about, it was beyond my reach, but I wondered about Moi.

The Highlands, Moi Girls Eldoret - would take top candidates from Rift Valley, Western and Nyanza provinces, a whole half of the country because most of the rest of the Girls National Schools were centred along the Capital or Central Kenya where missionaries first landed.

Highlands was built by the barons of the colonial era who owned ranches of wheat, barley and maize to supply the crown. It was originally, a school for white kids, exclusively.

This was not a school where you will falter with school fees for there is a long list of kids waiting who are equally sharp and with parents ready to write a cheque not for one term, but for 4 years and may donate lab equipment too, most who feel they have unfairly got the Provincial Boarding School 1 calling letter.

Not a school where you do not show up to pick your kid on closing day. I mean, I knew how we do. This was forever beyond our reach.

So I told Dad I had committed myself to the Convent and would not be going to either school but instead would go to Mukumu Girls High School. Mukumu, although a provincial school, was a more plausible choice. I was under the wings of the nuns, infact I had already started my life there, I had part of the school play with me.

I realised if we falter, I could miss out even on this chance.

Dad started walking with my calling letter to every office of anyone he knew in the city begging for fees. He reckoned it was easier to convince his friends with the Moi figure than the mind boggling Alliance Girls fees. He was on the street talking to anyone who cared to listen, sat among the social whirlings of Luo men in the CBD angling for a deal, and the self-styled political analysts who usually gathered to discuss Raila Odinga around Uchumi House, City Hall and Ambassador Hotel.

He would pitch up my calling letter and after the debate people would contribute.

His optimism was bordering delusion and lot of people offered him advise to take me to alternative schools because they felt the begging would not be sustainable in the end and could posibly interrupt my education. They gave him numbers of head teachers in Provincial Boarding 1 schools like Lwak, Ng'iya or Ulanda that were doing well in the Luo Nyanza region.

For most of his circle, Moi Girls, Eldoret was a school they only read about in the papers when exam results were out and had not heard of anyone's kid they knew who ever went to such schools.

After completing Primary School, I started visiting my maternal cousin Sammy K'Opiyo who had just graduated with a Bachelor of Pharmacy degree and had just started work. I admired his academic achievements as a man who beat the odds to become a most sought after medical professional in the country.

Daktari's mum (my mother's sister) died when he was still very young. Lacking proper guidance, he decided not to go to school, instead ventured into the mining fields of Macalder in Nyatike, Migori County. Our uncle Steve Osieyo would hear none of it and he took Sammy to our grandmother back in Ugenya. Sammy was forced to go back to school where he emerged a top student ending up in Moi High School Kabarak and the University of Nairobi. Pharmacy was still a profession for the very few. By the time he was finishing his course, Sammy was attracting job offers from leading organisations.

He lived in a massive 3 bedroomed house, own compound and Dad only allowed Philip and I to visit him after visiting himself and confirming it was a safe place.

The irony.

My cousin Dr. Sammy K'opiyo had no idea how we were struggling, we never told anyone about that, and in that December when I visited him, and showed him my results, he was so proud of me that he told everyone about it.

Then mum appeared.

Although Dad had made very good strides in getting me fees, Sammy wrote the cheque that paid for my first term fees at Moi Girls, Eldoret, Dad banked his money to be used in subsequent terms.

Mum visited Sammy and so we reconnected there. She offered to take me to High School.

Dad did not even resist her taking me. He instead pitched for himself.

"Tell your mum time has gone by, her kids are growing old, tell her to come back home."

A message I conveyed earnestly and mum stopped that train and its occupants with;

'Tell that man, the only room me and him can share is a morgue when one of us is coming to confirm the other is dead'

I walked into the gates of Highlands resolutely sour faced, I recall not being happy because I did not have Dad next to me, and I did not have his entourage of boys blasting into the school; we did not listen to any Franco or Okach Biggy.

My mother and I were impeded by a wall of silence and unified only by a common desire to be elsewhere. She tried to give me an embrace and it was awkward because I couldn't remember when she ever held me. There was pain involved anytime it came to her.

It was a beautiful school; aristocratic in colonial architechture, and resembling a university complex.

After processing I was selected to a dormitory called Sergoit named after the lumpy silhouetted hills in Uasin Gishu Plateau whose crowns flare majestically with haloes as they catch the Rift Valley setting sun.

The dormitory came with parquet floors,fire place,hot water and bath tubs and TV set in the common rooms. Form 1s only shared 4 per room and as soon as you hit form 2 you got your private room.

The standards in this school were higher than all public universities in Kenya and was the most cosy place I had ever lived in.

I was very unfamiliar with that sort of bounty.

The head girl's apartment was also in Sergoit. This student was living a better life than most of you today as I write - 602 sq feet apartment, en suite bath, and tub, living room, dining area, even a foyer to welcome guests.

At Sergoit, in the room I had been assigned, I met two ladies who had arrived earlier than me and were settling down unpacking and placing their stuff in the closets.

At the edge of our bare and new mattresses were neatly folded sheets, blanket, bed cover and pillow which the dorm matron had placed, a very sharp contrast from Mukumu where you reported carrying your matress, bucket and wares like a refugee fleeing war.

Highlands was definitely a place I would not wither at.

After exchanging niceties, mum said, "Meet Deb, she is a very friendly lady."

We were climbing down the stairs for me to accompany mum to the gate because we were done.

All the tense chit chat had piled up like a dry kindling waiting for a matchstick which I provided at the end.

I asked her, "How do you know that I am friendly?"

"I gave birth to you, that's how..."

"You don't know the first thing about me, Pam!"

"You could at least call me mum."

"Don't be ridiculous."

I surprised myself, because a few years earlier, I completely adored this woman who now I could not wait to leave my sight.

And my attitude towards her most definitely polarised us even more when she was probably now trying to meet me halfway.

We did not hug when we reached the gate. It was a very awkward goodbye and I walked back into the dorm, did not unpack my stuff, I just lay there on the bare matress and dug my face on the sponge.

The cuts had outlived the scars and so I began to sob.

My roommates who had never been to any boarding school, infact they hailed from the prestigious Testimony School of Eldoret from their uniforms, a private school, consoled me. I could hear them say;

"It's probably her first time in a boarding school, poor girl already missing home."

THE UNRAVELLING

By sheer coincidence, when I just began my life in Moi Girls, Eldoret, Dad was lucky to land himself a job with a leading law firm in Nairobi. He basically did administrative and other operational tasks. Apparently, the good lead partner in the law firm, Mr. Ambrose Rachier thought the business of begging to take a child through a national school was unsustainable.

With a steady source of income, but still could not quite afford deposit, Dad moved us into a guest house in Eastleigh.

He rented two rooms because Mikayi's kids had now joined us.

Life was better, we could afford three meals a day, he was able to take all 11 of us to school consistently and this is a lot, one of us was in college,4 in High school,2 in Primary and the rest were still in Pre School.

Dad still contributed to his children's lives, even the ones who had left with their mothers.

As a standard, all of us even in our adulthood remember that every opening day of school, he would call everybody's mother and schedule an appointment to meet at the city center.

The first ones to arrive were quite unlucky because it meant waiting for siblings from different areas of Nairobi. When we were all gathered up, he took us to Masters Café, a decent restaurant by our standards and he got us fries, burgers and soda.

Thereafter he took all of us shopping for our school needs.

Dad did this consistently without fail for as long as he held this job.

He did quite well that he even built a homestead back at home.

You see, Dad had built his two wives simbas in his father's compound and was supposed to move them eventually, but they stayed there a long time because life was happening to Dad in Nairobi including marrying my mother, Nyasamia, Nyaseme and was now single again.

Dad eventually started visiting the rural area and was being admonished to move his homestead, to build a proper home.

His elder brothers had even identified a piece of land where he could build for his two wives. The other three so called 'Nairobi wives' (including my mum) had acquired a life of their own. So one December, he decided to move his homestead. We were present as his children which means children from the Mikayi's house, Philip and I.

Festivities started in the morning with prayer and the slaughtering of a lamb in the weak morning sun. Blood sipped into the thirsty cotton black soil.

Dad's elder brothers pointed out where the Mikayi's home would be built, where Nyakendu's home would be, where my mother's house would be, Nyaseme, Nyasamia respectively if they ever decided to return.

The main house would face the gate with the cow shed at the heart of the compound.

I noted though, that only the Mikayi was present, our second mother Nyakendu was nowhere to be seen.

A spear split the earth, tilling and burrowing the earth to lay foundation for the Mikayi ensued.

The second spear was to hit the second apportionment for the home of Nyakendu but Dad refused which symbolised he wasn't going to build a home for her, effectively leaving her at his father's compound as an outcast.

A fierce wind swept across the bare land, it came from nowhere, a gale born in the moment out of a clear sky and we had to hold on to our buckets and lesos.

Defiantly, Dad moved on to my mother's apportionment.

Dad's elder brothers inquired why this was so. He said he wasn't moving forward with Nyakendu and had told her severally to go back to her village as the marriage had ended.

His brothers insisted he must hit the spear and Nyakendu must move to her new home.

Dad stood his ground.

One of his elder brothers, I recall, did not take this particularly well and stood up straight at him placing the spear on his hand. Dad pushed him away, he lost balance, fell and when he got up he charged at Dad and a scuffle began.

The two men wrestled to the ground amongst cries from the builders and the witnesses who had come to the ceremony.

Outside the gate, an old woman who could barely walk upright was also dirging and chanting, she so happened to be Nyakendu's mother and was asking why Dad wasted her daughter's time all those years to do this to her.

Nyakendu had gone back to her village a day earlier and informed her people that Dad was building his homestead and that she wasn't invited.

I recall the old woman, she could not even shed tears while she cried,she used a whistle to cry and when she got some strength, named the cows Dad had paid for her daughter.

'Nyasoko, Mier and Nyawich.'

With her were three baffled cows tied to the Otho, which she was demanding that Dad must take to fully divorce the daughter and were replacements for Nyasoko, Mier and Nyawich.

Dad said he was not interested.

The insults started.

Dad was asked how it was possible for him to abandon his wife yet he was out there collecting kids from all over that did not belong to him.

That was a tension point and everyone kept quiet, the question sank into the ground.

Dad said he was not bringing a prostitute to his new home and the people who had been 'visiting her hut' at night should continue to do so,he had left her for them.

"The people who had been visiting her hut in the night" was a calculated arrow directed at someone in the compound. Rumour had it the particular brother who was most incensed, had been visiting her hut a little more than was comfortable, a little too late than is usual for a brother in law.

'If you have abandoned your wives, who will take care of them? Who is supposed to feed them? Because somebody will!' Came the answer from one of his brothers.

Maybe he was referring to a common tradition that it was okay for your brother to sleep with your wife if you were unable to give her children. In a traditional setting this would happen if you were impotent, dead or just missing in action. That was the essence of wife inheritance. But Dad was a modern chap who no longer identified or subscribed to the old ways. What happened was nasty, messy and embarrassing because homes should not be built in that kind of acrimony.

The Mikayi's home was built, my mother's house was built which was ironic because she wasn't even interested unlike Nyakendu, she was out there living her best life but Dad was here busy building her a home.

Nyakendu left our village and dissapeared to a centre near her village; she was a migogo and was no longer accepted in her Dad's homestead, she was now to live her life as an outcast.

In the years she was married to Dad, she never once had a child. And that was also fodder for more speculations on her that her womb had been cursed and she could not bear any children, "she is damaged goods." Dads friends said, "by the time a woman stays this long barren she has tried everything including having kids with your brothers so the offspring is not far off."

I believe these are the reasons she was discarded, because she did not bear children, she did not do her assignment. Women came after her and bore kids even boys, that's how women who had been out on the street were actually getting a home - I felt sorry for her.

I was in my teenage-hood, and started struggling with identity – The words Nyaseme had planted in my mind kept ringing and I was questioning a lot.

What did she mean I should be returned to my people?

Dad and Philip were my people.

I noticed that unlike everyone in my family, I had very big eyes, I had full dimples and the most distinct of them all was the gap on my teeth, I also had a high forehead and light hair. I explained to friends who asked, that I took a lot from my mother's side.

I wished I could look more like my siblings.

It did not make things easy that mum also disappeared after her first stint of taking me to school, I thought we were starting to build something but I also recognised that my attitude on that first day stunk.

I realised I needed to make amends and draw her in again.

I wrote her many letters about life in general, performance in school and my thoughts.

She never responded.

I was constantly in problems while in school, I was in so many disciplinary meetings and each year of my high school I faced a suspension.

I was very strong willed, very strong in opinion and beliefs most which were non conformist. I was very clear in thought and communicated them in the most aggressive manner, years and years of reading books to do with nationalism, Marxist and Mao dogma had me existing in a revolutionary rebel mode in a High School that had rules to be followed.

I was constantly working hard to be in trouble.

At Sergoit, my school dorm, I had a huge photo of Raila Odinga, something that was against the rules in school. It was also in bad taste as Moi Girls High School happens to be in Rift Valley, a turf of Kalenjins who belonged to Moi's tribe. In fact, the school was named after the very president Raila was opposing.

Moi in his wisdom of lack of it, changed the name of Highlands to his and I had a problem with that.

Several attempts by the dorm matron to have me remove Raila's photo failed since not a single prefect could stand up to me.

My argument was if you have Moi, if you have Mandela, I may as well have Raila, No?...Yes.

They let me be.

Raila's father, Jaramogi Oginga Odinga had passed on leaving his party of Ford – Kenya.

The natural next leader was Kijana Wamalwa who was the then Vice chair but Raila would not hear of it, he challenged Wamalwa for the seat and when there were irregularities during the nomination, Raila walked out of the party and formed NDP effectively migrating with all Luos from Ford K to NDP.

The death of Jaramogi Oginga Odinga also made Raila the defacto undisputed leader of the Luo community.

During holidays all my dad talked about was how Raila was going to annihilate his opponents in the 1997 election, the first time he ever vied for the Presidential seat – He came third after President Moi and Mwai Kibaki but retained his National Assembly seat.Lots of teachers gave up on me, in fact most preferred to steer off my path.

In Highlands unlike most if not all Kenyan Public Schools then, corporal punishment had been banned from inception and all teachers could do is counsel or send you to the 'naughty corner.' You can imagine how happy I was, I pushed the limits.

During a lesson especially on Literature, I would raise my hand up to ask a question or give my critical thoughts but mostly teachers would choose the next hand up and ignore mine, and carry on as if I did not exist - they always knew I was going to come up with a controversial view, it always made the class laugh.

First week when I joined High School, it happened to be the term when countrywide drama festivals occur.

How the school came up with a play was all dormitories were tasked with writing and producing a play, which we would compete on within the school and the winning play then represented the school for the countrywide competition with maybe modifications from teachers and change of actors from the school's pool of talent.

On my first night, as my house Sergoit was practising their play, I watched keenly and saw nothing worth calling a winning play. I then introduced myself to the house and wrote them a new play which I personally took charge of. It won and went ahead to represent the school.

Four years in a row, I won best actress. I had graduated to actually writing scripts and poems, and would represent the school in all these disciplines and excel.

As the school was a Moi project, he visited a lot - I was the one who wrote him poems and presented which was hilarious because if I wasn't presenting a poem to him praising him, I was being judged in a disciplinary committee for terming him a despot.

There were teachers who wondered how I could be massively talented in the arts and creatives, could pass an exam without actually seating in class but be this conflicted internally.

An antithesis of my own self.

One such teacher was Mr. Bett who became my class teacher in my third year and also my Physics and Math Teacher.

"I want to know why you are so angry" was his opener one day when he summoned me during prep.

He approached me from a very different angle, not of judgement or reproach but from understanding and curiosity.

He was quiet a lot and I spoke a lot.

He continually did so and eventually I started opening up to him.

He confided in the principal, Madam Hellen Cheramboss and together they made it their mission to ensure I had a venting pipe.

I also was one of very few students who took up Fine Art, as I found it to be soothing. In fact, we were only two students in my year who chose art.

Students hated art because of the unpredictability of the main exam scores; when it comes to practicals it's hard to qualify methodology used to grade your painting or work of art as a creative since everyone perceives Art differently so in a system where everyone is chasing an A, Art is left for the risk takers.

My Arts teacher, Mrs. Bett happened to be wife of Mr. Bett (I know I struck gold).

I suspect they would discuss me over dinner, because Mrs. Bett would let me be, she was an amazing motherly figure who was kind and soft and patient in the art room, and in her I found solace.

Mrs. Bett belonged to the Art room where everything is creatively beautiful.

The art room was quiet like a gallery and every once in a while she would play soft soothing music as we went on our business of painting, I loved it.

She was always very calm, and thoughtful behind her thick rimmed glasses asserting a quiet authority.

There are days I would paint some very calm paintings and at times when rebellious spirits surged through me like tidal waves I would make some angry art.

She would quietly ask "What are you trying to project with this painting?" And I would be quiet, and she would quietly move on to the next student.

Teachers are such an integral part of a child's growth, as far as I recall my earliest heroes and influencers have been teachers from Mrs. Macharia who took me in for my audacity ,to Miss Nyamu the English teacher who first said I could recite a poem just from how I read a story book to the class both formerly of St. Anne's Girls Primary School, to Sister Joyceline Mukolwe who accommodated me when I was stranded, to Mr. Ram my English teacher at Primary who said he expected nothing less than a straight A from me, to Mr. Amboso my Drama teacher who said I could act, dance, recite a poem "You can do it all!" All from Mukumu Girls Primary Boarding School to Madam Cheramboss, Mr. and Mrs. Bett of Moi Girls High School, Eldoret whose story I am telling.

Where there is no hope, Teachers will still see a speck, a glint in a child and will try to nurture it, or they will mine it.

Mr. Bett spent many prep nights counselling me, talking to me and I recall on the last day of school when I sat my last exam, he had the following advise for me "You will go to college, study, do not join politics because you will be shot dead,' and we laughed...then he added seriously "you have a story to tell, ensure you tell it."

Dad also took on so much bills that he spread himself thin and since my fees were the highest, he started struggling at third year and many 'send homes' later, Madam Cheramboss decided to just keep me in school, she took me as a project that at some point I had to live with her. She also wrote to my mother a few times wondering how she could help.

Nobody in the school would have suspected this as she sought to protect me, and she was also protecting calls of being complicit when dealing with me. Already talks of 'Is Deb above the law?' were doing their rounds, but the truth is three teachers had inside knowledge and were handing me grace in my storm.

All disciplinary matters that I was called for, it's my Dad who attended.

Moi Girls Eldoret on a good day is six hours off Nairobi and we would travel the journey back together.

In the disciplinary meetings, Dad would seat pensively listening to the charges against me, his eyes firmly pinned on the ground, and would insist that I was a good girl, that I was going through adolescent stage and would pass the stage.

I felt sorry to have to put him through all this trouble, but there was a force in me that would not let me be; in the day I was strong and brave and was really popular but when night came I would be lonely and would cry a lot.

I recall one time on our journeys back to school he told me.

"Mami I am afraid if you continue like this you will not achieve your full potential."

"Full potential here means what exactly?"

"You will end up like me."

"And what is wrong with you?"

On my last year of school, I got into a nasty fight where I punched a fellow student who had christened me a nickname.

Principal Cheramboss sent me home. She said, "If I put you through a board, you will be expelled, I am sending you home to rest and come back to sit your final exam as a student and not an outsider, because if you sit as an outsider it will affect your whole life."

She actually gave me fare.

I walked to the Eldoret Bus stop to get a bus to Nairobi, while the various touts were jostling for my bag and attention, and I pretended I was undecided to make them work harder, I saw a bus written Homa Bay.

Instinctively I changed my route and got into the Homa Bay bus.

I was aware my mother had got a transfer from Kisumu to Homa Bay - I knew she worked for Care Kenya International.

From the day she dropped me in school, she never returned.

I needed to find out why my letters, or even the principal's went unanswered.

I decided when I arrived, I would look for the office and trace her from there.

I arrived in Homa Bay late in the evening. Care International is a very visible brand for its branding and for all the marvellous work it has done in Africa, I found it and luckily staff lived just next to the offices.

A kind man even pointed to where mum lived.

When I knocked, nobody opened the door - I pushed it in.

There on the sofa lay a child lookalike of mum, she at first looked at me blankly which is the mirror of how I looked at her... then she called my name.

It was mum.

In the years she had disappeared, disease had eaten her to the point she could not even go to work, she was covered in scars, on her body and in her body.

My first thoughts at her sight raced to Philip. My heart sunk to my tummy and I suddenly felt a strong urge to diarrhoea,my tummy rumbled that I had to physically hold it like I had been punched.

The once beautiful exuberant woman I knew lay in a heap of bones, her hair so light and wisp that you could see her skull, her bones were jutting out against a tight skin that looked like it had been polished with a dry cloth. Amidst a nasty cough she asked me why I was there and if schools were closed already.

I told her I had come to see her. I decided I could not tell her exactly why I was here, at least not now.

I asked what was ailing her, she alluded to the fact that she was being prayed for and that someone had bewitched her.

There was a disease encyclopedia next to her that she seemed to have been poring over. Shortly after, some church members arrived, settled in, and started singing hymns and praying for her.

She did not introduce me.

Night came, I asked what she would have liked to eat as her kitchen was fully stocked, I cooked fresh fish which she tried but her appetite failed her.

My mother had done well for herself, from the moment she got the paperwork I smuggled; she got a job in International development, first as a secretary but due to her dexterity, hard work and she kept going back to school, had risen internally all the way to a Project Manager. She lived in a huge company house fully furnished with electronics that we could only dream of in our little guest house.

My mother was also quite intelligent and coherent and was socially astute she knew her way with people, you would definitely choose her for a position and you would trust her to perform.

However, the improvement of her finances was mismatched to the improvement of her personal health.

She showed me where I would sleep and then told me I would have to take the next bus to Dad very early in the morning.

As we were folding up for the night, a Nissan matatu pulled up outside her house.

A very tall handsome well-built man, walked out and into the house. The manner in which he got in suggested he was the man of the house, I stayed silent and observant.

He sat, in spite of the fact that mum barely managed to stand and hug me when I arrived, she balanced on her feet, left for the kitchen and served him food.

He ate as mum lay on the adjacent seat, wide awake covered in a sheet dotted with dried peeled skin from her wounds, her eyes egg white and out of the socket most times.

Between watching news and barely looking at either of us, he asked; "Who is this?"

"This is my niece that I told you schools at Ombogo Academy, she is on her way to Nairobi tomorrow." The next morning, I was in a bus to Nairobi and to the guest house.

When Dad arrived in the evening, he found me in tears but he was more devastated than I was.

I will never know whether it was from how I described mum's condition, or the fact that I was mum's niece or that I was home on yet again another suspension.

But what came out of his mouth was;

'If you do not like how I represent you in your hearings that you opted for your mother, maybe you should advise me how I should do it, so I do better'

I expected him to beat me.

In Africa corporal punishment was and is still a very acceptable way of raising kids and dad was big on it.

I rarely got beat because I am a good negotiator and would try to reason with him and always got away with a warning.

The last time my father ever beat me outside the returnee incident, I was twelve.

It had to do with my absentmindedness, I had food on the stove cooking, I was immersed in a book and I forgot about the food.

I was a forgetful child, I always had a lot in my mind, had a lot of things happening at the same time in there, most to do with a better life that I was living than my reality. Most times in class, my mind would be out of the window into dreamland where things were more interesting and it took teachers giving me spot exams to ensure I stayed present.

The food got burnt.

Our Mikayi was present because this was after Nyaseme's reign but she was busy attending to other duties – She was disappointed but could not beat me. Among all the step mothers that I lived with, none of them ever beat me up.

The first rule Dad made if you were to marry him; Philip and myself were off limits, if there was any disciplining to be done, it was to come from him.

I recall nights when he would arrive late in the night and would wake me up and ask "Did you eat? Did she serve you enough food?" much to the angst of step mums who did try their best under the circumstances.

So the food here was burnt and Mikayi dared not touch me, left it for dad to handle.

It was funny because my step siblings were also watching and waiting to reinforce the fact that; 'Deb gets away with murder in this house.'

Dad's authority and consistency hung in the balance and he questioned what I was doing when I should have been watching the fast draining soup. I had no answer other than that I was sorry.

He smacked me across the face.

Suddenly, I felt lonely. I did not feel pain, I felt lonely.

Which was odd because I had spent my life seeing Dad beat my siblings and now it was my turn and my world fell apart.

I sat and said, "I have never seen Dad smack any of us on the face, he has smacked me like I am not even a child of this house."

Mikayi told me never to speak like that again.

Later on in the night, Dad summoned me.

I was seated across the table when he said, "Do you know that you made a mistake today?"

"Yes."

"What happens to everyone here when they make a mistake?"

"You beat them?"

"And so I beat you up did I not?"

"You did not cane me, you smacked me across the face, I have never seen you do that."

"I am sorry, it was a reflex reaction but I am not sorry that I disciplined you, you are not above the law."

Silence.

"Your mother says there are words that came from your mouth where did you get that?"

I could not even remember what words I had said in that moment of pain and anger.

Silence.

"If I ever hear you say that again, I will die a very sad man."

Whatever it is that I said secured me from punishment, the reaction it elicited would last a lifetime because Dad never ever touched me again, it did not matter what I did, he choose the path of dialogue.

Following the incident with mum and my visit, Dad was so devastated that he went to confront mum's brothers as to why she would introduce me as her niece while I was right there.

My Uncle,Steve who was now a big shot at Red cross had to locate me and have a discussion with me opening me up again to my maternal side.

Steve and I had a relationship from when I was a very little child. Lets delve into this relationship.

Steve was second last born in my mother's family, and my mother the last born, and at some point he ended up being my nanny for a while, right after he completed High School and was to travel back to California USA to study accounting.

As a child, I remember him as a very handsome and muscular soul brother of the 70s looking guy with a big fro and loved to put on tight muscular shirts and bell bottoms, he often let his first buttons open and you could see his hairy chest.

Steve was soft spoken, and had a most amazing smile, I liked that his teeth looked like mine, he had a huge diastema on his teeth.

He would bathe me,feed me and dance with me as I loved to dance.

In Uncle Philip's house where we all abode, I recall vinyl plates with faces of Franco, Seigneur Ley and Mbilia – Rumba was probably introduced to me while I was still in my mother's womb.

So one day, someone died, I believe I was two years old or thereabout and those days news of death came in the form of a telegram.

The post charged by the letter, so the message had to be precise and concise but also legible, you would find something like '*Dani otho*' meaning 'Grandma dead' and someone would have to travel all the way to the rural area and this time its Steven who travelled.

He left for Ugenya at first light while I was asleep.

I was probably too young because I do not remember this, but this story is told over and over again.

Steven was sent in advance with money for organising the funeral, but as he was his mother's second last born and last son, he stayed with his mama for about 3 months.

On the week he left, it's said I would stand every evening by the gate silently and look out to see if he would come back, and the next week, and the next... until I stopped standing by the gate.

Three months later, I was playing with a doll on the floor when I saw Steve, who was really excited to see me.

He spread his arms so I run into them as I always did, and he had with him a paper with all manner of goodies for me.

I dropped my doll and ran urgently...away from him.

And I stunned all the adults in the room and especially him.

I ran upstairs, into one of the bedrooms and banged the door in and it locked and I started to cry bitterly until I slept.

That day it was Steve's job to come intermittently to check if I was up by calling me by all the names he had christened me... then when he heard me shift, he pushed a piece of candy under the door.

I pushed it back to him, he pushed it back, and I took it then he asked if I could share my sweet with him.

I cracked it with my teeth and pushed a dirty piece of candy under the floor.

And he started singing and dancing on the other side and I opened the door and joined him.

Eventually Steve had to go to college but this time he said a very proper goodbye and it was all good.

So now present day, I sat narrating to him what happened in Homa Bay amidst interruptions from footballers of a club where he had been elected Secretary General (Reunion) while he shed tears.

I also went to visit Mama Mpenzi who I had not seen for dog years, she was as usual very happy to see me, she had not heard from mother in years; they had a sibling fight and mum had cut her off after writing her a letter.

I read the letter mum had sent her which was in Victorian diction, you would think she went to an Ivy school.

In this letter mum accused the sister of spreading rumors that she was HIV positive.

With tears in her eyes, Mama Mpenzi defended herself to me - I come from a family of people who tear really fast. I am one of them, I will cry for a book, I will fight tears at the Maasai Mara watching a pack of lions hunt and eventually devour a buffalo sending my kids in laughter, I grieved for Ragnar Lothbrok like he was my relative when the snakes completely subdued him.

Here, we cry.

I did not think it mattered though. I told her point blank that I thought she was indeed HIV positive but in denial.

Mama Mpenzi stared at me in shock from the audacity of how the words came out of my mouth, cold and hard.

Mum was in charge of a project called *Dak Achana* that was taking care of the HIV pandemic.

Care Kenya owned a simple magazine with cartoons called the Pied Crow and my mum was among the writers.

This magazine took care of community awareness, top agenda being the HIV pandemic.

I had gotten a hold of these magazines which were being distributed even in schools. The hardest hit areas were always the Nyanza region of the luo, for many reasons including polygamy, lifestyle, and as research indicated lack of circumcision.

At this time, Luos were dying in apocalyptic proportions – almost everyone in my Dad's little groupie was dead already – it became a national crisis.

Dad jolted awake by the emergency of mum's illness, and I think he thought time was running out, sent me back to revisit.

This time mum was so bad that she was barely speaking, her husband who was operating the Matatu was also away plying the Homa Bay/Kisumu route and would only come by on Fridays.

"Mummy have you thought about what you write about?"

"What?" She asked while swatting a cloud of flies that buzzed around the red sores on her body.

"Maybe we should test for HIV?"

"You think I am HIV positive? How dare you?"

"No I just want to rule it out."

Later in the evening I realized my visit wasn't helping as I was not a doctor and sought help, I walked to the calling box and called her sister who she hadn't talked to in years, Mama Mpenzi.

In a weird turn of fate, Mama Mpenzi's wealthy ex-husband with whom they had been estranged before I was born, had also died of HIV from wherever he was.

He was an interesting man, Mr. Wellington Opiyo. He was in oil and was based in Eldoret the city my High school was in, and one time when I was thrown out of school for lack of fees, I went looking for him.

At the BP Shell offices in Eldoret, after dismissing his guards and massive German Shepherds, he asked who I was and I explained myself, he let me into his office.

I don't know what Mama Mpenzi did to this guy, but in a low tone and looking worriedly outside the window as if someone would hear his words, behind his spectacles, he explained as if giving me a leakage to a very important exam.

He confided how my mother and her sisters were toxic, and that I must do everything in my power not to be like them, he explained that their brothers had spoilt them and they did not sce the need to live with or even respect their husbands and all of them were divorcees.

And that all of them would end up single and miserable drunks and finally banished them with HIV which would be the end of them. He sent me away with a 1000 bob note.

(I had been told Mama Mpenzi would deal him blows,and would batter him, he was scared witless of her).

He however died before Mama Mpenzi and she inherited a large part, if not all of his settlement which I found hilarious given how he felt about her, and Mama Mpenzi was willing to help heal her sister if to mend their deteriorated relationship.

She travelled that very night.

She arrived at dawn, I opened for her.

And when she saw her sister, she rushed to embrace her like a saviour - they both wept bitterly, and when they came up for air, their chests rose and fell at the same time, my mother's frail body shaking like a twig while at it.

Their pain was infectious, it wrapped itself around me, my tears threatened and I left the room.

Mama Mpenzi wailed like someone had died and neighbours who had been waiting for the imminent death of mum started wailing in their homes only to come and find mum looking at them curiously absent minded, white wide eyed, she was also speaking with a sloped mouth to one side like a stroke patient, her facial nerves were failing, her face was falling.

I heard mum tell her, "Sis would you believe the doctor told me last week that I am HIV positive, he must be lying."

With an increasingly concrete understanding of her fate, Mama Mpenzi made the decision to travel with her sister back to Nairobi.

Environments have a tone, the distinct tone here was death. It was in the shadows lying in wait and Mama Mpenzi decided to change the environment.

We travelled together, Mama Mpenzi hired a van, and her sister lay on her shoulder the whole seven-hour journey.

While in Nairobi now, the whole fold was able to visit mum who had reclused herself from the world as a tortoise to its shell, it seems she had intentionally cut herself from everyone in the three years I had not seen her.

The other person who saw her for the first time after a long time was my brother Philip.

When he saw mum, he was tagging at my skirt afraid of what was before him.

I stayed with mum at Mama Mpenzi's in Umoja 1. I applied salve on her chipping skin, I served her food, I did her nails, I gave her medicine.

Eventually she said she felt better and needed to get back to her home in Homa Bay, I guess she got tired of being the animal in the zoo people come to look at, and so Mama Mpenzi hired a vehicle that took her back home with her sister Anna to nurse her.

Mum died a month later.

The news was broken to me by Mama Mpenzi who I had gone to visit and was sleeping over at, I was now a big girl and could not fit in my childhood cot, I shared her bed.

She smoked for a while and amidst a thick puff said quietly to herself.

"Your mother passed on today."

Mum had arrived back at her house in Homa Bay and in a week she got worse, and was admitted at Gendia Hospital in Oyugis with Auntie Anna by her side.

Mum had tubes for infusing food, blood and water into her veins at this point as her condition badly deteriorated. She summoned Auntie Anna to get her water.

Anna went to fetch her water but also took the opportunity to walk to a nearby centre, got mosquito repellents to battle the mosquitoes that were forming a crown on her head.

She got back two hours later and found mum had yanked off all the little pipes. One pipe was dripping water on the sheets forming a bloated circle. The other pipe was dripping blood on the tiled floors with a quiet splat making a beautiful red abstract pattern.

Her white eyes were frozen in time.

I felt sorry for Auntie Anna because she had to stay the whole night with her sister's body as the morgue services only opened in the morning.

She checked her into the morgue then called Care Kenya and word spread that morning. It reached Mama Mpenzi by 9 am and she broke it to me in the night.

I did not cry but that night I did not also sleep.

It occurred to me that I had not walked in my mother's oversized shoes like how other girls do.

THE POWER OF WORDS

When mum died, Dad was in Homa Bay. He was in Homa Bay because Nyakendu had also passed on from HIV complications.

When Nyakendu died, she was no longer Dad's wife and wasn't living in Dad's homestead. And her people told dad they could not bury her since the cows dad paid to marry her had not been returned effectively still making her Dad's wife. Dad's brothers also alluded to the same reminding him of his stubborness when he was building his homestead.

And so on this day, Dad was in Homa Bay to collect Nyakendu's coffin when people saw him and told him;

"We are truly truly sorry, let us know where we can help."

He said, "No problem, I have already done everything, I am burying tomorrow."

They said, "but that cannot be, she just died this morning."

"Who just died this morning?"

"Your ex-wife Pam?"

He sat on the coffin he had just bought and he sat there a long time.

It was my duty to break it to Philip that his mother had died, the timing was awful because it was his final year in Primary School.

All the way to his school, I battled tears.

He was in class when I got there and when the bell rang for kids to go for break, my stomach was churning.

He spotted me and came running.

I am a wordy person but I could not find the long words for this.

I wondered whether to discuss the weather or how his classes were going... where to start, I just went for broke.

"Mum died yesterday and I thought to be the first person to tell you."

"Where has she died?"

"Homa Bay." - I looked for a reaction, there was none.

"Ok, I have to go now... its break time and we are playing football." He ran away from me, and I did not dare follow him.

He joined his friends in the grassless field that had brown dust rising up due to constant kids activities, none of his class mates could have guessed that he had just lost his mother.

Philip was a child who was constantly yearning for his mother who never showed up, carried a lot of unrequited love for her. Philip loved his mother, he really did - I always tried my best to replace his longing, tried my best to play all the roles a mother could, but he was steadfast in his love for his mother.

To date he still loves his mother.

But now, he was thirteen and his heart had been ripped apart.

He learned the price people pay for love quite early.

He had lost his capacity to articulate hurt, and it's on his behalf I sat on a stone near their school fence that was covered by lots of creeper plants, and really cried.

The complication Dad faced with mum's death is she had been married a second time by a man from Kano, the built and handsome man I earlier met in the 'Niece' Incident.

Mum had considered her marriage to Dad null and void considering he was already married to two women traditionally before, and two right after her.

She had moved on with her life to the point of building a home in this man's rural home, among the plain paddy rice fields of Kano.

They did not have any children though, she decided never to have kids again.

I want to believe my mum was not really a kid's person, she had me out of circumstance and Philip from duty.

But truly if she were born in my generation, she would be the ladies who chose not to have kids and are well fulfilled, because as some of my friends who do not have and do not desire to have any argue; Not every woman is born with maternal instincts, to my friends who find the idea of bringing a child into a convoluted world preposterous, to the ones who believe there are other ways of nurturing outside motherhood, to the ones who believe that motherhood supports patriarchy, to the ones who are completely scared by the idea of a 9 month pregnancy and the actual child birth process, to the hilarious ones who have kids then realise.. Naaah! I wasn't cut out for this!

So traditionally, it was this other man who was to bury mum.

But Dad wasn't having it that way especially that mum had a son with him. He had built her a home, and Dad said he wanted his wife to be buried where his children could visit and see their mother's grave.

The battle for mum's body was in the offing.

As previously stated, there were also ulterior motives, Mum had been working for a great organisation that took care of benefits, she had also invested in land and had bought a Nissan; the one that was being driven by the husband.

Dad saw it fit to claim the properties as he had been taking care of and was to take care of us for the rest of his life given we had both not completed our education.

When Dad confronted mum's ex-husband with a court order, he did not resist.

He said, "I do understand she has got kids with you and its only proper you bury her."

He however insisted on the property which he claimed he had contributed to.

That went to court.

Arrangements for burying mum eclipsed the funeral of Nyakendu, it was more like 'let's get this done with we have a bigger game coming up.'

If you recall, Dad had not built Nyakendu a house, and now he had to do it, hurriedly.

The days leading to mum's funeral passed me in a daze, we were there thrust in the midst of former aunties and uncles we really had no connection to except for Steve, Mama Mpenzi and my cousin Sammy.

They all kept saying how we had grown.

Kept praising Dad for taking care of us well.

I got reconnected to my grandmother, Deborah.

Mum was her last born and easily her favorite child, the two were very close and in her last years, mum was constantly at home with her mum during her leave days, whenever she was ill, it would be mummy travelling home to pick her and take her to hospital – She already seemed quite frail.

Mum's furniture were being rounded up in a huge truck, en route her Mum's in Ukwala, Ugenya.

Her clothes had been stolen by people, her once tastefully decored house was stripped off the accessories.

I travelled with Dad to the morgue to pick the body in a convoy of cars, snaking into the then Oyugis potholed road.

We reached Matata Hospital and were ushered in to the morgue to view her body in a single file.

I went in there with Dad. I saw her middle toe which looked exactly like mine, she also had on chipped pink cutex which I had applied on her while she was on treatment in Nairobi.

She was pale and grey and someone had undone her hair.

In death, she looked every inch the 36-year-old woman she was supposed to be.

I touched her forehead which was cold and hard.

I looked back to find Dad seated on the floor and had to hold his hand and lead him out.

'Tell your Dad the only time we get to share a room is in a morgue' The power of words she had told me taking a morbid reality. I was still a teenager.

Mum's body was transferred from Oyugis for a night vigil at her home in Homa Bay then eventually Sori bound where her body would rest.

The convoy from Homa Bay towards Sori was slow; dirges and Christian songs filled the bus we were in as it tried to navigate the long nasty road which had potholes the size of a valley, you were at times better off driving off road than on the patched road filled with pools of brown water.

It had been raining and lorries had gouged the ground too deep for clearance. You had to drive at a 45-degree angle, at times whole sides of vehicles suspended in the air.

Dad, Philip and I were seated infront of the bus. Behind was her coffin.

Traditionally among the Luo, when there has been the death of a significant person, all the cows are released from the sheds and come to meet the entourage. As we snaked nearer Dad's homestead, I could see the *'Otho'* on the left, which meant we had reached our destination. We met the cows and the howling villagers.

Young girls from the lake below were carrying buckets on their heads and due to the commotion, the waters spilled and sloched over the sides of the buckets.

Bulls with bells on their necks stampeding and being controlled by their herders and villagers carrying twigs and crying with their hands on their heads, the livestock in the confusion dropping enormous pats of dung flicking their tails and sending sprays of dung flying through the air.

Bewildered sounds of mourning mixed with cows mowing and bells chiming and vehicles honing and dust rising in the air as the majestic Nam Lolwe sparkled ahead, its cream topped breakers dancing all the way to the horizon.

Most times, the vehicles had to stop to let the way be cleared.

From the depth of his soul, beside me, Dad let out a cry and for the first time it hit me that mum was actually gone. I looked at Philip who was watching the ongoings in front of the hearse in silence.

Dad opened the door of the hearse and jumped out. He tore his shirt and threw his shoes, put his hands on his head as he led the crying party towards his homestead bare chested.

I looked at Philip, his face planted at the ongoings ahead, as the vehicles stopped due to the crowds all attempting to squeeze into our compound from the tiny gate.

I could see my mum's sisters and brothers already in the compound.

Mama Mpenzi dressed in a black Bui Bui was rolling on the ground, wailing, throwing dust and mud on herself.

I held my little brother's hand and I told him.

"You are very brave."

Minus the coffin, you may mistake a Luo funeral for an elaborate party. We conveniently hide under 'It's a celebration of life' Cows being slaughtered, chicken de–feathered, there is a whole industry for it, women have organised themselves to form catering companies popularly known as 'Jo-Kata' who arrive with pans, plates, spoons, stoves the only thing you need to provide is food.

Others come fully loaded with tents, chairs, a PA system.

Musicians, DJs and entertainers are also contracted for the night after the burial where mourners will dance themselves limb till the morning, it's called 'Disco Matanga.'

It's also an elaborate location for fashion statements, where the close relatives may get tailored clothes, shoes, complete with stunners, some actually import and some will print tee shirts.

If you have money, you can spare your guests the tears and hire professional mourners. Depending on the rate, they can cry periodically or they can cry interminably, they can sob or wail while being overly dramatic, they can cry with emotion or without - it depends on how fat your pocket is.

Africans consider mourners guests who have come to help them see off their loved one and so its their duty to feed them and make them comfortable if It means going into debts.

A Luo funeral has become a flex or show of financial muscle or influence.

I know that I have a hilarious friend who started a blog about Luo funerals where he would every weekend try find out what influential funeral was taking place, would sponsor himself to the event, and would report live and give reviews on number of people who attended, but most importantly the quantity and quality of food that was served, you can't believe how popular his blog was. Woe unto your people if Callisto deems the funeral a struggling one, if he keeps steady at this, I am sure he will be soon paid to attend funerals.

It's very common to find the moment a person dies, a fund raiser is immediately created to cater for the hospitability of the event.

People will have a budget of anything from 1000USD dollars all the way to 10,000 USD depending on how popular, famous the dead is and how influential the family is, its so entrenched that we now have Insurance covers for funerals where you pay a premium and if your loved one dies, you are paid the sum that will take care of mourners' food and entertainment.

Luos take the insurance for food and entertainment.

While it's a culture and its African to be hospitable, thoughts on helping the sick or needy while alive will not be as forthcoming as on their funeral. Also, nobody ever thinks of the bereaved family after the funeral.

People will spend lavishly on funerals and orphaned kids will have to drop out of school immediately thereafter.

It's also a popular venue for politicians to sell their manifestos since there is a ready crowd who will not demand that you pay them, they take the opportunity to clout chase and promise that they will take care of the bereaved family or kids which they rarely do –It at times gets out of hand when rival politicians and their fans clash at a funeral unleashing violence on each other, people flee to all directions, people have suffered bullet wounds in funerals, corpses have been left desolate while mourners scamper.

There were all sorts of people at mum's funeral which reflected the kind of person she was.

Her relatives, friends, colleagues, partners at work, neighbours in places she had lived, revelers where she would party, there were Dad's relatives and friends - She was a fun human being and she was really loved by many.

We were seated at the front as hosts of the funeral.

Speaker after speaker from mum's social and work life spoke and emphasized on her love for her son, her only child and hoped the child would be well taken care of.

Relatives shifted uncomfortably on their seats anytime someone referred to 'her only child.'

Finally, the Care Kenya representative who was also her boss gave an official speech which also referred to my brother Philip as her only child.

Dad who missed a good opportunity to remain quiet and let sleeping dogs lie, grabbed the microphone and addressed the crowd making it clear that mum had two children and not one, and admonished me to stand up.

The crowd craned their necks to have a look at me.

It was a fantastic display of a reject. We stood on mum's grave as the soil hit the wooden casket and my mind was far away.

I was looking at Dad, my relatives and everyone who said they were close to our mother and I thought to myself; 'What a bunch of cowards'

Because on one particular night, on her last days while at Mama Mpenzi's, Mum insisted on watching the news with me, I noticed she kept peering at me and not the TV, I waited for whatever she had to say because she did that a lot when she had something to say.

We always sunk into deep ponds of uncomfortable silence despite that we were both consummate extroverts. It always seemed like she was pondering on how best to design her words, how to present them.

We had careful conversations, everybody aware of their emotions and triggers and treading not to get there. I watched news without hearing what the newscaster was saying because my ears were waiting for her.

"You are a very sharp girl, how come you have never asked me who your real father is."

I thought I did not hear her correctly.

"What do you mean real father? I have a father."

"Your father is a man by the name Alex Minge, and he is Ugandan, look for him."

I had been kept in the dark by everyone in this funeral, like a mushroom, and fed plenty of manure.

FINDING ALEX

Back in the 80s, Uganda was facing civil strife and anti-Museveni soldiers were being hunted and killed on sight. They poured into Kenya as refugees.

In Africa we have come to recognise that war brings with it refugees from all walks of life, you have the refugees who are desperate who will end up gathered in squalid tent camps and the refugees of means, the ones of means will latch onto a holding country while processing papers for asylum in the west, some will rent houses and hotels in posh areas and will carry on the good life they had at home.

Such was the life of one Alexander Minge Tendo. A boy in a family of 8 to John Mark Minge and Jajja Tamalie Naku.

Alex, who went to Kako Senior Secondary School and Fortpotal College was a researcher but also served as a top spy for the Iddi Amin Government till it was toppled by the Tanzanian forces and Uganda rebels, and he had to flee to neighboring Kenya.

As a researcher and a spy, he had swam in money back home.

In Kenya, he did even better as he could also play spy for the Kenyan government which needed information on the new Uganda under Museveni.

He was a refugee who lived like a king with access to the State house as and when.

Alex was a dedicated fan of Rumba and especially Franco Luambo Makiadi.

He was the greatest at everything he did, he was a great dancer, a great dresser, generous to boot, charming, hilarious – so dedicated was he to his Rumba that he would go up the stage, take the mic and sing along the Congolese tunes much to the admiration of women and reverence of men.

He is described as a happy go lucky man, very popular, fun loving and extremely generous.

Alex had been a great dresser and reveled in donning designer clothes, got the newest cars and only hung out in the most exotic of places, a true lover of the finer things in life.

My Uncle Philip thought he had money, until he met Alex in the Rumba clubs of Nairobi, Alex stood and announced in the microphone that all drinks were on his tab.

They became close friends with Uncle Philip and soon Alex was visiting Uncle Philip's house in Buru Buru.

Uncle Philip's little sister, my mother, caught his eye. She was at this point 16 and in High School

The two had a brief affair that resulted in to Uncle Philip's sister conceiving. Alex's family were already getting asylum to Sweden and he kept travelling back and forth and missed this particular detail of his life.

Mother tried her best to procure an abortion, resorting to crude methods like grinding bottles and drinking them up with water, taking concentrate tea but nothing seemed to work.

The child was determined to live.

In the 80s and presently, most of Africa is still struggling with pro-life and pro-choice, whether it's a moral or personal choice issue and the safety thereafter.

When my mum found herself in the predicament, there were no known methods for safe abortions, no framework and it could not even be conceived in hospitals. The victim would overdose on quinine, drink concentrate or literally gorge the fetus out using a cloth hanger. Such attempts saw lots of women die or have their reproductive organs affected all their lives.

But they mostly accepted to take the risk because it was an easier route than the shame and stigma associated with a school going pregnant girl, Judgment the parents would have to go through and worse, schools would not accept back a girl who had conceived; it was literally just over.

The other prospect is you would be married off to an old man last in the pecking order for he would have to take care of a child he did not sire.

It would be preposterous for any young man to take and marry a woman who had a kid in their teenhood, pointed to loose morals and upbringing.

My mother's family was one of professionals with high standing in the society and nobody wanted to be caught in the spy web as they had a nascent awareness of how Alex made a living.

Despite her puny interventions, she was unsuccessful in terminating the pregnancy and her mother travelled from upcountry to salvage the situation.

She insisted the child be born, she would take the child with her to the village so her daughter may continue her education. She would be transferred to a different private school.

I was born some 8 months later on a Saturday afternoon when the sun was up, so the name Achieng suited me quite well.

They say I came out bald, curious, and with very strong lungs and my grandmother took me immediately. She named me after herself.

My biological father's name was Alexander Minge Tendo.

And so my birth certificate read Deborah Achieng Tendo.

Grandma took me with her to the village as an infant to allow her daughter finish school and pursue her dreams.

My mum went on to complete high school at Khalsa Secondary School in Nairobi before taking up Secretarial studies at Graffins College then located along Moi Avenue near Jeevanjee Gardens. She was still living with her brother Philip

Osieyo. Every so often my grandmother would travel with me to Nairobi and uncles and aunties would insist that I be left behind for a bit. That is why and how Uncle Steven Osieyo babysat me.

However, when George Auko met mum I was in the village with grandma.

As their relationship matured, women who were eyeing George Auko in the family were telling him that Pam had a child from a previous relationship, she denied vehemently.

On mum's side, uncle Philip told his friend that indeed there was a child in the village and George insisted they must go upcountry and pick the little girl, George Auko was taking the whole package.

George Auko insisted he must meet me and must raise me. It is said he fell in love with me on sight and made a pact with the family never to reveal that I was the daughter of a spy, but his very own.

At this very moment as we were burying my mother, all these collaborators were standing by mum's grave, unaware she did not die with the secret.

Mum died having played a number on Dad who also wasn't aware that I now knew.

THE PANDEMIC

In the period of 1992 to about 2000 there were a lot of deaths in Luo land due to the HIV pandemic.

It was the peak of the pandemic just before ARVs came to our rescue. And I am saying our rescue because if HIV did not infect a Luo, it affected a Luo. We were all in there, in the thick of war.

Every Friday, there would be processions snaking into the hinter lands from the cities carrying AIDS corpses.

The TB wards were full to the rafters.

Coffin business was booming.

This was the period when you could not cough incessantly, you could not suddenly just lose weight, you could not have red lips - tongues would start wagging about how you caught the virus and people would start avoiding you as there was little information on how the disease spread. The stigma associated with HIV in the 90s was deep as it was damaging and its effects far reaching.

All the fun, making merry and reckless living by the parents who bore children in the 80s eventually ended up in millions of orphans in the 90s. Most of us, the Luos born in the 80s have a story that will be woven around the scourge. If it's not your parent, it's your relative or a friend to your parent.

My dad's group of men who would chase bands all over in the late 80s early 90s would later converge in a pub in Nairobi called Safe life in Huruma Nairobi.

At Safe life, the legend Okatch Biggy would perform between his tours, and even when he was not performing, the pub would now engage different luo bands be it DO Misiani, Osito Kale or just play Luo benga, and it became a popular spot for men; they would converge there every weekend.

Dazed nights of dancing, reckless risky behaviour, and flowing alcohol, the place was home to all sorts of people from all walks of life be it the lower class, middle, upper middle or upper - here they all converged as Luos, and Luo music bound them and momentarily they could be village boys again speaking our language and dancing to our community folk songs.

We as luos are famed for loving a good life and in our idea of a good life, alcohol, sex, music are never that far away.

Safe life's owner went across the borders to Uganda and imported light skinned women to wait in his pub, to spice things up and waylay competition as business was booming.

Ugandan women then, unlike Kenyan women, were famed for being demure, soft spoken, polite, they were still kneeling for their men while serving them, even in this bar. Men at Safe life would request for extra seats where their egos would rest. It was exotic and it was a new experience, a new injection into the already murky cesspool.

As expected, revelers started mingling with the waiters, sexually interacting with them secretly and it took maybe one or two revelers or waiters who were already infected with HIV.

Two years later revelers started coughing, waiters started falling ill, a year later revelers started reducing as they were in hospital while the waiters started crossing the borders back to Uganda gravely sick.

In a matter of months the pub morphed to a fund raising joint as every week someone who was once a patron had died. Most of them fell ill, they died including the owner and Safe life was closed down.

So much for a pub named Safe life.

All of Dad's crew died except maybe two. Okatch Biggy, their star, also started ailing,

Several scare fake news announced his death, he released a hit lashing back at his detractors and confirming he was still alive.

'Okach alemo.'

He always sang standing, then he started singing part standing and part sitting, then eventually he would be brought on stage already on a seat while coughing, then his voice died and then he died.

What was sad about this period was innocent women who were at home tending to their kids, but whose husbands were revelers in this pub got sucked up in the vortex.

The women started ailing, and dying one by one leaving thousands of orphaned Luo kids of my generation.

A harsh epitaph on their lives, futures mortgaged and destinies rerouted.

The cost was along all walks of lives from mechanics, to drivers, to professionals, to cabinet ministers and civil servants and to lecturers in universities.

The lecturers not only took the disease home, but to female University students who were both fraternal with their lecturers and fellow male students and the Universities faced a brain drain.

It was a crisis that President Moi had to declare a pandemic.

In my family we had lost our mother and Nyakendu to the pandemic.

And I recall Dad's elder bother, the one who was most adamant that Dad had to build for Nyakendu.

He started falling ill.

He had about 4 wives – His third wife who ironically was a medicine woman started falling ill.

I remember her because she had a dark spirit to her, it was said she reversed barrenness, she was quite wealthy as women from all walks of life settled at her homestead to try get a coveted child.

She had no child herself.

She died leaving Uncle with two wives and Uncle added a young wife to take care of him immediately.

She first got ill and died, then Uncle's second wife got ill and died, then Uncle's Mikayi got ill and died.

Then Uncle died and his young wife followed dutifully.

A whole homestead with no parents and in excess of 15 kids orphaned.

A lot of NGOs and aid from the first world countries came to the rescue from around 1999 and I cannot emphasize here the sigh of relief when the community started seeing people who had been transported to the rural areas awaiting their deaths to save on costs, start re emerging in the cities looking healthy.

The deaths became less, the gaunt faces on the streets lessened and although the stigma held on for quite a bit into the 2000s where we had cases of polygamous men with HIV taking the ARVs and not revealing to their wives that they were sick and couples had to be forced to take the test together in the rural areas, due to the trauma of the 90s we could only hope it would get better.

In my generation, the stigma is even less, some of the kids of the 80s were born with the disease and have lived to tell the story, but even among the new infections.. it's not uncommon to see people go public about their positive status, or even take their ARVs publicly to kill the stigma.

I once asked Dad how he had escaped this net.

'I don't do Exes, I don't share women and I got circumcised,'

'But you always wanted mum to get back'

'Not for that, for you people. I could not continue further with Nyakendu because there were no kids in the first place so she had to go but the moment I heard the rumours of her ways, I never once stepped in her hut'

I think he just got lucky, that's all.

NYANANDA

Deborah Nyananda, my grandmother died exactly three months after mum's death. Nobody thought she would survive mum's loss anyway. She just had to follow her girl.

Dad attended the funeral as an in -law, the only one of two, a role he took on with so much grace -he was a Luo, arriving flamboyantly with an entourage of 30 complete with vans and traditional regalia.

He made an appearance so grand that anyone who did not know him had to recognise him and the fact that he once married in that homestead. And it was natural that he would do that. After mum passed on, Dad ordered all her household, clothes, literally everything to be swept from her house and given to my grandmother as the least she could have to remember her last born.

My maternal grandmother was very tall, with a long neck and a great hourglass figure. She loved her bottle and her cigarettes. She also loved her radio from where she would listen to Soukouss and it was funny as hell.

She was a great cook who I thought was crazy. She would not use a spoon to serve food, would just dip her bare hand into the pot and fish out the largest morsel of meat into everyone's plates.

Nyananda's home was open to orphans, all her grandchildren whose parents were going through financial problems or who were just not into the idea of raising kids.

She was well taken care of by her sons, had tapped water and even electricity as early as the 80s in Ukwala, Ugenya. She had a constant supply of milk and food and workers who tilled land for her.

She had taken me from my mother and named me after herself. Because she knew she would raise me comfortably but fate had it otherwise. She died without my asking why she did not insist that I be returned to her following the end of my parents' marriage.

I guess I owed it to her that I even got to live and that was enough.

She also had a moment of embarrassment when it was obvious she received dowry from my mum's second husband yet mum wasn't divorced from Dad, but nobody would ask as mum's death completely destroyed her.

My mother's family was shrinking exponentially. From a family of ten, already four members of the family had died. The first born, Uncle George, died of liver issues . He was famously known as 'Apong Kor'. As most of my maternal uncles, he was a bear of a man, standing at an astonishing 7 '2 inches. With eyes hard as flint. Never lived a day sober. Under his bed always was a 5 litre jerrican of traditional alcoholic spirit which he would gobble down like water and set off to work in crimson red eyes. He was so big that crowds parted when he approached. Always looked bewildered like he had walked right out of a hurricane. Most of the time wearing long socks, boots and at times shorts in the colonial chief fashion.

He was so big that he had his own *Duol* where his wives would bring food to him. He would thereafter take an afternoon nap and his legs would hang for his height ran out of bed. Cockroaches that would feed on his food left overs would at times nip at his caloused toes.

He would snore and you would hear him several huts away and when he turned in bed, the whole hut seemed to turn. A man of men.

The second born, Uncle John the trade unionist, died of a heart attack. He went to bed and never woke up.

Auntie Miriam, the third born, had been first to die while at child birth.

And mum their last born, of HIV.

During grandma's funeral, I observed that Auntie Annah, Auntie Apiyo, Uncle Washington and my great Uncle Philip, who were present for their mother's funeral were not looking good either.

Uncle Philip, the party master who was once friends with Dad and where mum and Dad met, went on to lose his job; went bankrupt.

He decided to contact the woman he was dating before with whom things did not work out for obvious reasons and who decided to leave the country to England with his son. He only needed an invite into the UK and would figure out life by himself. Philip sold all his belongings and flew to the UK.

At the immigration, they questioned him and the lady who was to pick him did not show up and when she was called, she denied any knowledge of him. He was deported back to Kenya and he deported himself away from people. He crawled into a whisky bottle and never quite came out.

He downgraded from Buru Buru where I had been born to some middle class abode, to mid lower to lower and finally ended up in a slum in a one room where the toilet and bathroom were outside. Degenerated from drinking Single malt whisky imported from Ireland, to cheap vodka and finally chang'aa in the slums.

During mum's funeral, he was frail and sickly and coughing. He had caught the virus.

During grandma's funeral three months later, he could barely walk.

Then he disappeared.

A stranger went to Mama Mpenzi's salon one day and told her that neighbours noticed chicken jumping from his window with maggots on their beaks and on breaking his door, they discovered his body.

The song Les Rumeurs was played a lot at Philip's funeral. You guessed that right. It's a Luambo Makiadi Franco classic.

Franco had also died in 1989 and the world turned grey

for a lot of his fans. Franco was at the climax of his career when towards the late 80s, he suddenly disappeared from the limelight.

Rumour had it he was ill and was recuperating in Belgium. After a while he turned up and had done an album called Tojour OK with his protégé Sam Mangwana.

Dad held out the cover of this cassette to me and was in shock. Franco had lost massive weight and looked terribly ill.

In Africa, you didn't just suddenly lose weight like that. Tongues started wagging. HIV was wreaking havoc in the Congo and he did a song called SIDA to sensitise his fans on the scourge.

Franco was last seen at a concert in Switzerland where a leaderless TP OK Jazz was playing. From his sick bed in Belgium, he demanded to go and perform at the concert, and his aide drove him across the bridge into Switzerland.

He hit the stage and could not stand on his feet - he was given a chair and handed his guitar.

With clothes that wore him, and sweating profusely, he attempted to hit the strings but his hands could not. He attempted and managed and what came out were some very wild notes that the band tried to blend to. He only managed to play that one song, was helped into a car and straight back to bed on palliative. He died a week later.

I was a child but I recall Dad grieved as if he had lost a relative. The airwaves were awash with TPOK's songs and we did not need to play our cassettes. The radio did a great job of transporting us from the 70s with Cheri Bondowe, Lisasa Libonga na Langi, to the early 80s Salima. The Mid 80s Mario and Mamou to the late 80s Tojours OK. It was like when an elephant dies.

After his death, a song he wrote on the stigma he went through was released. In Les Reumeur, Franco struggles to sing. He left the world letting us know what he thought and how he felt after having given us many wonderful songs. The song addresses the stigma.

This song played a lot in Philip's Funeral.

PRIVILEGE

I exited Moi Girls High School having left a mark both as an artist and probably the most turbulent student. I left having understood the power of privilege as this was a school with kids from some of the wealthiest families in the country. You got in and realised just how poor you were. You met kids who never once ate school food which was way above even what I ate at home, and would have catered food delivered from Sirikwa-then a five-star hotel every single evening. Kids of government officials who would be visited by flagged cars with sirens and body guards. Kids whose parents' security detail would arrive in school a few days prior to secure the area. It was a boarding school but Asian kids would be picked by dark windowed SUVs for the weekend to return on Monday. Kids who on closing day were travelling to the US to their families.

I left understanding why, in Africa, an election is a matter of life and death; systems that create smooth paths for some and broken glass shoals for others. Highlands, being a school after Moi's heart had a swimming pool, grocery store, state of the art sanatoriums, heated water while there were students in less privileged schools with not as much as a roof above their heads in class.

There are a lot of arguments out here that kids in institutions need to be uniformed so privilege and poverty is concealed. Institutions that go out of their way to construct an artificial borderless class system. I am not a believer of that. The dichotomy of the human experience dictates otherwise. No need to hide your reality only for kids to get shocked as they enter the society- it's a good thing for kids to be exposed to where they stand so they work harder in school. So they aspire. So they dream.

You have to learn early in life the invisible codes and boundaries. Commit to memory the protocols and idiosyncrasies because your survival depends on knowing them as well if not better than your own dreams and wishes.

Equally, kids who are privileged may not know just how lucky they are until they encounter the poor kids.

This is how it balanced out. Kids from extremely poverty stricken areas worked extremely hard and got good points while some of them were intimidated to the point they went further behind the marks that got them in the school in the first place.

Most kids from privileged families just performed averagely or were suspended quite early on for habits like drinking, smoking or sneaking out of the school. This is because they saw no need to put in any effort. They had it all anyway.

As a Luo, not only was I a poor kid but also a minority in a majority Kalenjin School who also happened to be in power. I can never say that the school biased me or the few Luos in subsequent classes. However, it was plain to see that because of Kenya's tribal politics, a lot of Kalenjin kids' futures were secured. Most left for universities outside Africa while we were waiting for calling letters to local universities on student loans.

Class played out even in the ruling tribe, because I schooled with some Kalenjin kids from really poor families and who struggled with school fees just as we did in the ruled tribes.

Let your kids know early on where they stand. In Africa and capitalist countries, they are not the same.

You cannot solve a problem that you do not admit exists. Which could be why some people may not want to talk about it. It may get solved.

The universe with its comedy once again had me in Fine Art. Being a special subject taken by very few students, it was slotted as the last national exam in my year and that meant two of us would remain in school long after every candidate had left.

I handed my painting to the invigilator.

I looked outside through the art room windows to the red brick tiled roofs of Moi Girls, Eldoret. The compound was deserted as Chernobyl, and in that moment, a blazing ray of sun struck the glass and filtered into the room through a small window opening. The opening broke the beam with its edges and scattered embers all over the art room.

I schooled here, where Courage, Honour and Industry are the motto, and nobody could take that from me.

I walked out of the school by myself.

Unlike other kids whose parents came driving vehicles to carry their stuff, I left everything. My box. Sets of uniform. And only walked out with my paintwork and drama certificates.

EAST-LEIGH

When I completed high school, I joined Dad who was still living in a guest house in Eastleigh. The guest house had a television at the reception where we would gather a few minutes to 9pm to follow politics together.

A lot had happened in politics while I was in school:

Raila's NDP had joined the regime he once shot from the hip.

Moi had to incorporate him to deal with the voices of dissent and to retire peacefully as he was on his last term - more like shaking hands with your opponents to live in peace.

I saw my Dad move from hating Moi so bad to now praising him for making Raila a minister in his government. I kept asking him, "Have you forgotten about all the reasons you had a problem with Moi? The corruption? Torture? Tribalism in state corporations? You were in a cell yourself because of Moi, no?"

He told me, "You hold on and see how we play this. This is Raila!"

In a twist of fate, President Moi bypassed his Vice President and nominated Uhuru Kenyatta his successor. Uhuru Kenyatta is son to the first President from whom Moi inherited the presidency in the first place.

Uhuru was a political greenhorn still wet behind the ears who had kept off politics all his life. At 43, he had not been present in the first or even second struggle and Raila would hear none of it.

Raila amassed all of Moi's powerful ministers from the major tribes and led them to protest the move and walk out of Government to form a party that came to be known as NARC, and when everyone thought he was vying for presidency, he nominated Kibaki who came second in the previous election and a Kikuyu like Uhuru so the vote would be split.

It was a master stroke.

Kibaki won the election, effectively making Uhuru the opposition leader and Moi left state house disgraced after a 24-year rule.

Dad was so happy. He cried.

And so we always watched the bulletin on this TV that was placed in a metallic box and padlocked with a mesh masking the screen so you watched a screen behind the mesh because of the crime rate in Eastleigh then.

Eastleigh is strategically near to the CBD and was a haven for illegal immigrants in Kenya in various stages of trying to sort out their papers. It was also a hub for criminals. An underworld where anything went – If you needed a gun, Eastleigh is where you went. You needed a kidney, head to Eastleigh.

People who could not afford to pay rent as landlords may ask for details or were on temporary stay, would end up in guest houses. They were the equivalent of motels in the west famed for runaways and fugitives.

In these guest houses you would find Bibles whose purposes far underweighted the occupants' mission. Nobody was interest in whatever Paul had to tell the Corinthians.

Occupants were here for illegal deals. Money laundering. Sale of guns. Crack. Cocaine. All of it.

It was also the hub for ladies of the night who, just as it happens in major cities around the world, took a one-way ticket to try make it in the big city. A haven for job seekers. Refugees and the people who were living hand to mouth and could afford accommodation only for a day.

Literally fifteen of the twenty rooms in this guest house were rented by ladies of the night - two were by us. The rest were for ad hoc customers.

It was a ground floor building, with all the rooms facing each other and a narrow corridor in the middle that ended in three communal bathrooms and toilets that were permanently revolting. Dwellers unable to deal with the toilet's filth urinated in the bathroom and so it had a permanent warm stench.

The toilets were unbearable. I recall walking down to a relative to use their toilet as Dad preserved the long calls to the CBD and Philip to school.

And the toilets were placed just next to the rooms. Someone gets in and you witness every gurgle and rumble. Every fart and every splutter. Every gush, some silence, then the sound of water from a bucket because they did not flash.

In the day, the guest house would be dead silent as all occupants were asleep from the previous night's shenanigans. Save for the caretaker, one Mr. Wahleed, always unable to sit in silence as long as someone was within earshot.

From the evening, it would come alive as occupants woke up, sent for food and started cleaning up and sprucing themselves for the night. The air would be filled with dizzying scents of cheap perfume. Then around 8pm, they would all be gone again.

Depending on business, they would start arriving one by one at 10pm in the night like soldiers from a war with their clients. At times the ladies would come high as kites and fight like cats outside the corridor. At times, the fights would come from disagreements between them or with their clients on the consideration to be paid. At times, the police would raid the guest house making the girls escape, flying through windows.

On knocking at our door and finding myself and Philip, the police would wonder what we were doing in there. They once questioned Dad if he was trafficking underage girls.

My earliest neighbours and friends when I completed high school and was looking at adulthood were hookers. Most of them had not quite gone to school and would hire my services to read texts or for general advice. While most of them were conflicted, they were all very good natured human beings.

Baseline, they all came from a place of struggle. They all had a story.

I sat with them during the day when Dad had gone to work in spite of many warnings from him not to, listened to their stories; from the HIV orphans who dropped out of school, to the ones thrown out by their brothers after attaining the age of 18 and could not find jobs, to the ones coming from abject poverty and needed money to take their kids back in the villages to school, to the ones who felt they were bigger than their village and needed a break but had not gone to school.

I would listen to their stories as they bleary eyed rolled a joint or spread cocaine on their gums or on the table to sniff from straw.

Women paying a very high price for very low living.

They had all sorts of pills. From the Blue pill to Viagra to pills they dropped in a drink that would turn a client to a zombie. They would then withdraw cash from their ATMs, bring the client over to the guest house waiting for midnight to withdraw a new day's maximum limit before leaving them on the street.

They had not come to Nairobi on a juvenile sense of adventure. They were in the city to survive.

Unlike some countries in Asia that I have seen, sex work is a means to an end in Kenya. They are on their way somewhere. Some of them actually got into relationships and vacated the guest house. Some left to the coast which is the tourism hub that opened them up to international sex tourism and they immigrated to the west. Some got men who took them. Some went to school and are pursuing corporate careers.

It could be the shame associated with the job or that it's just plain illegal in Kenya. Either way, the lack of regulation exposed the ladies and clients to untold risks.

Much later in life, I attended the wedding of one. I was probably the only person who knew the process that took her where she was. It was very special when we hugged that we cried.

I woke up in this guest house as usual one morning and our little room was quiet. I was cleaning up when a man approached my door.

He was of Somali origin from the texture of his hair but dark skinned.

He did not know his English but spoke in Somali and motioned in a clenched fist pumping his fist out.

I had no idea what he meant and I did not feel any threat at all.

"What is it that you want?" I enquired boldly.

"A shot," and discreetly showed me some dollars.

I had no idea what 'a shot' meant.

As I was still wondering what he meant and approached him at the door so I could see outside if Wahleed, the caretaker, could maybe help him buy whatever he needed, he gave me a mighty push back to the room and on to the bed.

All my alarms went off trying to register what was happening. He only had on a short and was fumbling with it releasing his member. I fought hard and screamed but could feel his hardness on my thighs.

I do remember the hookers storming our room and one of them, the one whose wedding I attended much later in life, picking a pan from our stove and hitting this man on the head and he collapsed on top of me.

She pushed him away and pulled me from the bed and we fell on the floor in a heap. She pulled the blanket from the bed and covered me and started crying on my shoulders while I was quietly processing the movie that I was watching.

Another lady rushed back to her room and came back with a bottle of Vodka and put it in my mouth. I had never tasted alcohol before.

The bitterness travelled in my mouth and I could feel it burning my throat all the way to my intestines.

That very afternoon, I wrote a long letter to my Dad thanking him for having chosen me all my life. I packed my clothes, a Romeo and Juliet book I had hidden when auctioneers descended on us, and a book I had been writing in my free time which never saw the light of day because that was the last I ever wrote anything creative. I packed them and my feelings in a nylon Nakumatt paper bag.

I showed up at Mama Mpenzi's but I did not tell her what had happened.

* * *

Dad moved from this guest house the week after and came to Mama Mpenzi's to look for me.

He moved to a proper estate by the name Olympic which was a two bedroomed house with a living room. Kitchen. Store. Two loos. Backyard. Front yard. Gated. He explained all that to me and told me to get back home. I told him to give me time.

It was the home I needed for so many years. But it was too late now.

I was happy for Philip though because he no longer needed to hide where he lived from his friends - Philip never had a normal kid's life where his classmates would visit him at home over the weekends.

Mum's benefits were released by Care Kenya and all of it had been assigned to my brother because on record she only had one child. Dad protested it and went to court to demand that I be added. I honestly thought it was a waste of time.

"Philip is still in school. He will need this. I don't. I will make it out here on my own."

He would hear none of it.

He went to court and proved I was my mother's child and I was given a portion of her benefits. The court also ordered for impounding of Mum's car from her ex-husband and Dad took it.

As Philip was still a minor, Dad was his administrator. I was yet to get my National ID but I was eighteen so I was a co-signatory for my portion.

Dad became a permanent fixture at the bank as there was no mobile banking then and you could only withdraw a certain limited amount a day.

I was now at Alliance Francaise pursuing my French classes before joining college.

One of the reasons I needed to learn French is I needed to understand Congolese Rumba Music and also hoped once in my lifetime I would visit the DRC and France and see the Tower of Eiffel with my own eyes. I loved the DRC for the music it blessed me with. And I was fascinated by the history and geopolitics of it. I loved France and largely Europe because I was born an artist. I hoped to one day visit the Louvre Museum and see the Mona Lisa, the many works of Picasso and the painters of the Renaissance works with my very eyes. Presently, I have travelled extensively but these are the two countries I am yet to visit. I guess I am saving them for last.

I had read too many books for my own good. I knew I wanted to travel the world. All that I read I needed to see. Whether it was Broadway in Manhattan, the centre of my long time theatre dreams. Or Hollywood from Jackie Collins books. Or the streets of London following the footsteps of Sherlock Holmes or watching my beloved Arsenal live. Or Paris. Milan for the fashion. Art and culture - I had read it all. I could see it.

NEW MONEY

As a co-signatory, it did not occur to me that I was now in a trap. Whenever I went to college, I sometimes found Dad standing outside Alliance Francaise, cheque book in hand waiting for me to append my signature here or there. He always had an explanation around school fees for my siblings that he needed to pay. I thought that action really stripped him of his ego. To save both of us this discomfort, I signed off all the blank cheque leaves and forgot about him and the money.

When you turn eighteen in Kenya, you will need to show up at the government registry with your parents' IDs or death certificates and your original birth certificate to apply for your own Identity Card.

I had gathered three friends and we had an ID date. We wanted to get our IDs at the same time. We went to Makadara Government offices for this purpose.

We submitted our papers for vetting and consideration. Thereafter, they would have to take our finger prints, pictures, signatures and give us a waiting letter that we would use to collect our IDs.

My friends were called in one by one and they were all cleared as I waited. They completed and were given dates for picking their National Ids.

I was made to wait a long time. We got so impatient that two decided to go ahead and get a place for us to eat as I was still being attended to.

Eventually I got called - but not to have my picture or finger prints taken.

Handcuffs were put on me and the officers promptly started questioning me. They held my birth certificate against the light and asked if I could see anything. I was trembling, but I could clearly see the father's name had been rubbed and my name had been rubbed too. They then asked me why I had forged a certificate of birth.

I did not have anything to say. All I could do is cry but I figured it out pretty fast. I gave them Dad's number and they called him to the place urgently. Due to the traffic in Kenya, Dad took longer to arrive and so I was bundled in a van used to transport villains to court houses and all I could see from the cracked floor was the tarmac of Jogoo road rushing underneath.

By the time I was arriving in the court house, Dad was already there with a lawyer. I was intercepted before facing a judge and was released.

Dad and I had a strange nonverbal discussion as he gave me fare back to Mama Mpenzi's. When I got back to the estate, that tea was with everyone and I did not have an explanation.

Dad later organised for me to travel to the village. I had my finger prints taken and my papers straightened out and I got a new birth certificate and a new ID. The original certificate that had been rubbed traced to Pumwani Hospital. It had my name as Deborah Tendo and father's name as Alex Minge Tendo.

Dad was still working with the lawyer. He was also swimming in mum's benefits from CARE and was doing well in the city.

Little by little I started hearing, no actually- I met Dad with a new lady, a former flame with whom they were rekindling their love. They had a child together also in the 80s.

I was living with Mama Mpenzi waiting to go to college and also studying French. Dad was paying for it. The Mikayi had also moved in with Dad as this was a proper house.

Our Dad was the kind that takes a woman in her entirety. All he needed was to fall in love. He will adopt you, your kin and kith and will take your debts and liabilities as his.

His old flame, who was having trouble in her own marriage grew very close to Dad, moved out of her matrimonial home and soon her family became Dad's.

It was around this time that Mum's Nissan, just three months into Dad owning it, burst into flames mid journey.

He had packed up the whole family of my step sisters and they were upcountry bound. They were all just lucky to come out alive.

Neither Philip nor I was in the Nissan. I only watched this on the news and was relieved to hear everyone got out safe but had all their luggage burnt to the ground.

I was out looking for scholarships to study out of Kenya and had applied to study literature and performing arts in the UK. I did send all my certificates of performance and I was accepted. In fact, the college agreed to part pay my scholarship and I approached Dad with this prospectus.

Mama Mpenzi at this point had run out of the money she inherited from her husband's death, moved back to the salon. Back to her day to day struggles.

Dad dismissed the prospectus and I instantaneously knew he was either financially constrained or had no money at all paying fees and taking care of about 13 kids at different stages of their lives.

He started delaying paying the fees at Alliance Francaise and I had to defer some modules and drop out momentarily.

And this was also the point I got a call up to college which meant I had to work to sustain myself and study on Education loans.

He had at this point left the advocate he was working for and started his own company that did tenders. Ad hoc tender agents scroll all day through papers to see if there is a company tendering. You do bid then involve a lot of canvassing. If you win the job, you source for financing either from banks or well-wishers. A bank will finance only if you have a good credit score or history.

Well-wishers are the easier financiers but demand a huge cut so you end up doing the running around and gaining little from tenders as a broker.

Borrowing money against a Government Tender Local Purchase Order (LPO) was another big risk. It was known to everyone that the Government of Kenya does not pay anything in or on time. The banks on the other hand knew how to demand debts on time. A combination of these factors would put many brokers in dire financial strains. Dad was confronted by all these and I became a collateral damage through college.

All these came by Dad - I was struggling through college. He was struggling with finances yet again.

Arts came naturally to me, and the fact that I had studied French was an advantage since the French Cultural Centre owned an auditorium and has been an amazing supporter of the arts in Kenya to date.

As I was a student at the FCC, we had a free pass on opening nights to watch a play.

The casts and productions were a far cry from what we did in school. They were so magnificently high end and the actors seemed very sophisticated with high tech lighting and sound systems. Pulleys. Automatic curtains.

I also went to the National Theatre and watched plays that based themselves mostly on set books with students as audiences.

One day, at the French Cultural Centre, I gathered courage and went backstage to try meet whoever was in charge and I was introduced to performing arts legend, Sammy Mwangi.

I did not have to read a script twice. Sammy gave me the leading role in my first ever professional play called 'After you with the Milk' and I went on to act many, many professional plays with Heartstrings ensemble which has produced revered thespians in the country among them Vic Ber, Ken Waudo, Daniel Ndambuki, Phelix Odiwuor (Jalas), Angel Waruinge. The list is endless.

Would you believe that we performed in a US embassy sponsored play, as the US embassy is a big supporter of creatives in Kenya and were offered a six-month part scholarship in an arts college in the US together with my then mentor Anne Mwalagho and four others.

I could not make it because I could not raise the air ticket. Accommodation was also not provided and I had no one to go to and the chance to ever see Broadway with my eyes vanished.

Two of us however had their families conduct fund raisers. They left and never returned.

I grew up to love sports. During Rugby matches, I would procure beer from the factories and resale at a profit - I made very good cash because I got good tips. Some of the rugby fans always forgot I had their change and kept ordering for more beer.

I would have loved to do this in Gor matches. However, soccer is not a rich sport in Kenya. Rugby is.

Whatever I could get my hand on that legally made money, I did it. When you are in the hustling game, you form a network of people who provide these jobs or people who work these jobs and when something is up you will always get a call, "Hey we have this happening this weekend, are you game?"

Whether it was promotion of new brands and products. Or waiting in events. Gate collections. Even modelling. Never mind I have never grown past 5'8!

I remember when the Ugandan singer Chameleon performed in Nairobi, I was among the dancers. Kenyans thought we were his entourage from Uganda. We had been put together that morning, taken through a mock rehearsal and let loose. When we jumped onto the stage, we wore some leather shorts and tank tops and worked the stage in no particular routine.

I happen to have a very deep voice which I inherited from my mother and was a favourite with voice overs on radio. My little brother was also about to finish school and I made it my job to ensure he was fine. The lucky thing is that CARE offered to pay Philip's fees till he cleared high school so that was not a problem then.

I graduated college and there were no parties held for me. Dad attended with my step sister Lillian who I was very fond of.

Lillian was my step sister from the Mikayi's house.

Lillian was sharp as a razor in school. But was also a natural rebel who locked horns with Dad throughout; was a victim of Dad's cane most holidays. As with all my siblings, she loved her Rumba and was a great dancer.

I got my first job at a law firm, BA Achieng Advocates along Standard Street and so I left my acting career to concentrate. Although it was my passion, I decided to abandon theatre because the financial returns were measly yet I came from a struggling family.

As early as while in college doing these odd jobs, Dad had already started asking me for financial help. In most African countries, stage theatre does not pay as much. In fact for a long time, even acting in movies did not pay much.

Nigerians revolutionised this followed by South Africans and Ghanaians due to the specific countries really consuming their artists content, which was never the case in Kenya.

I had struggled through college and now my little brother was to go to college and with no funds, I had to make the decision to concentrate on work that will ease the financial burdens at home.

I recall Sammy Mwangi calling me for scripts and me telling him I could not give him my best since I now had a day job that needed my attention. He wondered if I could go for practise in the evenings after work and I told him I would think about it.

I had won first runner up in the best actress category for the National Mbalamwezi theatrical awards with Heartstrings Ensemble. The late Lorna Irungu of Phoenix Players beat me to win the best actress and Sammy was keen on the top award coming to Heartstrings the following year.

"The world moves on, Deb. And your space will be filled up with a new artist."

"Talent is not a sweet. It doesn't end, Sammy! See you when I am retired!"

We laughed about it but I have never been on stage again.

On the first month before I got my first salary, Dad would stand outside the building, wait for me and we would have lunch together. He would update me about Raila Odinga.

It is funny how daughters yearn to move out of dad's house and immediately they get their own house, they relish going back to his house some weekends. You start missing your Dad the moment you move out.

After working a year, I went to visit Dad and he took one look at me and asked "Mami, are you pregnant?"

I was expecting my first born son.

When I had my son. Dad had saved up money and came visiting with all sorts of gifts. He carried my son in his arms and played with his cheeks like a dotting grandfather.

HUSTLE

The other reason why I did not get back to Sammy is I secured a new job in the legal department of a leading security organisation in the country.

Then I was moved from legal which I studied and thrust into operations because the directors felt I was under-utilised, I was immediately transferred from the City to pioneer the organisation out of Nairobi in the organisation's expanding programme.

Heartstrings had no branches outside of Nairobi. The new job offered better pay and I did not have to deal with dusty files at the courts' registry, draft deeds and sit through Industrial court room hearings. The legal profession was never my calling. It was Dad's.

I jumped straight into the world of Logistics, Security and Supply Chain with my mission in Operations and Expansion.

Dad was vehemently opposed to me leaving the city. He claimed he would be lonely. He said it was comforting for him to know I was just a bus or a building away.

He said my personality was too big for the little city I was moving to but I promised him that I would visit Nairobi every month.

At around this time, he landed a good tender and got a windfall. First thing he did was to buy a second hand car– his first ever car. A Premio, off white in colour – His premio was the most loved car on earth. I had never seen a car that is washed twice a day. In and out.

His weekend to do would be to clean his car in the morning. He would wash it with foam. Then wash it with plain water. Then change the cloth and dry it up. Then he would spray it until he could see his reflection on it. Then he would get in and polish everything in it till it shone.

He would finish with laying old newspapers on the leg rests so that anyone who got in did not dirty the carpets.

I am on the cumbersome side of life. I drop things. I leave bottles uncorked. I press toothpaste from the middle. I will probably knock a glass by mistake. I am terrible with keys. Dad and I struggled when it came to meticulousness. Dad hated me to get into his car because I was always eating something, and would leave a sweet wrap. Or crumbs of cake. Or would spill soda on his seats.

He hated that mid journey, I would see someone selling sugarcane and there would be no peace until he parked and I got a cane. He hated the whole operation of my eating sugar cane. How the juice splashes. How it drools from my lips while I fill him in with stories. The cane peels and where I would place them. Then the husk after I am done with juice. But most of all he hated the stickiness of my fingers when I was done and I loved telling him stories while lovingly touching his shoulder or hand as he drove.

He would listen to my stories while halfway dodging any contact and also checking if I was spilling anything on the car seats. In these moments, he absolutely loathed me.

Before I got into his car, he would politely ask for my shoes which he would give my younger siblings to clean.

You would see the pain in his eye whenever he had to drive over a puddle of mud and water which is 100% the case if you were living in Nairobi, a city where you would encounter a pot hole so big it could change the song playing on your stereo.

He would curse if a fellow motorist drove roughly beside him and dirty water splashed on his car. He now had a permanent paper bag in his car specifically for me to deal with my waste.

He gave his car a name - Sibuor Marach

Anytime I would be in the city, I would meet him up.He would always come with his former flame. We would have dinner then we would set off to Rumba concerts and dance the night away.

We had Rumba favourites where we hopped on our feet once they came on. We were constantly at the DJs trying to influence the music with a list of Franco songs that needed to be played.

When there was soccer we would both wear a Gor jersey and head to the stadium. A lifetime of supporting Gor yet I was the one who bought his first customised jersey.

We would get in together in most Gor derbies with rivals AFC Leopards. But when the teargas came, we would run in different directions and meet later in an obvious Rumba joint. At times we would lay low below the stadia seats amidst heaps of bodies when stones were crisscrossing the air between rival fans.

He was still a dye in the wool Manchester United fan while I went for North London's Arsenal, much to his chagrin.

I chose Arsenal when I was about 15 and he really protested. But I told him we needed to have variety in the house for the sake of debate because at that point he had influenced everyone to support Manchester United.

I also loved Arsenal as it had more diversity in the players' races. I had a crush on Thierry Henry and the club was also supported by my favourite cousin Sammy who had also been influenced by Uncle Steve our maternal uncle.

We had terrible fall outs whenever United lost and Arsenal won. He would simply ignore my calls all week long.

It was not uncommon to see my Dad and myself on the dance floor dancing and making merry. During slow songs, he would embrace me in his arms and I would rest my head on his chest.

We confused a lot of suitors. They thought he was my sugar daddy and women thought he was out with a very young girl. It suited both of us whenever we were not interested in whoever was trying to court us.

It was always hilarious when I introduced him to suitors as 'Meet my Dad.'

Dad would call me on a weekend and ask, "When are you coming to Nairobi?' and I would tell him 'How about now?" And I would fly in.

He would give me options of where we needed to go dance. He would momentarily disappear from the festivities to check on Sibuor.

He never ran short of stories.

Dad was still a magnet even in his 60s. You would find women in their 40s asking me to say hi to him, greetings he would take with so much zeal.

He was born on the 20th of June.

You needed not mark it on a calendar because on 19th June midnight you will receive a text from him. It's my birthday. Send me a gift. - Such a needy guy.

Acknowledging his birthday meant so much to him. I guess he missed being mothered, having lost his own mother at birth and it's for this he named most of his girls Achieng, including myself. Because his mother's name was Achieng Nyongalo.

At around this time, my sister Lillian had also finished her training at the Railway Institute and was struggling to get a job.

Dad had requested that I talk to my former boss in the law firm to take her in as a secretary. And she did. Because if I was good, Lillian was better - she was eloquent, neat and diligent.

Lillian had also met a man who she decided to move in with as soon as she got a job. Dad had opposed the marriage just like all our marriages. Dad never wanted any of his girls to get married. It was always a push and pull. The best strategy was always to get a job, be independent then show up pregnant. He would have to tow the line fuming.

There are times when Dad would follow our older sisters all the way where they were married, steal them and their kids and bring them back home. Our first born sister really suffered this.

If he suspected you were not happy or were suffering in any way, he was going to do everything in his power to get you back home and yet he also had moments when he was not doing so well himself.

It was very common to arrive home and find Dad living with grand children and his daughters or daughter.

And so he vehemently opposed Lillian's marriage.

All of us went to Girls boarding schools and had very little interaction with boys until college for me since I went boarding in my formative years.

I think for my sisters like Lilly who never moved out of Dad's grip past high school, she literally just started dating whoever was available near home. I was lucky I moved out even before college and got my first boyfriend while in college. He had little say about that.

Lilly's husband came from deep in Kibera slums across Olympic estate where Dad lived. And Dad hated it. He was a young man who had nothing but seemed to have potential and Lilly so desperately wanted to leave home. She spoke to me to also assist her husband get a job which I did in the same industry I was in. I could see she was desperate for it to work because as long as the husband was unemployed, Dad would never respect him or their union.

One time I travelled into the city and went to visit Lillian at her home. She had lost a considerable amount of weight and I noticed her eyes were yellow and all this while she was pregnant with her second born. Lilly had been diagnosed with anaemia during her first pregnancy and was advised not to have any more kids. She however went ahead and did. A naturally rebellious person who danced to the tunes of a different drummer.

Immediately after having her second child and several tests later, she was found to have cancer of the blood.

We had various challenges as a family. But this here was a big problem. It blew a tornado in our hull. Lilly fell ill and was on chemotherapy. She was constantly in and out of hospital as she gave cancer the battle of her life.

Ridden by so many sick offs and absenteeism, my former boss called and informed me she would have to let my sister go.

Chemo took toll on her and her husband took the exit toll.

Their marriage had fast turned brown. Curled up on the edges like an old photograph under the bleaching force of disease.

Dad hired a taxi, went to their tin house in a promising slum, picked Lilly and her kids and moved them in with him.

Lilly was in a step to step salsa with cancer for almost two years and when the footsteps of death gained on her, she refused to take any more chemo and opted instead to travel and visit the people she loved.

She visited me in my house outside Nairobi and we spent a weekend together. She was bald. I shared my wigs with her and we reminisced on the little childhood we had experienced together. Her being my step sister from the Mikayi's house, she had spent most of her life with her mother in the village and only joined Dad, Philip and I later in life.

Lilly died in the still of dawn in her bed at our father's home.

On that morning, Dad was still downstairs preparing to leave for the day when Lilly cried out for him.

Dad climbed upstairs and sat with her on the bed. Held her hand ever so softly. Dad called Mikayi who was preparing porridge downstairs.

"Lilly *tho*."

They both sat next to her as her hands grew cold like a cup of tea outside in the winter.

Dad then settled in the living room, called Philip and George to come pick their sister to the morgue. He then called me in tears and said, 'your friend has just left us.'

Lilly died at the age of 26.

In her coffin she looked like she had found the peace that so eluded her in this life.

Among the Luo in a traditional setting, an unmarried woman with children cannot be buried in her father's compound. If she dies, she can be interred outside the fence because customarily at a certain age, girls are considered not being part of the family and are called *'wagogni'* as it had happened to Nyakendu.

It is actually shameful and frowned upon that when your husband cannot bury you, the family has to cover the embarrassment by asking your elder sister to bury you as a co wife. Times have changed and nowadays, families set aside family burial grounds where any member who dies is buried whether lady or man. Married. Bachelor. With children. Without.

Lilly's husband never showed up for the funeral and his children remained my Dad's lifetime responsibility.

I was rising steadily at work from supervisory to junior management and had made it to head of department. I was required to now drive a company car.

I had never driven a car before as my previous position gave me the option of a driver.

I was terrified. But I needed the job.

Philip was also a full time student at Kenyatta University and needed sustenance money and it was all on me.

I called Dad and asked him if I should come clean and tell HR that I could not drive and so I was unqualified for the job.

"Mami, do not ever say that you cannot do something." He shot back.

I was now in Nairobi for further training on my new role and was required to collect my car at the end of it all.

Dad knew of an abandoned piece of land that played the role of an ad hoc football pitch for kids and at times it harbored street children in one of the estates. And he advised that every day after training I should meet him there.

I did.

So he carefully explained to me parts of his car *Sibuor.*

"This here is the steering wheel." It was the first time I saw him not mind that I got into the car in dirty shoes.

"Today you don't even mind my shoes? Am I dealing with a clone here? Where is my Dad?"

I teased him punching his shoulders.

"Be serious this is not a joke. Cars kill people. You are the most forgetful and clumsiest person I know."

"Ok so I am learning to drive here? In this field?"

"Here and in driving school. I just must be sure you are doing the right thing."

So I joined a driving school for a crush course.

I would go for training. Then the driving school in the afternoons. Then meet up with Dad in the evening and we would head to the field together for me to do endless laps in his car.

I was right there terrified at first when the car started moving. With Dad giving instructions by my side. At times helping move the steering. All the time reminding me to look at the road when he spoke to me. At times getting frustrated when I took long to grasp something. At times even mocking me.

"*Wengeni dongo ka torch to okinen?*" 'There is nothing special about everyone you see out here driving Mummy. You can drive.'

He had a way of praising me from my childhood

"*Ma be Achieng wang'e dongo? Ma Nyawasaki ma riek ma tiende oke? Mamana? Ma in?*"

My ego would shoot up and in these moments, I could change the world.

My fear dissipated and I was now driving around the abandoned land freely by myself while he set up stones that I would pass through. Try to flash park. At times I would drive straight to where he was standing instructing me like I was about to knock him and he would run for his dear life while cursing me.

I only worried about actually going to the road.

Meanwhile HR kept calling asking that I pick my car. It was ready and I kept informing them that I would go. When it was no longer tenable, I filled in a leave form to get some grace time to finish classes at the driving school.

When I hit the road with my driving school supervisor who was also an acquaintance of Dad, I was somewhat confident on the pedal but scared stiff when a different car approached me or felt the anxiety when a convoy was behind me and could not overtake.

The most hilarious thing is as we were doing our road tests. I could spot Dad's brown coat on the edge of the street. Waving an envelope probably carrying Tender documents assuredly.

I eventually picked my official car, with my Dad waiting right at the bend.

My organisation's workshop where I was picking the car was right in the thick of traffic and I was not sure I could navigate once outside the gates. It is interesting when you are an individual that exudes confidence, nobody really goes down to vet you and the head of workshop did not even do a test drive. Handed me the keys and moved on to other important things.

When I drove out, Dad was outside. He hopped in and sat on the passenger seat next to me and we did rounds so I could get used to the car.

Nobody at work ever found out that I learnt to drive on the job. They are probably reading this now.

I looked at him in traffic in disbelief. At some point he told me, "Do not ever tell anyone that you can't do something."

These words that he liked to tell me had put me in trouble quite a few times in my life.

When I was 13 years old at Mukumu Girls Boarding, the teachers would announce prefects at the beginning of the year and they would be called out in the parade and given a badge.

On that day, the notorious ones like myself would be behind the parade being naughty and engaging in our own agenda. Which is what I was doing on this day with friends. Suddenly the pupils who were standing close to me all turned and looked at me and that section of the parade also did and the parade went quiet. I had no idea what had been said in front and had no idea why everyone was looking at me

I only heard the Headmistress Sister Joycelyn Mukolwe's voice, "Is Deborah with us?"

Apparently I had been chosen the school time keeper, which was okay only that I did not know how to read the clock.

On the week the clock was being taught I was out of school for some reason and so whenever I sat a Math exam, I would score all questions except for the clock which I never bothered to even respond to. Just left it blank and because in boarding nobody really checks your past papers as a parent would, the issue subsisted.

Instead of saying I could not read the clock, I walked courageously and was given a bell and a clock to manage the entire school.

In another incident, I arrived at Moi Girls Eldoret and during the first week nights, different club masters were walking in dorms trying to recruit new members into their club.

Mrs. Kurgat the swimming teacher came to the dorm and asked; "How many of you have come from Nairobi?" I raised my hand up.

"Give me your names. Tomorrow morning please show up at the swimming pool."

Mrs Kurgat's assumption was that if you were from the capital city, surely you must have interacted with a swimming pool. She did not know Nairobi has the rich and also the very poor. I had never been in a swimming pool all my life but I never said, 'I can't swim,' so I showed up.

Both incidents ended up well, fortunately.

On the time keeping, my desk mate Marylin Monroe Nyamuok happened to have a digital watch which I used till she discovered I could not actually read the clock and taught me. On the swimming, I was permanently not feeling well during practise until I confided in my desk mate Zippy Asewe who after laughing hard, decided to teach me how to swim over the weekends when everyone else was swimming for fun and four years later, I left the school as the swimming captain and her captain.

During competitions, Zippy would cheer loud and emotionally because she knew the back story.

Now when it came to driving, it did not matter how good a driver I became. If I was driving Dad, I was perpetually a student he would give instructions. Inform me that a car was approaching. Even criticise the music I was playing.

I realised that was him just being Dad.

I was deep in soccer which I went with him. I was deep on the night life which I went with him.

I was also deep on the alcohol.

Dad had stopped drinking after Nyaseme left and he would live the rest of his life sober.

But I had picked up Vodka and Gin and later Whisky which he was lovingly concerned about.

I would be effective at work and took on very heavy tasks in Operations but I was also heavy on the bottle.

I would be the person who would travel from one city to the next and this time not following Okatch Biggy like my Dad did, but Musa Juma like my generation was doing. In Luo land, we don't run short of stars. We will create one if need be.

I was never the person who would drink and fall on the ground. Or drink and not be able to drive.

I would drink and be deliriously happy.

I would drink and would experience clarity. I actually sat some exams high and passed exceedingly well.

At times I would drink, retreat into my car and cry. I became the happiest unhappiest person when high. I reached the point where I could drink a whole bottle of Whisky by myself and still function.

I would never miss driving into the city on Dad's birthdays and I would pick him up and we would hit the night life together. Then drive back to his house where I would sleep next day all day.

One evening I woke up at home and found him downstairs obviously listening to Agao Patrobas on radio for his amazing Rumba show. While at the same time also watching Fred Machoka the blackest man in black Africa who also hosts a Rumba show and so depending on who played his favorite hit, he raised or lowered the volume.

When I was settled down, he asked,

"Are you ok?"

"Yeah I'm good Dad."

"I am worried about you."

"What? Why?"

"I know you handle yourself quite well. But I feel you should reduce your drinking."

I laughed it off. But he was steadily looking at me.

"Really. Are you being serious right now Dad?"

"I have been worried for a while actually. You are not on a good path. You remind me of my past and at times you remind me of your mother."

***

In 2005, I was already an adult and very active in politics and yes you guessed it right, an ardent supporter and follower of Raila Odinga.

Apparently for Raila to support Kibaki, there was a memorandum of understanding that one of the things Kibaki would steer was an amended constitution within 100 days of power.

Part of the compromise that led to that win was the coalition supporting a constitutional overhaul that would see Kenya get a new constitution anchoring an executive Prime Minister who would be the leader of the majority party in Parliament. The constitution was to also include devolution, which Raila had always championed for. Once the coalition won and given Kibaki's status on the wheel chair, the luminaries around him went back on their word. Part of the coalition led by Raila felt shortchanged and opposed it. A referendum was scheduled with the symbols banana for Yes and orange for No. Raila led a section of leaders in opposing the proposed constitution.

The orange team humiliated the banana team 57% to 43% and Kibaki decided do a cabinet reshuffle, firing every last cabinet minister who was in the orange camp led by Raila Odinga.

Raila formed a party called the Orange Democratic Movement.

In the following year, 2007, Raila vied for the presidency for a second time through ODM challenging Kibaki's NARC.

Africa and especially Kenyan politics are about coalitions. This is entrenched by the tribalism that is so deeply rooted within us. Every tribe somewhat has a figure head who forms a political party that they use to negotiate.

So towards elections you will find a motley collection of parties with baffling acronyms to match, that have no use other than revolving door politics. Short-lived parties that are as forgettable as their chairmen.

The biggest negotiator is the one who has the most fanatic support or whose community votes as a bloc because some politicians demand a seat on the table but only hold a handful of followers like a string of beads with very few beads and lots of string.

Luos have always led in this front and it always gives Raila a vantage point in negotiations on who is going to be the flag bearer but he had made pacts with similar figure heads from other communities and his bid this time was very strong.

The three tribes that vote as a block are Luos, Kikuyus and Kalenjins.

Anytime two of these come together, or anytime you manage to split the bloc of either of this, it is instantly a winning formula.

Raila was going it with the Kalenjin figurehead William Samoei Ruto who had inherited a fanatical support from his previous mentor, President Moi.

Dad had bought a calendar that had Raila's face on it complete with his kitchen cabinet.

He pushed the envelope further by buying Raila's portrait and hung it up like his house was a business.

"God is great! But Raila is on earth!" He often declared.

Raila was headed for a massive win.

The morning of the election, Dad called me at 4am and wondered why I was still in bed - I told him I am an essential worker and needed not wake up at dawn to vote, I would just bypass the queue.

Fuming, he demanded that I send him a photo of my inked finger.

Voting in Kenya starts at 6 in the dawn and ends at 6 in the evening. So on the election day, you ensure you have all your supplies because results trickle in at night and you will be up all night monitoring.

The results started trickling in and Raila was firmly ahead. We were over the moon. Next day, Raila was ahead by over 1 Million votes and looked unassailable. Celebrations started in Luo populated areas. I drove some 7 hours into Nairobi because I wanted this moment to catch me while with Dad.

Found my old man upbeat. Trying new dancing styles. Ironing clothes getting ready for the swearing in. We left to the store in the evening and shopped massively for party stuff. Alcohol. Drinks. Meat for a mighty barbecue next day when finally the dawn of Kenyan politics would change.

We went to bed beaming at the possibility of a first ever Luo president in Kenya. Having missed this opportunity when

Jaramogi gave the mantle to Kenyatta, and Raila having given the mantle to Kibaki and in both cases lived to regret as they were discarded the moment power was aligned.

We woke up.

Kibaki had not only caught up with Raila but was steadily rising.

Kibaki's numbers were rising like a jet, while Raila's figures were being drip fed like an antibiotic.

Although not for this reason, I was glad to have travelled to Nairobi because Dad was on the throes of a heart attack and we had to call a medical officer to see him.

Kibaki was hurriedly declared president in the night.

He was then sworn in unconstitutionally, and unceremoniously, in the privacy of State house and not publicly as was the norm.

In the run up to these campaigns and historically, lots of politicians had built popularity fanning the flames of anger and resentment between tribes with the same algorithmic precision of ethnic war torn countries. Politicians who understood instinctively what excited the vulnerable base the most and supplied it with precision. Politicians who are ill qualified but hide conveniently behind tribe.

That very night, the country plunged into violence and chaos.

This election costed Kenyans 1,000 lives and thousands displaced especially Kikuyus who happened to live in Luo and Kalenjin lands.

In Kisumu, the Luo capital and emotional city, angry citizens burned and looted shops and the CBD looked like a picture straight out of Darfur.

Raila's supporters felt robbed but worse, the era of controversial electioneering was back in pure unadulterated fashion without the basc alloy of hypocrisy, when we thought all that was behind us with the ousting of President Moi.

I could not go a day without wanting to punch somebody in the throat.

Dad was sick for a long time. The twinkle in his eyes dimmed.

They were born four boys and one girl in his family.

The girl had died earlier.

He had already lost two brothers. The first and second born.

And so they only remained as two siblings. Himself and Uncle Kasera whose home shared a fence with us.

Uncle Kasera was a man of quiet demeanor. Very kind but a strict disciplinarian. He was an old man with the youthful eyes of a dove and Dad followed him. I never really knew where to place him as he hardly ever spoke.

He looked like a half cast, extremely light skinned and with a jet of white hair.

Death snatched him from under the carpet in a matter of hours – He was healthy. Then he fell ill at night and by morning he was dead.

I heard of this news from my brother Philip before I heard from Dad .

As Dad was now the only living member of the Nyongalo house, he was in charge of this brother's funeral. He was now the patriarch.

I called him. He was on the road upcountry. Philip was driving his car.

He picked and just started to cry.

He was saying, "I am now truly alone."

I assured him. That was not possible.

I recall during Uncle Kasera's funeral, Dad was withdrawn. He looked tired.

I recall asking him what the issue was and he said he was having stomach problems. The doctors had asked him to give up on salt and meats as he was having ulcers.

PHILIP

My brother Philip was now a grown man.

He had gone to University and was in Tech. He grew up to be what I call a passive introvert.

He will talk if there is need to or if you are familiar to him, otherwise he will definitely be on the quiet side of things. More the listener than the talker.

He will be quiet until someone starts a conversation then he will be very involved in it. He never liked to be in the centre of the room, but participated fully on the flanks. He grew up to be a most kind and considerate human being, quite hilarious if you are close to him.

Philip had spent all his life with Dad. I left when I finished High School and he did the same. Philip had been my son. I became his mother when I was five, the moment mum left. Always putting his needs before mine. Under my wings. Looking out for him. Protecting him and in our bad days, when food was really low I would give him my food and face the rumbles of my own gut.

He developed the love for soccer and is a diehard Manchester United fan to date. Also patronizes Gor. When he joined High School, it was his first time in a boarding school. There was nothing more important to me than to ensure not a single visiting day passed without me seeing him. On every closing day, he would have fare back home.

Every end month, I would be in a bus upcountry. The bus would arrive at 5 in the morning. As I did not have money to lodge, I would sleep in the bus till dawn and as they prepared for the journey back, I would alight and make my way to his school.

I was fresh in college and had no job but as I pointed out, was in the theatre and would take up any opportunities to earn a living. I would definitely be carrying his favorite food which at that time was French fries and chicken.

He would be perched up near the gate expecting me. We would sit under a tree and spread the food and would eat. Then we would talk all day long. The bus would leave at 5 in the evening so I left his school at 4pm. At times due to the vagaries of travel and not sleeping, I would spread a cloth and sleep under the very tree we picnicked at after we ate while he waited for me to wake up.

His birthday happens to be in June. He would definitely be in school. I would buy a cake and take it all the way through this journey to school. I never wanted him to miss a single birthday. He never did for as long as I was working.

The first time I visited Philip in school, when I alighted at his stop, opposite me was a hospital that looked familiar.

I wondered how I was connected to the hospital since this town was not in my route ever until Philip joined this school.

As we were having lunch, it occurred to me. This was the same morgue where mum had laid. The morgue Dad and I visited some years earlier to collect her body. Thankfully, Philip had been in school and did not accompany us.

Going to see Philip thereafter was always really special to me.

The moment he checked into Uni, he told me he needed to rent a house near campus so he did not have to commute back even when school was out. Which he did and just like me, he never ever moved back home.

In contrast to Dad, Philip was never a ladies' man. You would really struggle to even get that sort of energy from him.

Ladies hardly really bothered him which was sad because he is really a loving guy. All that love going to waste. I am known in my family to keep asking about people's romantic relationships. I am really that auntie and my nephews and nieces are always telling me about how it's going. I am aware of all the highs and lows of their relationships. All heartbreaks and I am the one to introduce the subject to their folks to secure a softer landing when they need to bring someone home. I am also the one who takes care of sex education. Philip was always adamant. He wasn't interested in dating. I felt this was a trauma of some sort and that needed peeling. Not that I was any better in that department.

I left High School without ever exchanging a love letter with a boy. During school innings, girls would spruce themselves up in their best uniform, do their hair and since it was always in the weekend, I would be in my room reading a novel then later in the afternoon, I would be seen in untucked shirt and shaggy hair making my way to the swimming pool for an afternoon of swimming and reading by the pool.

In the evenings of an inning, as the climax of girl boy relations ensued around the buses during goodbyes, I would be making my way back to the dorm. White faced. Red eyed and with shrunken type 4c hair. I never ever went out of my way to catch the attention of boys. Never bothered.My friends would wonder what was wrong with me.

"Deb did you see Fredrick?"

"Yeah? What about him?"

"What do you mean what about him? That guy is the IT!"

"Well. He is a fine actor, he is alright."

"Alright? Something is wrong with you!" They would declare while laughing.

I was a consummate tom boy. In all honestly, the nearest I got to boys' letters is me drafting love poems and catchy romantic messages on behalf of my classmates at a bread fee which they would then send.

In my usual mama bear fashion, I felt it was my responsibility to introduce my brother to his first drink. Sat him down with my step brother who was named after Dad. The two of them reconnected later in life after High School and refused to let go. So if you are to see Philip, you must also see George. George is also one of my favorite human beings -Did I mention that already?

There is power in naming kids after certain individuals. I believe this because George is a carbon copy of Dad. In mannerisms and in ideology which is both sad and amazing and probably why I love him.

I explained to them that they would have to decide if they are beer, or whisky, gin or vodka drinkers.

I told them about being a social drinker and not a functional alcoholic and all the rules including, you are not Rambo when you are drunk. And, do not drink and drive.

I bought them their first beer and sat back with my whisky to monitor how they evolved as the beers kept coming.

They drunk 12 beers in total and were still sober, and ended up carrying me to the car. Life was happening to people whether I made the narrative or not.

Philip graduated in Tech and is an IT guru - all these things that don't make sense to creatives and humanities guys like me.

One day he told me, "You have mentioned about looking for the Ugandans. Where did you reach with that?"

I had confided in Philip about my biological father. And he was not surprised given he was present anytime this issue came up subliminally and he advised me to search for Alex.

"I hit a snag. The photos that are appearing have to do with white people."

"Where are you searching?"

"Google."

"Have you ever heard of Facebook?"

"I think I have – this global village thing?'

'Yes you will need an account. I will set it up."

So my brother registered me on Facebook and all he did was send me a password. He uploaded one of my worst photos when I was looking emaciated as a profile photo.

I peered at it and called him and he immediately started laughing knowing I was going to protest the photo. Because that's Philip. The dark humour guy.

To date he is always threatening to post TBTs of our childhood when we were emaciated especially if I happen to post a filtered photo of myself he will start with;

"Madam. Who is this? Where is my sister?"

So me looking at my Facebook profile for the first time.

"Of all photos, this Philo?"

"I think you look cute. I have sent friend requests to all your relatives."

"Who said I want to be friends with relatives?"

"Look, you write unnecessarily long texts. This is the forum for you. You can write long opinions there and nobody will have a problem. But the main focus for this account is for your search. I am sure one of them is on Facebook."

I joined Facebook really late and the first thing I looked for was Franco. Arsenal. Raila Odinga and the Mighty Gor. I found it fascinating that other people I was not aware of also felt these three were the best things since bread and butter and I could connect with them.

It's quite easy to understand how social media becomes addictive. Here you are talking to complete strangers of common interest and most if not all of them understand your passions more than even your blood relatives.

I later sat down and went on a search for the name Minge.

Now, in Uganda the word Minge will come with an accent at the *e*. But this could also be an English name with a silent e so when I searched;

Alex Minge – White people.

Alexander Minge – More white people.

Every last search that popped up was white. I scrolled through and hit a dead end. I hit a snag.

Philip and I are very close. We speak quite a lot or rather I call and I speak quite a lot.

"Filter the search to specific countries."

I was clueless on that.

He instructed me to go to filters and make it Uganda or if I had heard that they moved to England or Sweden filter it to the countries.

I told him I would do that.

The truth is, while I was interested to know, I wasn't sure what I intended to derive from this knowledge. Of course I was curious about my features and those of my children and if there were any family genetics and trends that I needed to be aware of. They had a right to know their heritage.

I wanted to know why I look the way I do. Why I think how I do.

Who am I? Who is the other half of me and how much influence does this side have on me?

I was also laden with guilt for this search because I wondered how Dad would feel about it. I never dared ask him about this matter. I was quite sure it would hurt him. He prided in me being his child.

I recall when I joined the theatre, instead of using my surname, I used the surname Alexandria as my stage name. This name was stemmed from information I had that my real father was called Alex and I wanted to own a part of that and so I went by the name Deborah Alexandria. My first ever appearance on stage was a hit in Nairobi and I appeared on the papers quite a bit.

Dad would come across it first because, well, he loved reading the papers.

We were meeting for lunch in the CBD when he brought up the issue. He was visibly hurt and actually concerned that I wasn't using my surname (His name).

"Where did you get this name Alexandria?"

'I just came up with it.'

"Why?"

"Well it's a stage name. Creatives do that quite a bit."

"Don't you like your name? Are you ashamed of your name? What is the problem with your name? Why not even your maiden name, Achieng?"

"Good lord Dad, it's just a name!"

"Yes and a name is everything. You need to use your name so you claim your talent with your identity."

In the next play I tried to change my name but Sammy said 'you only get into the business with one identity and should never change it.'

Dad always sulked when I showed up in any papers with the Alexandria name.

I am not sure he knew what I did right there. Maybe he did but did not want to walk down that road and I took full advantage.

I wondered what sort of person my Dad was.

I only deduced that if he was Uncle Philip's good friend, he must have loved life.

I am a lover of life myself but in a measured way. I am self-aware when going overboard. And it's on this basis that one day I woke up on the 1st January 2015 and decided that I would never drink again.

I recall posting this on my social media and my friends really laughed.

The did not know just how resolute I can be.

The first weekend that followed this decision I was with Dad as usual combing Nairobi for fun and I ordered a soft drink. He asked if I was ill or on medication and I told him I had quit.

He scoffed.

"Really? What happened?"

'Nothing – I just quit.'

He looked at me more carefully this time and knew instantly I meant what I said and he only said.

"Wow! Now you will bore me to death!"

This is a question I would have to answer from many people and I still do answer this question.

Teetotalers around the world will tell you if you are a party goer, and you show up and you do not drink the questions you will have to endure.

"What happened?"

"Are you on medication?"

"Did you have a life changing experience?"

"Did you get an accident while drunk?"

"How do you deal with stress?"

"How do you have fun?"

"Are you a spy?"

Anytime I join a party or event and I am offered a drink and I say "I do not drink," people's faces fall on the floor.

"Not even a bit? A tiny winy little bit? Let me give you just a shot."

Ok taste."

"What about weed? I know somebody who knows somebody. I can fix you. Weed is herb. Medicine."

People who drink somewhat feel the non-drinkers are not at the same frequency of fun as they are and its hilarious. Because I am a natural extrovert with inexhaustible energy.

Then comes the friendly bullies.

I have had friends buy bread on the table so I accompany with my juice. "Get her juice and bread too."

Or when the bill comes, 'Deb you are sober. Calculate!'

"Deb you are sober. Check our bags we are going to the floor."

And the perennial "You are the designated driver."

I used the filter that Philip gave me and clicked on Uganda.

And one black person popped up with the name Minge.

My heart pounded it filled my head. And then I told myself to calm down. This is a whole country and Africans do share names. I then checked his profile and if we looked alike.

We did not.

I however sent him a chat.

'Hello there. I trust you are well - My name is Deborah. I am a Kenyan and I am searching for a family in Uganda with the name Minge. Specifically, Alex Minge.

I have been searching a year now on the internet unsuccessfully until I got into Facebook and decided to give it another shot. You are the only person who has popped up with the name and I am inclined to engage you. The family I am searching for left Uganda early 80s into Kenya and finally to Europe on political asylum. I know this is a long shot but if you know anyone that matches this description please advise. Thanks a lot and sorry for invading your privacy.'

I read it again carefully before pressing send.

And it was sent.

My Facebook page was new and so not so much activity was happening there.

But one day I logged in and found notifications and friend requests from people in their tens.

The Minges were here.

PEARLS OF AFRICA

I was some years late. My biological father had died in Sweden in 1993 from TB complications in what was suspected to be AIDS.

I felt disappointed more than I felt hurt. But I also got to the stark realisation that I was biologically a statistic as an HIV orphan.

It's true that dead people are faultless and people speak only well of them.

But I know it to be true that my biological father was a great man just by how people poured onto my social media page and tried to connect with me.

I got DMs from Sweden, England, America and even Uganda.

His sisters especially were truly enchanted and quickly really tried to make up for the lost time. He was a married man and had a family when they had to flee Museveni's rule.

I therefore had a half-sister and two half-brothers out there in Sweden and in the US. It was a lot of information to take in and I did not honestly know how to process it all.

My aunties needed to know how I was. Who I was. How my life was. How it had been. How my mum was doing.

So far, you know it's a long story. A story you really cannot start narrating to people you just met.

And this was the thing even when I started dating. The men I would most connect to were the ones who took time to write back and forth. To go on several quiet dates for conversation.

The ones who were patient enough to peel me off one by one.

I was never the person who would be asked 'so tell me about yourself' on a first date.

My Ugandan relatives were well meaning and I told them what was necessary; that I was fine. Dad raised me. Mum died. I have a little brother. I had gone to school well, was married and I had kids.

Photos of my father came through and I saw my forehead there.

I saw my last born son's forehead in there.

I saw my bulging eyes.

I saw my gap in there.

I saw my height in there.

I felt fulfilled. I felt my body come to meet my soul and I felt whole.

There is a particular cousin of mine in Sweden, who has grown to be one of my favourite relatives. She is a carbon copy of me.

Now, that startled me.

In fact, when they were made aware of me, when they saw my profile photo they all said, "But this is Nakaiza."

I also connected with my step sister, a most adorable woman who planned to travel to Uganda so we could meet.

I connected to my step brother who, in his true genes, was pursuing a career in Music.

All this was happening but I could not open up to Dad about it. It was cowardly of me as I should have brought it up because eventually, I made the journey to Uganda to stand at my biological father's grave a year after this reconnect.

I kept saying, "We are just getting to know each other. It's not like I am changing identity."

Uganda and Kenya border each other and so it was a bus journey.

I crossed the border and it was my first time ever in the Pearl of Africa. Uganda is a beautifully green country and from the moment you cross the border, the air becomes sharp as if it has been washed clean.

Clouds were gathering into fists and soon, the highway was drenched with torrents of rain; silver drops of water dancing on banana fronds then cascading on the ground. As night approached lightning ripped the sky apart bathing the tropical forests in its eerie momentary glow.

On the roads you also realise how militarised the country is. The ouster of Milton Obote in 1971 changed Uganda, a once peaceful country that had then had its fair share of political strife and civil war from the 1970's flowing into the 1980's. The ouster of Milton Obote by General Idi Amin was the game changer in this landlocked East African country. The ouster of General Amin with the help of Tanzanian soldiers later brought in a series of short stint leaders, including a second Milton Obote rule, and the military rule under General Tito Okelo, before Yoweri Museveni was elected in 1986. He was a guerrilla warlord who, as I write this book, is one of the longest serving presidents in Africa.

Every regime change drew bloodshed, displacement of people, death, refugees, an enduring long witch hunt and unending suspicion amongst the populace. Refugees and mass movement of people brings about children born during war by dysfunctional families and victims of instability back home.

The Minge family was among those being witch hunted for being very close to the Amin regime. Their lives were interrupted. The family had to leave massive wealth behind to live a refugee life with the little they could salvage.

Museveni, over time, brought a semblance of stability over the last forty years and for that, Ugandans always voted him back.

However, there is a generation; my generation of kids born in the 80s, the abazukulu, who were not there during the civil strife and feel he has done the most and needs to handle the mantle to the younger generation.

They want him out.

Out of the din, a single voice has risen above all others by the name Bobbi Wine who bears the hope of the youth in Uganda. He is pitted to compete Museveni's son, General Muhoozi, when the oligarch retires.

The bus drove along the winding roads and every once in a while stopped by the police who would have everyone alight and check our papers.

Twelve hours later into Mukono where vehicles move at a slow painful grind due to the traffic jam, a sub urban town just outside Kampala, I looked outside and was momentarily entertained by little boys who were playing soccer with a nylon football, wearing tshirts written Messi, Ronaldo and Aguerro and not their local star, Sserenkuma.

As all my siblings were out of the country, my cousins, the Tamales, picked me up. Some of the most gracious people I have ever met. They filled me in on who my father was and all they said was consistent with everything people told me previously.

It so funny how I would meet someone and they would hold their mouths and say, 'My goodness!' at my resemblance to Nakaiza and my aunties.

All except two of my Aunties lived in abroad.

I met my Auntie Evelyn and her husband Mr. Tamale (now late) and they gave me a befitting welcome.

I met my Auntie Robina who was taking charge in the family compound.

She saw me and she shed tears.

She led me to my fathers grave and I stood among banana plantations there and read his name.

Next to his grave was his father's and his mother's.

A huge feast was prepared for me.

Africans love their food. And Uganda is right there in the stew.

Ground nut soup, matoke, chicken, you name it.

They all reminisced on Alex Tendo Minge with so much reverence and they told me my grandmother would have been knocked off her stool if she was around for this.

Minge is the family name. My father's name was Tendo.

He was Alex Tendo Minge.

He died in Sweden but Ugandans insisted his body be transported back home, and they all travelled with his body, and buried him home with his people. I am told the funeral was a state like affair as people whose lives he had touched whether in Mpererwe or in Kampala or Nairobi or Europe all insisted on a moment to give a eulogy.

I was given a family name Tamalie and they sang traditional songs as we sat in the expansive compound.

It was a beautiful day.

I went back to Uganda a year later to meet my step sister who had travelled from the states for this specific purpose. When we hugged, we cried and she did not really want to talk about our father.

She said she was yet to deal with everything and I understood her.

We went out partying where we discovered we were both really talented dancers. Little wonder where that came from.

I definitely had to sit with Philip and tell him how it went down.

I saw that he was a bit insecure about my depth in this pursuit; his words were.

"Oh you travelled to Uganda? I thought you only wanted to know if he is alive. And sadly he is not, and have you told Dad?"

The fact that I had not told Dad and wasn't about to bring it up meant I definitely had some things I needed to work on. I felt guilt and I also felt ungrateful.

Later on in my work life, I met all my Aunties in England. I met my only Uncle, Godfrey Minge Kisuulo, in Uganda. He keeps posting my face on his Instagram and reminding everyone of Alex. I met Nakaiza in Sweden and all my cousins and all I can say is they are always drawing me in while they are also aware I lived a different life and I pay patronage to it. I can see always that they are giving me that space.

They are all wonderful people.

BIDDING

Dad was very steady with his company that was about tenders. I think it contributed very little to his pocket because myself and elder sisters had to chip in to ensure he was okay.

All of us now had jobs.

One time he called me that he needed some money urgently.

He needed a lot of money.

I did not have that kind of money and decided for us to talk so we see what could be done.

Apparently, an acquaintance who had won a tender needed financing and sought Dad to look for financiers.

Dad was to get a cut from it and since he was known in this field he made a few calls, checked in with some people who agreed to finance the job.

They gave him millions of shillings, which he faithfully handed the owner of the tender. All these transactions well documented.

A week later, they were to work on the tender together so he is in the loop of what was going on.

His acquaintance who was in Mombasa to clear some vehicles sent him the paperwork to begin the process. He of course had to call the company to ask for some guidelines on requirements.

A bored receptionist at the other end of the call told him the bid had already been awarded several months prior, contract signed and work had began.

Dad's tongue turned into leather.

He thought it must be some kind of joke. He frantically started calling his acquaintance who said all was well and that he was travelling to the city the next day.

He did not turn up.

Dad called him. He came up with an excuse.

Four days later, this guy had not showed up in the city and Dad decided to travel to Mombasa himself with cops to arrest him.

They arrested the acquaintance but that is the far it gets when dealing with con artists in Kenya.

They are anticipating an arrest and will take care of it in advance. They will pay someone in the system and so he will be arraigned in court. A bail put on their head, he will pay the bail using part of the loot and will be out back to freedom. He may even go to Dubai for a holiday and post on his social media.

Politicians in high places who have cases to do with integrity, even murder, are elected as long as they have power, influence and money.

Leaders forge papers and make the cut to run for public office.

The case will drag on for months, years even and at some point you will realise you lost money and is still losing money paying lawyer fees and you will most certainly give up.

For a man of my father's puny earnings, it was a case to nowhere.

But the financiers expect you to do the due diligence and these are not people who you owe money and imagine they will waste their time with courts.

I saw fear in Dad's eyes.

We had to look for money real fast and I was looking for any election gigs for a quick buck.

Around this same time in 2013, some election gigs were ongoing and Raila Odinga was vying for the third time still with Orange Democratic Party. The violence that had broken in the 2007 election had drawn the world's attention to Kenya. Koffi Annan, Desmond Tutu, Graca Machel and Ben Mkapa all converged in Kenya to oversee and midwife a coalition government as the country was dangerously sliding towards anarchy.

Raila became Prime minister while Kibaki held on as President. Since both Raila and Kibaki were in government, Uhuru became the defacto Opposition leader. This was a marriage of convenience just to ensure the country held on together.

In 2011, ICC knocked on Kenya's door to deal with the violence of the 2007/8 election. And among the accused responsible for the mayhem was Uhuru Kenyatta who had been on Kibaki's side and William Ruto who had been on Raila's side. William Ruto was a core principal in ODM and carried with him a basket full of loyal Kalenjin votes who had voted Raila to the last man.

The Kalenjins resented Kibaki when he took over from Moi.

In the five years he had been president, Kibaki re installed the Kikuyu hegemony and got rid of the Kalenjin one. A second loss to Kibaki was painful and they had reacted resoundingly. Most of the violence was between Kalenjins and Kikuyus, in Kalenjin populated Rift valley where Kikuyus had settled during colonial era.

William Ruto had expected that ODM would defend him. The party went silent. It was the first time the ICC had arrived in Kenya and with its reputation of hanging warlords, shivers were all over waiting for spines to climb up to because at any point in a politician's life, they have said something that fuelled violence. Laden with his votes he joined his co accused Uhuru Kenyatta to form TNA matching for the next election together.

A Kalenjin and Kikuyu vote together was massive as these are amongst the most populous tribes and they were glued on an emotional sympathy platform. Raila was going against Uhuru Kenyatta and William Ruto.

Dad was as invested as he usually was, bought himself an ODM tee, renewed his membership, got a calendar with Raila's photo and attended virtually all major rallies.

I was playing my part. All my social media pages had Raila's face on them.

The logic was we would be crazy as a country to elect ICC suspects actively attending hearings in Geneva.

I was now attending political rallies with my Dad . One to note was in Uhuru park where Raila was received by a mammoth crowd after being away overseas for treatment.

Dad and daughter - seated on the grass, in the blazing Nairobi sun, sharing a maize cob waiting for Raila's entrance.

This was a common goal and conversation that had seasoned our lives.

When Raila's convoy arrived, Dad was overcome with emotion that he left me standing and charged towards his hero's limousine.

Emotions overwhelmed him. He tore his shirt and joined the crowds that were dancing right in front of the motorcade bringing it to a stop. At this point, if the SUV carrying Raila was to crush them, they would have died martyrs.

Let me break it down in local colloquialism.

Juogi is a mystic spirit in Luoland and so far only two phenomenons have been able to infect the community with this supernatural feeling where an outer body experience overcomes you. You feel invincible, strong and can die for your cause. Only Raila and The mighty Gor are able to elicit *Juogi* on Luos. The people were washed with it. They were shedding tears. Were lying prostate on the ground. They were kneeling on the ground arms in the air. A euphoric experience without parallel.

This is the religion of true politician followers, looking like mounds of sand on a shore, a million indistinguishable bees in a hive. It is either that or the force of a people so opressed that they find a way to channel their pent up emotions in a common figure, to the point they deify them.

I was standing a few steps back in the charged atmosphere, always looking out for Dad and if he was okay. At one point in that crowd our eyes met and I saw that guy who was cooking and would switch the stove off when Raila was speaking on radio as a little child, but now white hair was beginning to show on his beards and his face was beginning to wrinkle, and yet he was still doing this. And this was probably the closest he would ever get to this lifetime hero.

The 2013 election was held on a Friday.

I had driven to Nairobi previous day and was now voting in Nairobi. The one mistake Luos always did was to travel upcountry to vote.

Whilst in Luoland, it was obvious whoever got the ODM nomination at the primaries was going to win. That was not the case in the cities where we spent most of our lives anyway. In 2013 we all had to move to the hotly contested areas so we give our party candidates a real chance.

I woke up early, queued with Dad while he read a newspaper the whole time, then voted and retreated back for a night of result monitoring.

In our minds, there was no way under the sky, two candidates who were actively facing trials at the ICC for the violence of the previous election were making it to office.

The election results started trickling in.

Raila was leading with a million margin but nobody was celebrating because we knew better. We held on.

Day two Raila was still leading but Uhuru Kenyatta had closed the gap to a half million margin.

Subsequent results continued to come in. And the gap held on.

We went to bed happy, pregnant with cautious hope.

Dad was permanently in the toilet with a running stomach shouting from the toilet "Wachopo adi?"

His pressure was up but there was no way of deterring him from following the tallying.

In the night, when the house was dead silent, I heard the television give that jingle that is produced when election results trickle in. I woke up, and found he had been to the washroom and thought to check on progress. The half a million gap held on and there were very few areas still to submit their results - I reprimanded him and told him to go sleep for chances were that we had a long celebration the next day.

The first person to see it was my little nephew, Lilly's son.

He had just woken up and wanted to watch Nickelodeon. But everything was about the elections.

"They are stealing the vote!" He cried out.

A county called Tharaka Nithi showed up with massive votes and bypassed Raila.

We all woke each other up and stared at the TV in disbelief. This was so familiar. Yet it hurt like it was new.

By morning next day, Supporters of Uhuru Kenyatta poured on the streets while Raila's supporters went dead silent, nursing internal injuries from wherever we were.

Raila issued a statement to his supporters for mass action and for the first time in my life, I joined protesters on the streets.

What I saw when my Dad arrived home after protests when I was a child, I became that when I got home. Torn clothes, teargassed eyes and the bewilderment of injustice.

Nobody else in my family has ever gone for these political protests and people did not understand how a woman would fill an official leave form at work to join protesters on the streets.

The day Uhuru was sworn in, I cried like a little girl and Dad had to call and console me.

Elections in Africa are such a terrorizing aspect because of the winner take all stance. The us vs them. This tribe vs that tribe. That is followed by unequal distribution of resources, public theft, favoritism on the part of the winner. People cry because they know for the next 5 years, they will be in the shadows and that is a lot of time for them and for their children given our life expectancy is only 60.

The only consolation here was that Dad's favourite team Gor Mahia was performing.

As I was on social media, lots of communities to support Gor had been formed for the sole reason of revamping the club which had been facing low turn outs due to mismanagement and lack of funds.

During my Dad's youth, Gor and AFC were doing quite well because the clubs rallied up their communities, it was their pride to be associated with their community club and had to show up and support it.

But this later came to die with the rise of companies who set aside budgets and could sign up the best footballers, fees that community clubs could not as community clubs depended mostly on donations from notable members of the community especially those gunning for political seats.

The quality of players determine performance and the league started seeing the rise of company football winning leagues as community football languished behind.

This killed the morale of fans coupled with mismanagement and soon, the stadia were empty across the country because in Kenya, only community clubs attract a following.

Company clubs are not able to attract crowds as much since the masses do not identify with a company if they are not employees. And how many employees are actually interested in soccer, let alone fill a stadium?

This situation was reversed by my generation. The third generation of Luos, who had grown up in the shadows of our parents supporting the mighty Gor passionately.

Campaigns to have fans go back to the stadia were started in a movemet dubbed 'Jaza Stadi' steered by seasoned sports media moguls Carol Radul and Joe Gidi.

Facebook communities organised themselves into branches whose sole aim was to recruit fans. Once a branch recruit, you would be registered and during matches the branches would organise for fans to attend.

Many initiatives were started courtesy of these branches and social media also played a big role in hyping.

Fans started attending matches once again and especially where Gor or AFC was concerned.

The turn out attracted sponsors and the matter of affordability or quality players was sorted. There was a betting company that also sponsored live transmission of matches on TV, something even the age of my Dad did not. This helped create awareness as people seated at home would see the attendance and catch on to attend the next match.

Gor was on a breeze.

I attended every possible match I could, was involved in many social fundraisers and fan opinion shaping of the club. I attended some matches with Dad . In some I was dealing with gate collections as I happen to work in an organisation that also handles valuables in transit.

I was in the thick of Gor, thicker than my father ever had been in his lifetime. It came naturally to me. Mid debates, I was able to discuss the legends of Gor without missing a beat. The winning goals. The violence-related episodes. Past glory days and I would go deep to the astonishment of many of my peers.

It was because I grew with it from the soil.

Gor Mahia FC is a heritage for me and for a lot of Luos my age. Its juogi would suck you in and it would take everything in you to climb out.

Match day for Gor - In my generation, from as early as the previous nights, you would see banners in various night clubs with Gor colours basically trying to lure Luo fans.

Mid concert you would find the main act calling onto us 'Where are the Kogallo fans?' and we would all stand up in unison and shake the club down. On the morning of a match as early as 6am you would start seeing fans going about their business in replica jerseys, with fantastical names imprinted behind the jerseys that could be their original or a fictional name meant to project some form of message or for comic relief because we the Luo are hilarious, names like 'amit moloyi' 'Jaber ma chon' 'tija tek wek gomba' 'Hooligan' 'Rateng mor kich' 'Akinyi Teargas.'

A Gor fan would turn and you would start laughing at whatever is written behind their jersey. We are cool like that.

From 8 in the morning you would now start seeing fan groupings picketing up and down streets hyping up their team carrying banners or paraphernalia symbolising the team.

On TV the fact that Gor is playing AFC would make top news with fans called in to give commentaries.

The officers in charge of security would give a briefing on the security situation and how security has been beefed up to deal with any wayward fans in case their team losses...or wins.

Because from fans crazy reactions post match you could never really tell whether Gor has won or lost. Are they happy? Or are they angry? Because whichever way the police would have a day-full of running battles.

At times Gor is the only way for Luos to express their pent up political frustrations.

The officers in charge of traffic would give a briefing of no gone zone routes and the timings where cases of mayhem may arise.

From around midday the people who do not care for football retreat to their homes or somewhere indoors so as not to get caught up.

The atmosphere is now charged to carnival heights. The isukuti drums are thumping and in the stadium the Ohangla is at fever pitch.

Fans pour from all parts of the city dressed in green or stripped blue.

Once at the stadium's compound, they part ways after several insults and exchanges that always seem to threaten to a kerfuffle but never graduate to one.

The stadium is full to capacity. It is song and dance and a few dramatic gestures from fans who storm the pitch amidst jeers from fans.

Raila Odinga's motorcade glides in sending the stadium to a frenzy. With him are leaders from the Luhya community in a show of unity, and any other leaders of the day that he is trying to woo for a vote.

At this point, the Luo nation is aligned.

The players arrive in the stadium and line up.

In unison, all Kogallo fans stand up on their feet and place a hand on their chests and the other in a fist of defiance to the air and the Gor anthem follows in a mighty thunder that consumes the stadium and the environs outside it.

Every flora, every fauna sits still. From outside in traffic the thunder catches on and motorists honk their horns.

Adrenaline runs high. The hair on your back stands.

Kogallo?

GO-OO-OR MAHIA!

Kogallo?

GOOOOR timbe duto ywakni

It is kick off time.

THE DREAM

There was this night I was out with Dad . We had a mighty great time dancing to Kenya's best Luo Rumba artist Johny Junior. Dad had taken a liking to JJ when he did not feel like going for Congolese Rumba.

We left the club around 3 in the morning and set home with Dad insisting I remove my shoes before getting into his car. I had hop skipped a puddle to his car and he feared I may have stepped on to mud.

I complied and got in bare feet with my shoes in my hands.

We reached home, I bid him bye going upstairs to wash my feet.

He had to sit at that hour to watch a repeat of the news that he had missed.

Raila had faced obstacles this way, blockades that way and bridges burnt behind, had re invented himself and was vying for the presidency a fourth time.

"But the TV is not going anywhere? It's a repeat you can still watch this tomorrow."

"Raila cannot wait!"

I went to bed to sleep.

I had a vivid dream.

I was walking along a narrow street with high walls and vehicles were hooting incessantly. There was a narrow pavement and roads were cabro'd as in the ancient Rome.

Cars were squeezing past me and so I walked very carefully on the narrow pavement. The crowds were Asian from the dressing.

On reaching the corner of this street amidst the crowd, I saw my brother George Auko Junior.

He was crying inconsolably. Something had gone terribly wrong. "Ginho (short for Georginho) what is it?"

"Deb. Dad has died!"

"But that is impossible! I was with him just tonight. We have danced till morning."

"Dad has died Deb!' '

I did not even need him to elaborate further. My heart fell on my stomach.

I fell on the ground and I started to wail and so here we were. Siblings on the corner of a crowded street with high walls, seated on the road wailing.

A most unlikely lady friend of mine showed up around the corner too. She recognised me and rushed to me.

"Deb what is it? What has happened?"

"Lydia. My father has died."

"Noo its not possible." She was grief struck and joined us on the floor wailing.

I suddenly woke up. My pillow was wet. Tears ran from my face into my ears.

My heart was broken and I was going through pain at that very moment that I had to put my palm on my chest. And in this bed, at home, I could hear Dad making a fuss downstairs about something that had not been done right.

I was so relieved to hear his voice that I started crying all over again.

My little sister asked if I was suffering a hangover or if I was ill.

I told her I was having a bad headache.

I woke up and went slowly downstairs. My heart was heavy to carry on my chest.

And there he was seated, looking at the TV for different views on the fact that Raila was vying yet again.

He hardly looked at me, but I looked at him very steadily.

He felt my eyes on his cheeks and now looked at me.

"Are you ok?"

"Hangover."

"Hangover and you don't drink. Hangover that makes you cry? Gosh Cynthia, get your sister some pain killers from the shop."

"I do have painkillers in my bag. I will just go up with a glass of water."

"Painkillers in your bag? Is your life really that painful?" '

"It is Dad . It is. Especially this morning. Its really painful."

To which he laughs while I look at him seriously and I see him.

I really really look at him.

The young guy who wore a skirt while washing clothes is gone. And now here sits an aging man wrinkles on his forehead and on the corner of his eyes. His lips are thinning in concert with his hair.

He is shaven but you can see sprouts of white hairs attempting their way out of his scalp and beard.

The square and bold shoulders. The beaming chest and youth is now gone and replaced by drooping shoulders. A small chest. A robust but a smaller Dad.

What hasn't changed though is the paraphernalia and morning cleanliness tools.

On the table is a chewing stick, a toothbrush and a cup of salted water indicating he is yet to start his OCD rituals and so he has not showered. Even that early in the morning and on stale news Raila is speaking on telly and my Dad listens intently to the point he tilts his head so his right ear leans towards the telly.

Raila himself is not the man I saw when I was a child.

He no longer has the somewhat long beard he donned, and keeps dabbing one eye with a hankerchief.

He has a slight limp when he walks.

I realise I am not that child anymore too.

I do go for Gor matches. I do go to the bar to listen to Franco. I am a Raila activist. I am about 160 pounds with a bit of a tummy from child birth.

Its been a lifetime.

"Dad!"

"Ehe Mami am trying to concentrate here."

"I love you."

Without looking at me he said, "I know that."

I started up the stairs and shot back, "You are so entitled!"

I flew back to my city and my heart was heavy. I was in pain and was mostly balancing tears all flight for no reason at all other than a bad dream. I reached home to the warmth of my kids and later that night Dad sent me a text.

"Nyawasaki..Are you ok?"

"Yes I am."

I later on called this friend of mine I dreamt I had met and narrated the story.

"But that would be unfortunate Deb. What I know about such dreams is that the person ate a little too much."

"No he did not. I was with him."

"I said a theory not the truth. Hey! Get over it. It was just a dream."

I also called Philip

"Old man probably overfed."

I called George. We could not even hear each other as he was partying and the club was noisy as hell.

"Who has died?"

"Why are you partying on a Monday?"

"What? Who has died on a Monday?"

I just hang up to which he called back twice and also gave up.

In Africa we do have those standard dream interpretations where, when you dream someone died, they overfed. If you dream people are in a party eating meat, someone is about to die. If you dream you are eating meat and especially tripe someone very close is about to die. If you dream of a snake then someone is planning evil. If you dream of a frog crossing your path, you are probably pregnant and so on and so forth

That whole week a dark cloud hang over me but it eventually dissipated.

After Uncle Kasera's death, the con job and Raila's third loss, I realised Dad had lost lots of weight and generally the zest for life.

He complained of a stomach issue, for which he had gone to hospital severally and they told him he had ulcers and gave him lots of medicine for it.

He saw several specialists who all agreed he had ulcers.

This diet change coupled with his tummy issues, had him lose lots of weight.

Weight loss was a good thing but there is weight you lose and you look healthy and weight you lose and you look emaciated, troubled even like something is eating you from within. He had also lost the zest for life.

He however still woke up early, went into the CBD to keep himself busy. We spoke severally and I did not know what to make of this ulcers that wasn't going away.

I was indeed aware that the con job costed him severely but Dad was the kind of guy who recovered really fast from setbacks.

I took him out during this time for a drink. We actually went to watch Manchester United not of the time of the likes of York but the new Manchester United that could lose balls, could be up 3 then loose 5-3.

It did not make matters easier for Dad who needed shots of happiness in the arm.

Sir Alex Ferguson had retired and the tears at Old Trafford were out of control.

On my side as an Arsenal fan, things were not easier as even obvious cups like the FA cup were no longer ours to lose. We had to really fight for them.

English Premier league was stressful.

The league at home wasn't any better.

Mismanagement of funds in Kenyan football was having a whole generation taking foreign leagues more seriously than our local league.

As I was now an active Gor Mahia fan and was very well versed with foreign leagues, we started comparing our football to the English Premier league even if at a small scale.

We came up with ideas on online ticketing, serious branding, management and copy writing of merchandise advertising, which we tried to sell to the club to adopt.

Our ideas fell on deaf ears.

Gor was lucky it already had a steady fan base who faithfully paid cash at the gate. But we were still out here with the begging dish even with help from sponsorship. On the other hand corporate sponsored teams with little to no fan base were managing themselves just fine.

Pointing out to mismanagement of the club, we held elections. We tried to choose progressive youth in the office who would push our agenda. Unfortunately the soccer cartels in the sport were so entrenched that it would take a whole government to intervene, something the government cannot do since these are community based clubs.

Of course there is always someone or people benefiting from dysfunction and they will do all within their might to gate keep status quo which on every election came out very strongly from hired goons meant to threaten, discourage and disrupt free and fair elections so we always got the same people back in office and the new faces we injected into the office were soon swallowed up by the system.

Culture beats strategy all the time - so frustrated were some of the new office bearers that they resigned just a year into the office. My long time friend Chris Omondi resigned as Secretary General when his manifesto could not see the light of day due to cartels.

Two botched elections later, fans got disillusioned, started preferring to stay home rather than attend live matches and support the team.

Fans figured the money they were paying to watch matches end up in people's pockets rather than to better the club and even players were struggling.

Comparisons to Tanzania's Yanga and Simba did not help as these were clubs just across the border that were doing big things including purchase of land and building their own stadia, something that could only remain a pipe dream for our community club, even as I write this book.

A second cycle that happened in my Dad's generation was now happening to us. Fans started deserting matches and the club struggle started afresh and was stitched to the zipper.

Fans now either watched soccer from their homes or just concentrated on the English Premier League.

The English Premier League has a large taking in Africa and in Kenya with majority supporting Arsenal and Manchester United, a distance third would be Chelsea then Liverpool and lastly Man City.

You could attribute this to mismanagement of local soccer and basically what they are consuming on television.

On a day Manchester United and Arsenal are playing, the tension is always plausible. To the amusement of Chelsea, City and Liverpool fans who over the last 10 years have been winning the league unassailably while the two clubs struggle with succession.

If you ask kids in Kenya about soccer, they will know more about Manchester United and Arsenal but will have no idea who the coach of Gor or even AFC is. Most adults will struggle to name the coach of our National team Harambee stars.

So here we were once again seated in this pub that also doubled up as a band joint.

Dad and daughter, watching soccer.

He could only take water as his tummy would not let him be – I was taking ginger tea.

He was ill at ease as I observed that even when his favourite song played, he only danced from the seat and would not stand up despite several pulls and nudges from myself.

Next day I called Philip who happened to be in South Africa and told him the old man would probably need a thorough check up, a full body check up so we know exactly what the problem was.

The ulcers drugs given to him were probably not working as he seemed to only sink further and further into whatever was eating him up.

A few calls here and there and as his children we decided to take him for a full body check and several tests for all organs, get the blood, heart, liver, kidney, throat then go deep into the problem area, the tummy, get a full test on the intestines.

We also have a nurse in the family who gave it a nod and said it was the best way forward.

Our brother George who was now a banker in the CBD and our main contact in Nairobi took him for the tests which he was only happy to do as he also needed to know what was ailing him. I was always laughing at Joju because CBD was Dad's hustle ground. That only meant any little issue he has, he shows up at Joju's office like he used to do mine till I relocated.

Although he was a graduate of Enviromental Science, Joju ended up a banker. An African's degree is a metaphor of just how little formal education can do for you. Few people practise what they study in college.

Dad was never a sickling.

Dad had never been admitted in hospital. All his life he never once slept in a hospital.

Dad even escaped the HIV scourge despite risky behaviour and his serial polygamist status.

He was king of self medication.

Good health came to him like oxygen.

Dad's results finally came in on a Friday.

He went to collect them from the labs.

When he got the results he had first sat down and tried to make sense of them. They made no sense at all. There were all these medical jargon in there that he did not understand and so he folded them carefully and neatly as he always did paperwork.

He walked across to the hospital to present them to the doctor so he could get a diagnosis.

He was feeling positive because finally his issue would be resolved.

On this same Friday afternoon, I was seated with my husband, listening to the beats of Rumba.

He was filling my glass with water when he started to talk, "so Dad's results are in. I just got a call from Philip."

Sirens shot up in my ears... "Why did Dad not call me himself? When did he call you?"

"He called me earlier. I needed for us to sit to discuss this. Deb, Dad has Cancer. Colon Cancer. They are saying it could be stage 3 or 4 but more tests will be needed."

A DARK BLUE RIBBON

I once read that when humans are facing a danger that they are not able to control. When they are about to die like when they see a truck approaching them on the wrong way. Or when a plane is about to crash and you are in this plane; your body gives you a natural pain killer and you see or hear sounds like you are under water. Life goes in slow mo. You might even faint since the body is trying to shield you from inevitable pain.

As my husband was saying those words, I could see him through tears in my eyes. His face wobbling and floating on some sort of water. Thereafter, some clarity came to me and I wondered where Dad was at this point. What was he thinking?

He was not with me. Yet he had just received news that he had cancer. He had cancer and he was all alone.

I stood up and gave him a call.

It rang for a long time.

A nervous laugh is what I heard on the other end. Assuredly. Resignedly.

"Mami.. hehehe."

"Where are you?"

"I am home."

"I am coming."

The thought that Dad was seated in a room, all alone and someone broke the news to him that he had cancer was death for me in the first place. I wondered how it landed.

How did he feel? Did he sit at a nearby bench and think things through? Did he believe it himself, that he had cancer? Did he get in his car and cry? How did he drive home? What was he thinking in traffic? What did he think about people going on about their lives outside on the streets, yet he had cancer?

When I saw him. I hugged him and I was crying like a little child and it was his turn to console me.

But he asked me, 'You know a lot of things Mami. Where does Cancer come from?'

I wanted to tell him that after Lilly dying of Leukemia we should have all been wary especially as a family. But it was a tad too late now.

I looked back at all the doctors who diagnosed ulcers which we had treated for a year now. Specialists who recommended lifestyle change and had us buying loads of ulcers medicine.

I felt bile really rising.

'Dad, I have seen people who have healed from cancer. We have cancer survivors all over.'

I believed these words. I believed these words with my all.

I called Philip who was holding his emotions. Talked to my sister who is a nurse. We all agreed we needed a second opinion on this.

I don't know whether we expected to confirm beyond reasonable doubt or just by some miracle it would be that Dad got the wrong result. That he got someone else's result. Someone else's cancer.

One of those very slim margins of error where a mistake like this happens.

We took Dad to a cancer specialist.

It was confirmed beyond reasonable doubt that Dad had colon cancer which had advanced to stage 4.

We had gone through cancer as a family with Lilly. We had a stark and morbid idea of what lay ahead.

He especially had an idea of what it meant.

Lillian went through chemotherapy. Went through her loss of hair. Went through several really painful procedures on her spinal cord and in the end she said she had enough of it all and chose to live her life palliatively to the end.

Lillian's greatest worry as she told me was her children but she died knowing she had left them with Dad and Dad loved children.

Lilly always kept saying, 'Of all people in this family, cancer chose me because I am the strongest. All of you here are lilly livers none of you can survive what I am going through. and especially you Dad.'

And now here we were.

It's like cancer was listening in and said; *Ah, this is the soft landing. Let me perch myself here.*

The test confirmation straffed us like a single bullet.

We had to decide the best way to go about the problem.

We agreed unanimously that we were going to fight and looked for the best medical care we could afford.

Cancer is an expensive disease in Africa. The reasons people still die in relatively higher numbers of cancer in Africa is late diagnosis and misdiagnosis. We were suffering from both.

Dad had been ailing for over a year now. We had sought medical help and he was diagnosed with ulcers over and over again - Misdiagnosis.

When as a family we now decided to do a full test, we found him at Stage 4 - Late Diagnosis.

There were no equipment for testing of cancer and the ones there were really really expensive and three quarter of the population could not afford.

Cancer was not a disease that was rife in Africa. But it shot up just after the HIV pandemic and it has been attributed to lifestyle changes in diets, family planning but mostly also genetics.

There were very few public chemotherapy machines in the whole country by then and these were crowded, with people being scheduled and on the waiting list for up to three months.

When you have cancer, you do not have three months.

I know this because Lillian went through this system. The machines would break down and she would have to wait up to two months into a chemotherapy session.

The staff do their best under the circumstances but the rot is in the system. The ones in private hospitals were too expensive even to fathom.

One thing that you will notice about people with cancer in Africa especially the well to do, they always seek treatment abroad.

And this will tell you a lot about the faith they have in their own medical system above affordability.

This is your call up to organise yourself with your cancer patient.

We really did our research and it took us to the jungle of herbalists, medicine men, dieters and juicers who all claimed to have eradicated cancer.

I was focused on stories from cancer survivors.

India came as a favourite. It was affordable per chemotherapy session but had its downs when it came to accommodation because we would be living in a foreign country. Dad needed a caretaker and we were all employed and now more than ever needed to be at work to make money to fund the problem.

Our first born was a nurse and work was tight. Second born a teacher school was on. I was in Operations. In Ops we do not have time. George was a banker. Philip was in IT in South Africa. Fifth born was a teacher the rest were in school which meant they did not have the dexterity of navigating a foreign country with a sick person.

There was also the issue of money.

We were all working but most were in mid or entry level. I think I was the only one at that point in management level and the bill to complete chemo in India was comparatively easier than in Kenya if we could control accommodation.

Living in India the whole time made more sense than chemo and travelling back home every month.

We would need all the help we could to sustain twelve chemotherapy sessions, accommodation, travel and drugs.

It is interesting when your parents have grown old. How the guy who would line you up on the floor and give instructions or read the riot act or discipline you grows old and roles reverse.

They now start looking to you for instructions.

We decided to call for a fund raiser from all our social networks workmates and communities we were involved in.

So Dad sat there with arms folded as Philip who happens to be the first son, the wide eyed optimist he was, discussed the elaborate plan of what was needed and the task ahead.

The money needed seemed insurmountable to Dad, he kept asking if we were sure we would raise those funds.

I am not a churchy person as some of my siblings are and they all retreated back to church for help. My strength has always been in social capital. I also had a social media page where I had been very active and over the years had developed a family like community. Never mind it is Philip who actually created it.

I always kept sustained writings on Rumba Music. Soccer. Kenyan politics and Geopolitics in general and kept the company of like-minded people.

I wrote a lot about Dad. Posted a lot about our adventures be it in the stadium or out dancing or travelling. I would write about his OCD or would ruffle up his newspaper then take videos of his reactions once he got into the room.

Lots of Gor Mahia fans knew him. Lots of Rumba fans knew him and had met us together.

He had a whole fan base on my timeline.

I had never been the kind in all my years on social media to post my problems. I had never once come on my timeline to ask for help whether financial or otherwise.

Instead, I tried my level best to always lend a hand when I could, whether there was a death, an illness, a loss of job or whatever form of struggle, I would try contribute the little I could afford.

I feel people's pain so deeply. This has been taken advantage of a lot but this has also paid off even though it was not the aim.

I am the person who is happy to spend money. If I have money and there is a problem, I will give it. If I have money and there is a bill, I would pay - If I have money, I will look for ways to spend it.

It is easy for money to leave my hands. I put no attachment whatsoever to it and my father always said, "You will make money. But you will never be wealthy."

The truth is, that is what Dad was. And that is what my biological father was.

Both of these men were happy go lucky men who would have stashes of money today, would live in the moment and tomorrow would have nothing in their pockets.

My mum, though, was good with money. She died having invested. Bought a van. Bought two pieces of land and had cash in her account - After her death, the van was inherited by the man she hated so bad. The land she bought in Homa Bay, Philip has been unable to develop to date because Dad also inherited it and pawned the deed and it has been really complicated thereafter.

I took a photo of Dad and wrote a short message on my Facebook timeline.

I told my friends that Dad had been diagnosed with cancer and that we would be seeking treatment in India which would cost millions in Kenyan shillings and that I had some but not all of it and would appreciate help from them.

I do not know if Mark Zuckerberg is aware of the impact Facebook has had on humanity.

People talk about globalization, connecting, dating but does Mark know that Facebook has literally touched lives?

That you can be closer to a community on social media than your own family.

That social media can change your life.

That people we like to refer to as strangers on social media can actually feel your pain. Can be closer to you than your own blood. Can write a check. Can recommend. Can put in a good word. Can connect you to a resource.

I put up that post and in a matter of hours, a Facebook page had already been formed to start a fund raiser for Dad by my friends on Facebook.

They did not invite me to it as they felt I needed to deal with other issues.

I reported back to my family that I may be able to get maybe Kshs 100,000 from my Facebook friends.

I applied for a loan at my sacco. Applied for a loan at my bank. Sold my shares both at Safaricom and Equity.

Philip was busy organising the logistics for India which seemed really tough.

There was the option of going for chemo every fortnight and living in the hospital which was really expensive. There was also the option of living outside of the hospital and only getting admitted while on chemo which was the plausible option.

We also needed air tickets to India.

It was agreed unanimously that I would be the one to travel with Dad, set up, stay with him a few months then the next sibling would come then the next till he finishes.

It was a natural decision.

Of all my siblings, I had spent the most time with Dad outside Philip and Philip was not able to travel as he had exhausted his leave days.

I always sat to reflect on Dad's life.

In his lifetime, Dad married five women – Here he was going on a mission where most adults would be with their spouse as a caretaker for un interrupted sessions. He had to turn to us, his children to organise ourselves in spite of our active work lives to stay with him.

Our Mikayi was present, but she needed to be home with Lilly's kids, did not have a passport and even getting one was going to be difficult as both her parents had already died.

Nyar Denja had been present and never once left Dad's side despite all the women that came after her. A staunch Adventist who dreamt to be a teacher all her life. During dry days when Dad would not send her money, she would start a little nursery school in the village where little kids would go to sing. She was a follower. Dad led her all her life and even in this matter she was more following what we had to say than actually give directions.

With a hindsight, I don't remember ever hearing her voice. Or authority on anything. It was always Dad bulldozing agendas when we were young and she would fit in. And now Dad had taken a back seat. And we were now bulldozing the agenda and she was fitting in.

I remember as we grew older, even our voices grew louder than hers. It was not uncommon to find a situation where Lilly would argue her down and she would back off.

She was the model submissive, demure African wife who came to get married and would make it work if it killed her. Traditional African women defined by their resilience in suffering, their pride was in their staying power.

'*Dak law yuach*' They called it.

She would be absolutely terrified to find herself in India and it wouldn't help that she would be with Dad who hardly ever listened to her, when at this point Dad needed to sit back and listen.

The ticket we got would have us go from Nairobi to Doha. Then onwards to Delhi.

It would be Dad's first international travel.

I had a lot of leave days pending and claimed all of them plus extra which was approved.

We set up a date for the main fund raiser and invited friends over. We also had been collecting from our communities as previously stated.

I had cleaned out my savings. Took up my loans. Sold my shares.

I was throwing everything into this.

This was my Dad. My only Dad.

On the morning of the fundraiser my friends told me they had sent two representatives to meet me so they would hand over the cash.

I travelled into Nairobi ready for this hand over, then to meet a few more friends who wouldn't make it to the fundraiser. We were in the streets with Dad who had also been amassing his friends and contacts.

He was upbeat and kept asking me if we would hack this India business.

Hope is the opium of life – Hope is all humans need to get through.

The guy I was seated with about two weeks ago was very different from the one I was walking with in the CBD. He seemed stronger. Happier and the colour of life was showing on his cheeks you could see it through the creases on his forehead.

I kept going in and out of offices, meeting people at receptions collecting money and they all kept telling him, 'You got this.'

And then we sat in the cafeteria and waited for the representatives from my Facebook timeline.

They sat there, and handed us 1.2 million shillings, raised by strangers on Facebook 99% who I had never met. Never even had a face to face interaction with. Would probably not even recognise them if we met on the street.

There was something interesting about Dad's fundraiser.

The crowd consisted of young people from all walks of life. The age group was 35 and below.

Mostly there were friends, colleagues, and church members of my siblings.

I looked around for any people his age and could not spot anyone.

Looked around for his friends, who for years I had known in the various stages of his life. Friends who went out partying with him. Who they stood for days on edge discussing politics. Who danced themselves limb with him. His business associates – I did not see any of them.

Maybe they had sent him money. But they did not show up.

It was a sibling operation through and through.

I was proud of my siblings for coming up with an elaborate crowd.

Everyone contributed from their pockets while others had been sent to represent various interest groups.

When Dad stood to the podium to speak, he took the microphone and he kept quiet. He wanted to speak but the words could not come out.

Instead, he started to shed tears.

MISSION POSSIBLE

On the night before we travelled to India, I went out to dance, at a pub called Pots and Pans.

There was a band there that played albeit lazily, old Rumba music.

When they played the hit 'Salima' by TP OK Jazz I took to the floor and paid the band leader asking him to repeat the same song again in what is known as 'Encore'.

It reminded me of my childhood. It was nostalgic. It was symbolic I had a long journey ahead of me.

I arrived at the airport the next morning to find Dad already there with our Mikayi and my siblings.

We looked like a team headed to space on an impossible mission.

Medical tourism is all about citizens of third world countries seeking affordable medical care outside their countries.

There are several ways this is done.

The moment you are diagnosed, you seek to get a quote on what it means from both private and public hospitals in your country.

Usually for public hospitals it's a tedious process and the unpredictability of machines working or not.

For private hospitals, the costs are crazy. Ironically, you will find cancer doctors recommending hospitals in India that you could visit.

Rumour has it that these doctors have connections with the corresponding doctors in India who pay them a commission for getting them a client.

The moment you are connected to a hospital in India, you will write to them stating your issue while attaching your results. They will have a look and give you a quote based on whether you will be resident in the hospital the whole time. Or if you will need accommodation the whole time. Most people will go for the latter.

Immediately you go for the latter, a solution will be offered to you recommending accommodations that are associated or linked to the hospital which will be near the hospital and even transportation will be offered for anytime you need to go to the hospital.

You will live in these shared accommodations and pay rent monthly and they are like AirBnBs where you only buy your food but everything is provided for you. The hospital will give you a phone when you arrive which has data for communication.

It's a very well-oiled machine.

So the doctor in Kenya gets a commission. The accommodation gives the hospital a commission and your private taxi guy gives the accommodation or hospital a commission. All these are extra expenses that you do not need as they beat the reason you are in India in the first place. Very few people who go to India as medical tourists are actually wealthy. Wealthy Africans go to Europe, the US or South Africa.

The lower class have no chance and have to contend with local conditions. India is for the middle class who mostly benefit from well-wishers fundraising.

I cannot say we were even middle class. Dad was always oscillating between lower and lower middle depending on a deal he had hit.

He however educated his children and we were now earning a living. We managed a middle class standard of health care.

We travelled coach. He slept little. I was consumed in thought and played classic music.

We both cursed the fact that airlines did not take African music seriously. It is not African music if we do not have some Rumba.

The whole time hostesses kept walking up and down the aisle offering people alcoholic drinks but I did not order.

I had been sober that whole year.

"You know you can order a drink if you need to. No judgement. These are crazy times."

"I quit drinking Dad."

"Seriously, I can order for you."

"I am serious Dad. I no longer drink."

He summoned one of the hostesses carrying the various Vodkas, Gins and Whiskeys over.

The girl politely came and he said, "Give her a double of whisky."

I politely declined and the lady was somewhat confused. wondering if the old man seated next to me was bothering me in anyway.

She waited when I went to the washroom and told me, "Are you alright? Is the old man making you uncomfortable? We can offer you a different seat."

"That's my Dad."

'Your Dad is forcing you with whisky doubles?'

"It doesn't better get than that. I know!"

She was so amused.

While we cleaned our hands with napkins to eat in flight, Dad made his way to the washroom to wash his hands. And yet he used his folks and spoons.

Then he made his way back to the kitchen to wash his hands.

The flight attendants were amused and he made friends there fast.

He explained to them why he was going to India and complimented their looks.

They made it their job to make him comfortable.

He absolutely hated the food served because for him it had to be pure vegetarian while I went on to enjoy beef, chicken and ice cream for dessert.

He could not complain to his new lady friends, because Dad wanted them to feel like they were doing a very important job.

He gave them his phone so they could add their numbers. I was observing quietly with one eye closed and the other eyeing the motley of activities while listening to Mozart.

Then I closed both eyes to deal with the air compression and I told him while closing my eyes.

"Carry on whatever that is. But you are not getting married in this plane Dad."

He chuckled naughtily.

"If I was 30 these ones would be in trouble I tell you."

I just shook my head in a world weary way. *'Dhiang tho gi lum e dhoge.'*

During the flight, he was a permanent resident at the kitchen area. The ladies kept him busy with stories and even during moments when the plane was silent as passengers dozed off, they were chattering away.

We arrived at Hamad. And were welcomed by a nice gentleman who is the son to one of our family friends during Nyasamia's regime.

Souleyman Toure bought us dinner and shepherded us to the next gate, after Hamad, the flight from Qatar to India.

If you are a frequent flier, you can tell a lot about a destination from the gates.

There are gates you pass by and you see lots of Chinese looking like casual or construction workers. These are gates mostly headed to developing countries on predatory Chinese loans. Gates you pass by and passengers are on sunglasses, hats, flowered shirts mostly these are gates to the Carribean countries with islands. People who are going on vacation.

Gates you pass by and you see back packers from the hand luggage they are carrying. Heavy clothing. Hiking boots. Khaki trousers. These are gates heading to Switzerland or Nepal.

Gates where passengers are calm. Kids with head phones on. Mothers have back supports and are reading a book and men are mid business meetings on mini laptops. These ones are headed to Europe, the US or Scandinavia.

Then there is the sick gate. Loads of ill people. Some barely standing. Some with huge bandages. Kids carried by their mothers. Old men being chaperoned by what seemed like their son or at times the wives. The mood is forlorn. Everyone's face tells a story of long nights. Pain. Agony. And hope or lack of it.

Unlike most of the ill travellers, Dad was well on his feet – very strong and upbeat.

I wondered silently whether this was a first journey for most of the sick or if it was second or third visits.

We boarded a very long flight that would take us across the sea to mystic India.

When India finally emerges from beneath the clouds you will realize the air is foggy even when the pilot declares it's a clear day. Then the heat will embrace you. Then the sky which is never blue. At least not in the time I was in India. The sky is always forlorn, graying like its brooding to rain.

If you are from Africa all this is very strange – we are a continent of blue clear skies, clean air and the weather is tropical and can be hot and cold depending on season.

The other thing is the hooting in traffic. They do have traffic cops dressed in white but their impact if at all is minimal based on the decibel levels of the hooting.

And we were in Delhi. The epicentre.

Street families with begging dishes outstretched in traffic. Weeds poking through walkways and some beggars sleeping on the pavements.

Granted, Africa has its share of beggars and street urchins but the ones in India can be classified under family urchins. You find a whole family on the streets with begging dishes.

India is largely vegan but there is a lot of chicken being made in different styles whether its tandoori or curry.

The hospital-attached taxi received us at the airport and drove us to the accommodation recommended by the hospital and we were scheduled to go to the hospital the next day.

It was in a very good neighbourhood. You could tell from the cars that were parked outside homes. The malls around and the general tranquility.

In this accommodation were two other families from Africa who were in India for medical care. All were cancer patients.

There was a Kenyan and Tanzanian family. The Kenyan was a lady in her 50s who was in the last sessions of chemotherapy and had been in India for three months. Had struggled with breast cancer and had both her breasts severed but was still treating the cancer that seemed to move from one part of her body to the next.

She was a prayerful woman and was interested to hear about us. Kept trying to talk to me when it was just the two of us in the kitchen. She wondered why I had married an old man. I told her that this was my father which really surprised her because sick men in India are mostly cared for by sons or their wives.

"Where is your mother?"

"She died many years ago."

"And he did not remarry? I know a Luo man can never just stay alone. In fact they are the only remaining polygamists back home."

I laughed - 'It's a long story.' It's always a long story. Hence a book.

She seemed very set up and accustomed to her life in India. Had her shopping intact, and her part of the shared kitchen elaborately arranged like you would your own home.

She was being cared for by her sister. The second family was also from East Africa. Tanzanians. Their daughter had leukemia. She was only 12. The child had lost all her hair and her skin was devoid of warmth or color. She was headed to her sixth chemo and mostly sat at the couch covered in swathes of clothes. She looked like she was freezing all the time. She did not talk much. She was being cared for by her mother. Her mother was only just slightly older than me.

We never really count our blessings as parents to raise healthy children until we encounter parents raising children with special needs. Or children who are ailing.

The mother's face had exhaustion painted all over it. But her love was stronger than the struggle. In fact, she was so graceful that she made it look easy and I guess that is what mothers do.

It occurred to me that despite a difficult childhood, health was something I had never been denied as a child.

God gave us challenges we could manage.

I wondered if mum walked away when we were such healthy kids, what she would have done if one of us was this sick; would she have come back to take care of us?

The woman hardly talked. She kept steady in cleaning for her child – she looked the kind who had told her story over and over and was now just sick of telling the story and was more focused on hope and living one day at a time.

I thought about my children back home. I had left them behind to tend to my sick father for months. I did speak to them about it but I wondered if they felt cared for.

The room had amenities like WIFI so I was in touch with my communities.

Our first appointment at the hospital had to do with a major colonoscopy test done again to ascertain that Dad had cancer and to determine what stage he was at.

We already knew all this but the hospital explained it could not start treating a patient on a different hospital's results.

This test was really costly. And in India they will do that.

We were to go for the results three days later. Get a diagnosis and a treatment plan. In these three days I did my calculations and realised living in this posh palace wasn't going to be sustainable.

We needed to move to a more affordable accommodation because we were looking at months,not weeks and not days in India.

I shared this with my siblings. We did the math and agreed.

I had to also try and sell the idea to Dad who was pensive about leaving a secure and clean accommodation to the uncertainty out there. It was his first time ever out of his motherland and everything put him on the edge.

Once again I was looking at my contacts on Facebook and clients I had left at home. Asking if they had any relatives around Delhi who could help us find cheaper accommodation.

Several suggestions came up. The best and cheapest was an accommodation about an hour by train from Delhi.

It was perfect because Dad would be going through his chemo sessions for 3 days every two weeks for six months. So we check into the hospital when he is taking chemo then we retreat back to the rented house and recuperate for two weeks before the next.

I was introduced to an Indian by the name Neeraj Yadav. He was a resident of the town we were going to be living at called Gurgaon. He had been in Kenya himself once working for a tech company.

We chatted on text and I told him I only needed one room but we had to have electricity, clean water and security.

He already had a place in mind just near his own apartment.

I decided that on the day we were getting results, we would also be checking out of our posh accommodation, would hop onto the train outside Delhi to his city and start a new life there.

There was a bit of a push and pull when we informed our landlord that we would be leaving the next day. He had expected us to live in the whole time. Even tried to tell us lawfully we needed to give him a one-month notice. He called the hospital which warned us against leaving to unknown abodes and that they would not be responsible if anything happened to us. Our housemates were also against it. They talked of insecurity and the need to bundle together as Africans. Their concern was legitimate but I was looking at the money. A month of living in the posh neighborhood was a whole session of chemo. I was going for broke.

After push and pull, we carried all our belongings and set off to hospital for Dad's results and a way forward on his treatment while I was also trying to organize the way to the train to our new abode in Gurgaon.

Dad thought I was mad. The traffic and the drama outside was already terrifying him. It did not make it easier that most Indians do not speak English.

"How is it that they cannot speak English yet they were colonised by the British?"

"Because they have emancipated themselves from colonialism even by language."

We arrived at Dharamshilla Cancer Centre with luggage like we had just alighted from a flight and went in to see the doctor.

The doctor looked at us curiously.

"Are you the wife?"

"No I am the daughter,"

"Oh really? I rarely see Dads and Daughters here. It is always Dads and Sons or Men and their wives."

"Here its Dad and Daughter."

"You are the primary caregiver?"

"Yes."

"How old are you?"

"I am old enough."

Looking at Dad, "I will need you to step outside briefly so I can have a word with her."

"Anything you need to say, say in my presence. This is my daughter and she will tell me whatever you tell her."

"It is just procedure."

I looked at him. My eyes assured him. He stepped out.

"You are the primary caregiver?"

"Yes I am."

"So your father has Stage 4 cancer. You are aware of that?"

"Yes I have been aware for the last three weeks."

"Do you know what it means?"

"It means he has stage 4 cancer Doctor. Is there any other meaning?"

"It means without treatment he may have about six months to live. But with treatment he can live a year. And there is a slim chance of less than 1% he can live."

"We are here for the 1% because I have done my research have seen people who have lived. He is a very strong man."

Probably used to this wide eyed optimism, he carried on in a flat tone.

"The statistics I have given you, is he able to take them in?"

"Let's keep it at the one year and the 1%."

"By looking at the 1% means you are accepting to go the chemo way?"

"We are going whatever way will keep Dad alive. Is it chemo? Is there anything else?"

He took Dad's files, hang up the films in the air to reveal morbid pictures that looked like tripe.

"So here, that's the source. It has now spread here, this is the kidney and the liver and is well headed to organs so only chemo can help."

"Will help Doctor, will help not can help. We will go with Chemo"

And so Dad came back in. Searching my eyes for tears but found me looking jolly and confident.

And with as much fanfare as he could muster, the doctor

told him he had Stage 4 cancer and that many people did not make it. But some did.

He explained that Chemo would be rough. He would lose hair. Would diarrhea. Would lose weight and we both told him that we had nursed a chemo patient before.

Dad was set to begin his first chemo in a week's time after we paid the hospital.

Armed with college education and education from the streets, I was now ready to take Dad to the train station to look for a new accommodation outside of Delhi. I looked at Dad who thought I was out of my mind and while laughing I asked him, "Are you ready?" Because, consent is everything.

It was a room in a two storey building with twelve households. A lockable gate and a shared outdoor shower cum toilet.

It was a basic accommodation. But we had been in worse. Nobody was here for a four seasons experience.

We got a dull room on the first floor - with one window and separated in half by a wall to what seemed like a kitchen as it had a sink. It also had one bed with a beaten mattress.

It was painted offwhite and had a most benevolent fan.

India is so hot, that even the poor must have a fan, as you go up the classes you start seeing ACs outside homes.

This fan did not help at all aside from circulating hot wind in the room. Dad hated it. He said it compressed his chest.

We went shopping to start a life. A stove, two pans, two cups, two plates, two spoons, tea bags, soap and all basics to start a life.

We now did not have Wi-Fi but Neeraj bought us data.

Life reset itself.

Dad took the bed and I took the floor. Neeraj was gracious enough to lend us an Indian mat. I made a makeshift matress from my clothes.

I cooked, cleaned the room, washed his clothes and since the wash and bathroom wasn't to Dad's standard, I decided to be washing it on behalf of the entire flat.

Every morning I would wake up. Prepare his breakfast. Clean the room. Clean his clothes. Hang them then scrub the washroom and bathroom before he got in.

By 11am, I would be done with all that and would just idle interacting with Facebook friends, siblings and reading books on Kindle.

As we were on the top most floor, there was a roof above us that I would climb on. Reflect. Above me the foreboding Indian clouds that would not let the sun shine, and below me informal settings with man-made wired aerials jutting out of roofs.

Neeraj visited every single evening with his wife.

They were a young couple. He couldn't have been past 35 and the girl past 25 years of age.

She was young, trusting, naive and smiled a lot.

She did not understand English so the husband interpreted a lot of what we were discussing.

They both called Dad 'Uncle.'

We had a lot of animated discussions on the Indian culture. The gods. Their politics. I was especially interested to know why the divorce rate among Indians is really low. It was an expansive elaborate explanation about how at the wedding, their spirits marry and that the marriage is not only on earth but in the spirit world as well.

Dad really took on to liking the wife as a daughter. She saw him as a father and even on the days when her husband was working late, she would pass by to spend time with Dad and I would be amused while reading, as they told each other stories but neither understood what the other was saying. They both used gestures a lot.

When we had a power blackout, they would not give up these laborious discussions - they lit up a lamp and continued as it burned brightly between them, flattering their faces into masks.

On the day of his first chemo, I packed clothes that would last three days. We locked our little flat and we walked to the train station.

I would like to mention that for the Indian population, what they have done with their transport system and network is impressive. It is no less than what I see in Europe.

In the trains were students and the working class pouring into Delhi in the morning. Then evening leaving the madness back to more quiet countrysides.

The trains were crowded during peak hours and people always made room for Dad to sit. I have no idea why. Maybe as he was old. Or they knew we were here for medical reasons or that we were foreigners and needed a bit of grace.

But it always happened- As soon as we got into the train, someone would always stand for Dad to sit.

Unlike our room in Gurgaon, the Dharamshilla Hospital was a state of the art facility and it specialises only in Cancer. We had a tiny form of luxury when we checked in for the chemo which would last three days then we would board the train and head back and wait for the next session.

Dharamshilla is the cancer capital.

Forget the airport. Here you will meet all forms of cancer. The amputees. Bald heads. The ones holding bandages on their left breast. Old men walking on sticks. The ones being wheeled on chairs. The ones with bandages on their heads. Some walking along with the IV on their hands.

It was all manner of people in various stages of cancer and corresponding treatments. Shrunken people with reedy voices, delivered to the feet of the most dreaded disease, suffering far beyond the hangmen of medieval Europe, rule of the Huns or the charging lions in the Colloseum of ancient Rome.

There were mostly Africans and Arabs but very few Europeans. And lots of Indians.

So much for theories that meat causes cancer because all these were vegans.

My siblings had wired in the money for the first two chemos and we had to take care of some paperwork before being ushered into our room.

The private wing of Dharamshilla Cancer Centre will pass for a hotel only they have the medical equipment.

You are confronted by great views. Indoor washroom and bathroom. Smart TV. WIFI. An extra bed for the care giver and a menu for the day to choose from where they will serve breakfast, lunch and dinner.

The grounds were also great and I could take a stroll around the lush gardens when my patient was asleep. As it was at the center of Delhi, I could take a walk into Delhi's down town when it was less crowded during their holidays. And they had a lot of holidays.

Entry into this little hotel of a hospital ward was great relief for Dad who immediately had them looking for Kenyan channels for news. And the English Premier league. He made such a fuss that the IT crew had to visit the room to make it work. He was spending every last coin that was fundraised for him.

We watched a game of Manchester United and tried to follow politics at home.

Raila Odinga had just chosen Kalonzo Musyoka to be his running mate in the coming 2017 election which would be his fourth stab at the top most seat in the land.

Amidst a background of horrid times in Kenya where we were treated to some of the worst economic crimes of recent times, public officials looting money from organisations like the NYS, conduits walking out of banks carrying money in bags – It was horrible.

This time, there was no doubt in all our minds that Raila was breezing through the elections.

The nurses came in with the chemo fluids. Mixed them up in a bag. He had a change of clothes. And they settled him on a pillow. Set him up on IV and the chemo started dripping into his veins.

He fell asleep.

It was the first time ever in his life that he slept on a hospital bed. And it was in a foreign country and it was on the ultimate disease, Cancer.

I recall the hot Indian days and even hotter Indian nights when you did not know what to do with yourself and especially as we did not have AC.

India gets so hot that butter liquifies. So hot that you cannot close the door or windows when you go to sleep. So hot that without a fridge, eggs cook in their shell.

Every day was the same as the last. Unexpected weeds bloomed on the pavements and died. Strange insects scuttled and writhed to their deaths in the burning floor.

The sun made wind tremble in the air and made houses shudder and heave for breath.

We spoke a lot in the dark. We dug and reimagined our life together.

"Do you remember our discussion on HIV when your uncle Philip died?"

"Yes I do."

"You spoke too soon. I was spared off HIV and then given a worse disease."

"Why do you say so?"

"HIV positive people are living now and not dying."

"Cancer patients are also living."

"Most are dying. Also HIV is cheaper to treat than Cancer."

"You are right on the second point but only because its 2015. In the 80s HIV was expensive to treat. Do you recall telling me a story of your wealthy friends who would travel to Europe to get whole blood transfusions to clean their blood?"

"And they still died."

"If you were to contract HIV you would have contracted it when your peers did. And you would never have lived to see Raila being president which will happen in my lifetime."

"He will win 2017."

"I know!"

All we would do when it was impossible to sleep was to play some Franco. My brother had downloaded some TP OK Jazz that kept us going. We would play Massikini then Serment Kikame. Then Illouse. Then Laissez Passez. Sadole with Franco's thunderous voice vibrating and rising in concert with the heat from the floor.

I was also into modern Rumba of my generation like Fally Ipupa, Ferre Gola, Koffi Olomide and would every once in while bridge with those.

Somehow the bulbs made our little abode even hotter and we preferred to just communicate in the dark after dinner. Both of us lying in whatever positions on our mattresses, just talking.

Life is indeed a paradox. He talked a lot about mum.

He said that mum was the ultimate prize as she came from a wealthy and known family.

"You mother was a most beautiful woman. I had actually heard about her before I met her."

"Your mother had beautiful big eyes. That were lazy on the gaze, and oh my goodness her legs!"

He went on and on in the darkness.

"Yea. Her legs were legendary I hear."

"Do you know songs were made about your mother?"

"Yeah I have heard."

"So this is the story. Your mum and her cousin Apiyo were club hopping when at the floor, the musician Ochieng Kabaseleh saw your mum . And like most of us men, he had to meet her. Went to her table after the dance and asked your mum what her name was and your mum lied that her name was 'Zainabu'. She thought of this name because by then your Aunty Mama Mpenzi had married a Tanzanian guitarist who was Muslim, converted to Islam and was going by all sorts of names from Farida to Zainabu to Amina. She was yet to settle on a name that would stick because, unlike Muslim women, she was still smoking and drinking; your Aunty Mama Mpenzi."

'Mama Mpenzi is a legend Dad. You know that hahahaha.'

"Crazy woman that one,"

"I have not only heard but have danced to the song Zainabu"

"Nyaugenya Kager..that was your Mum."

"There was not a day I took your mother out for a dance that she did not wear the highest of heels, and balanced gracefully in them. She only wore dresses made of chiffon. She dressed like Princess Diana, she was like Princess Diana. I would walk with her in any room and she gave me instant profile. She was indoctrinated to Rumba because everyone around her listened to Rumba but her true music was country. Jazz of the 60s and she loved Elton John."

"That was pretty refined for an African woman in the 80s."

"She was hilarious and the queen of impersonation the moment a person left the room. She was a terrible dancer!"

"Noo! What?"

"Her dancing was horrible." He repeated dismissively "Are you judging her on dancing to Rumba only?"

"Actually come to think of it. She could do a good waltz or tango."

"There you go."

Silence.

"Are you at peace with her?"

"I am good Dad. I am at peace with everything."

"She was a good woman. She was a great person. A lot of people out here will tell you only the best things about her.

She may have not made the best choices in as far as you are concerned. She was young. But her heart was always in the right place."

"It is what it is Dad. I am in my early 30s and with kids. It took me marriage to understand her choices. It took having kids and a career to juggle at the same time. I may not agree with some of her choices. But I can come from a point of understanding."

"That's good to hear, Mami. She was not the model mother..."

He pressed on this ticking bomb and I cut him short.

"Talking models. You are not exactly the model husband Dad. What was your role in her decisions and ultimately how her life turned out or the lives of virtually all my step mothers? Have you asked yourself why you are here with me and not any of them. Have you observed that men your age are with their spouses and you probably married more than each of them combined.?"

Tension rose like a wall surrounding us. 'Do you recall the story of how Auntie Apiyo died Dad?'

Auntie Apiyo was my mother's cousin, age mate and bosom friend - her husband died and she got remarried to an insecure man who had a problem with everything. Auntie Apiyo got a job in Nairobi that would have her relocate from Kisumu and leave her un employed husband behind in Chiga, a sub urban abandoned land that her new husband had her move in to cut her off from everyone else.

But she never reported to work. Days went by and Auntie Apiyo never showed up for her new role.

It was my mum whose soul was restless and sent her to her cousin's house after everyone thought she had snubbed the job. In that abandoned house, mum called out to her and there was no response. She asked neighbors of the last time they saw her. They had no idea because the next neighbour lived almost a mile away. Mum got some villagers to break the padlock.

Aunty Apiyo's decomposing body was discovered pushed under the sofa. She was swollen that her decomposing body lifted up the sofa. She died with her arms up in a defensive position and rats had eaten her whole face.

The typical domestic violence syllabus that starts as a casual micro aggression. Degenerates to full scale physical violence then murder.

"Do you remember Auntie Apiyo Dad?"

"Yeah. But I was never going to murder your mother."

"You don't know that, she did not know that, nobody ever does Dad. A slap is well on the road to a murder."

He went silent and that was all the conversation we needed for that hot night.

In the darkness, in my sheets, hot tears welled my eyes and I buried my head in my make shift pillow so he may not hear me crying. I was breathing softly and with lots of control.

His voice cut through the darkness.

"I am sorry."

I shot back with, 'Go to sleep Diel.'

"I also need to tell you that you passed that exam."

"What exam?"

"The first exam to the first boarding school. I got your letter but we could not afford fees for two."

We had formed a routine of taking walks every evening when the sun was setting. The heat was bearable in the evenings. We would walk to the edge of the street, take the corner that revealed lots of beggars who would not bother to target us. We would then end up in the market that sold all sorts of wares from Saris, to knock off designer bags, to jewellery, vegetables which I would replenish if we were running out. We would then take the bend lined up with spices then all manner of shoes. We would have to contend with stares from Indians and children horrified, running away from us.

For a very globalized world and access to information, it is quite interesting that India still has people who stop and stare when they see dark skin.

These stares would annoy Dad. Because, just like the people staring at him, he had not had the privilege of a culture capital and was taking it as some form of racism.

With time he got used to the stares and would even wave at people staring at us. They would wave back. If you looked interested enough he would approach you and explain that he was in India to seek treatment because he had cancer.

Dad told people at the market, at the souk, at the store, in the train who cared to start a conversation with him that he had cancer. He told them expecting them to pray for him and there is a part of him that believed if they did, he would be fine. They had several gods that they worshiped and he figured if they were fine while not worshiping Jesus, then there was also something special about their gods. He needed the combined efforts of all gods. In a weird way, I always felt the more he spoke about it, the more he got it out of his mind -talking cancer away.

Indians are generally good people. We did not face any sort of violence whether physical or passive. They gave way. They stood for Dad to sit. They tried to understand what we were saying and they served us with smiles if only to say, 'Velkam to India .'

Every last street food in India has pepper so Dad never got the privilege of sampling.

Chemo had a strict diet regime that he could not veer off.

In one of those hot Indian nights, I had left the windows open and a slight breeze was sweeping into our little shack making the thin veil of curtain flatter above my face.

I thought I was dreaming when I heard Dad's voice in the darkness. "Deb...Deb..."

He woke me up the way I used to wake him up at night when I needed to Pee.

I kept still to hear if he will call again.

"Deb..."

"Dad ..."

"I just saw my mother."

"What do you mean Dad?"

"I have seen my mother."

"How. You do not know how she looked like. She died giving birth to you."

There is no photo of Achieng Nyongalo anywhere. All his life, Dad had no idea how his mother looked like. "I have seen her. She was standing above me, calling me, and beside her, around me were all my brothers, Maroko, Ojweke, Kasera and my sister -My siblings were shaking their heads and saying it's impossible. It was so vivid."

"Wow!" I sat up on my mattress in the darkness.

"How did she look like?"

"I don't know. I can't remember."

He also sat up on his bed. From the floor where I was, my eyes adjusted and I could make out the form of his light feet on the floor.

Dad was unable to sleep well as time progressed.

And I really appreciated it if he could even get 3 hours of consistent sleep.

His cells that had cancer had realised calvary was on the way. And they fought back like crazy.

And when cancer fights back, it's a battle at the cellular level.

Your body is in pain you have never thought possible.

When you have a headache, toothache or a wound it's easy to deal with the specific area.

From Dad's cancer war, the pain he felt was in the bones.

There is nothing you can do about that.

"Where exactly is the pain. Is it your head? Or tummy? Where?"

"It's everywhere."

You feel your bones grinding and for a man who was not accustomed to pain, it really took a toll on him.

The drugs to relieve cancer patients' pain is not expensive. It is damn expensive but they absolutely cannot do without it.

There was a time when the hospital had scheduled our next chemo and the next stash of medicines simultaneously only for the hospital to call and tell us we would be scheduled two days later. Unfortunately, the painkillers ran out. I thought Dad would survive the two days.

We did not sleep. Dad cried the whole night and curled in a ball like a child. At the break of dawn, I had to board the train to Delhi as it was not an over the counter drug. This drug had to be taken when it had to be taken and without fail.

Next, chemotherapy has its side effects which go anything from diarrhea, to vomiting, skin problems, loss of hair and lack of appetite.

He suddenly became a five-year-old who you would have to coax to eat. To sleep, to do just about anything.

He had also lost substantial weight and his hair was falling off.

We were half way through the chemo and were now running thin on cash.

I kept on making calls back home for money to be sent here and there and once again friends were responsive and kept on sending money through Western Union.

I could only access Western Union in Delhi and would wait for when we were on chemo sessions to withdraw. Would leave Dad asleep then venture out.

To this day I owe it to friends, colleagues, facebook friends who kept checking on us and would just randomly send money to Western Union to help with Dad.

I was common in that Western Union bureau conveniently placed near the Dharamshilla Cancer Hospital that I became friends with the owner. First time I went there, I was with Dad before we checked into hospital and they got acquainted. He then realised that I was Dad's care taker. He was so gracious that he would actually give me a call when he saw a transaction on my name. Or while Asians close shop at 1pm for lunch and back in the afternoon, he would wait in for us to come from the train.

While in Delhi, I also visited a longtime friend from my days in the theatre, Janet Kanini.

We performed a play together at Heartstrings Ensemble and she had gone ahead to pursue a career in the media; first as a travel blogger promoting the Kenyan tourism sector and finally as a news caster for lunch hour all the way to prime time.

Janet had been diagnosed with lung cancer stage 4.

She was on chemo but could afford to keep going back home and so we met on one hot Indian afternoon in a different hospital in Delhi.

Dad was going through a chemo session that would have him sleep for hours.

I was happy to see Janet. She laughed at how mysterious life was that one day we were young girls hustling at the Nairobi CBD acting for less than 5 dollars a show and now we were grown women with families, with kids and in India battling cancer.

We spoke about our children and how the future can be uncertain. Janet was being cared for by her mother.

Her mother had carried Kenyan food and apportioned some to me.

It was a wonderful Indian afternoon.

I also organized a meeting with the Kenyan embassy for India one time just after chemo to meet our ambassador.

The then Ambassador Bella Omino who was daughter to one of Kenya's most renowned politicians and also from the Luo tribe had previously met my Dad in one of his many calls for his previous lawyer boss.

previous lawyer boss.

She welcomed us to her office. I was curious to know if there was any benefit to Kenya from the millions of cash in India for medical purposes and the fate of patients who get stuck in India with medical bills.

She told me the situation was out of hand. There were so many undocumented Kenyans in India who went as students, dropped out of college and were unable to go back home for the shame and have to keep surviving in India engaging in shady deals.

Most ended up as alcoholics because alcohol in India is very cheap. So whatever pocket money they got was enough even to sustain them in houses and not dormitories.

There were also Kenyans in India who went in as businessmen but have over stayed their visa and are now living undocumented and surviving on shady deals.

She said it was difficult to track them and they got deported every now and then.

She confirmed that there are cartels in India collaborating with Kenyan doctors who on the first sight of cancer or any complicated disease will immediately sell the Indian idea which desperate Kenyans will take and will end up not only paying for the service but also commission.

Kenyan citizens who die or who are stuck in India with unpaid medical bills were one of the biggest challenges her office faced. She did not have a budget for this problem and could only negotiate with the Government of India to subsidise the bills. Unfortunately, most Kenyans went to private and not public hospitals.

We were also in a private hospital.

She invited us to her home over the weekend for dinner and wished us well.

Kenya was definitely in good hands in India. She was a very kind lady, who gave me her personal number to contact her in case anything went wrong.

I had exhausted my leave days and I needed to go back to work because that was the cash cow. And we needed a lot of it.

Philip was still held at work. But my brother George could get a month off work to push the next few chemos.

We set up a date. He got a ticket and was now on his way to India.

He arrived in India at the crack of dawn.

He was excited to see Dad and they kept calling each other 'Name sake! Name Sake!'

He arrived laden with a suitcase full of Kenyan food. Fish, roasted and smoked meats, vegetables, flour; both for porridge and for ugali.

Our Mikayi had done an elaborate job of packing food so George's tenure would be less expensive and more nutritious.

Dad was excited especially at the fish and meat because in India, you do not eat beef.

We hadn't eaten beef for months.

I cooked it with all my might and when I served, he could not eat it – He was having a bout of nausea.

George or Joju or Georginho or Ginho as I call him, is absolutely one of my favourite siblings. He happens to be the son of Nyasamia who named him after our Dad.

There was now three of us and our little house was busy, with me playing mother goose as the two men made conversations to do with football and Raila Odinga – Joju is an Arsenal fan. Another thing I have in common with him.

Joju kept recording videos of Dad dancing and posting them on his Faccbook timeline to the cheer of many of his fans.

Dad was only too happy to dance for the camera, as sick as he looked.

He kept peering at the videos and urging Joju on;

"Serve all those fans of mine. Post it now."

"Did you post it already? What are they saying?"

"Hand me that phone let me read the comments myself!'

TAJ MAHAL

I am a renowned adventurist and a wanderlust and I had promised Dad that if he fought hard enough and we reached half the chemos, I would take him to Agra to see a wonder of the world.

I thought to take both him and Joju at the Taj Mahal, so we break the monotony and routine of hospital or just chilling in our flat.

Some people need the constant flow of movement to keep them rooted. While people find travel tiring, for some it provides a constant barrage of novelty.

I had organised to get us a comfortable van that would take us in the four-hour journey.

I had narrated to Dad the story of the Taj Mahal, its many myths and theories, and he had gained an interest.

We both thought it was fascinating that a man would build all that to grieve his wife.

The story of Taj Mahal, just like Romeo and Juliet is, one that fascinates romantics but that's not about it, the building is an architectural marvel from its design to the amount of marble used in construction and the uniqueness for it keeps changing colour depending on time of day.

Once upon a time was an emperor by the name Shah Jahan who ruled India between 1628 to 1658. Jahan had a wife by the name Mum taz Mahal.

Mumtaz was the love of his life for about 19 years. Mumtaz

died during the childbirth of their 14th child and just like Queen Victoria, Jahan sunk into great grief.

She died while she had accompanied her husband in a military campaign at Deccan. Her remains were transferred back to Agra and Jahan started the construction of the Taj Mahal which took a record 22 years to complete and it is a show of combined Turkish ottoman, Indian, Persian and Islamic architecture.

Later on Jahan died and both their bodies lie inside the Taj Mahal.

The Taj Mahal is a testament of the human dexterity.

It took about 20,000 humans, and animals including elephants to get the job done and it's very evident.

I position it in the same pedestal as our African architectural wonders, the Pyramids in Giza to the Great Mosque of Djenne.

The Taj Mahal was built some 400 years ago but hasn't dropped its marvel even by a hue.

It's also evidence that technology has had the modern day human loose in skill and creativity.

It's a very protected building and during previous wars between India and Pakistan, extra scaffolding was employed to protect it from exterior attacks. It's a definable symbol of Indian design, architecture, culture, genius and dexterity.

We set off really early and waded through the town traffic. In no time we were on the highway - Dad, myself, Joju, Neeraj, the wife and the driver.

The sun was already up and like always shy and hiding under grey clouds. We passed expansive lands, rice paddies, farmers going about their business.

The road narrowed and we countered a few bumps, had a steady lonely 2 hours drive. Beasts of cows lay basking on the tarmac, some grazing by the roadside.

In Africa we consider cows wealth and pastoralism is still widely practised in rural Kenya. Cows play major roles. They provide meat, milk and this will supplement a diet during hard times. They provide cow hide and whisks that are both ornamental and decor. They provided free labor in tilling of land before technology took over. Cows were also currency and are still used to pay dowry, to pay school fees, to settle debts and disputes. Cows were also symbolic for rituals like death sacrifices to our ancestors, and for Dad who grew up in the rural areas, cows were gold.

But In India, cows are sacred. You cannot slaughter them. Fat Cows grazed by the roads aimlessly untethered and with no herds boys.

"If only I could carry these cows and take them back home," he sighed wishfully. He was in an altercation with our herds boy back in the village just a few days into landing in India because of cows. Our Mikayi was in Nairobi taking care of Lilly's kids. No one was in our home in the village except for the herds boy who was taking care of Dad's collection of twelve cows.

Nobody was supervising him, and one cow got lost. A cow getting lost simply means someone has stolen it, or your herds boy has organized for its sale with either a butcher or a distant location where it will not be traced and may end up as a feast in a funeral.

Dad lost his marbles and worked himself to lather. He made an international call to the village, despite that we had so little airtime and exhausted our bundles for the day.

"Otieno. ifuo seriously. Kendo aduogo deal kodi ." - Otieno you are such an Idiot. Let me get back I will deal with you.

"Dad, shouldn't you be more worried about why you are in India and not a cow that is lost in Africa?"

I was annoyed because I needed to communicate to work to extend my leave days and now I could not.

Anyway, he pressed his nose on the car window with longing like how kids look at toys as fat cows rushed behind us and continued to look smaller and smaller as we moved forward.

The earth is largely the same.

In all countries I go to, you will always feel a different beat and culture from the cities. Their architecture. Their music. Their people. Their dressing. But ultimately if you drive to the outskirts, and take a long drive into the countryside you will realise it's the same. You could as well be anywhere.

Scattered farms and homesteads hugged the surface clinging on to earth. Farmers tilling land. Expansive acres of crop. And the slow tempo of village life.

Buildings reappeared and the realisation that we were now approaching a city. More human activity and soon we were in Agra.

Agra is a touristic city built around the Taj Mahal, a tomb made 400 years ago, has built a city and keeps sustaining it. And we were part of the statistic.

Everything about Agra is about tours, travels, how to get to the Taj Mahal, curio shops with little Taj Mahals, hawkers with pictures and paintings of the Taj Mahal. We snaked in through the windy cabro roads, narrow pavements full of tourists most who were Indians.

It all looked very familiar.

We parked near the Taj Mahal as vehicles are not allowed in.

Niraj went in and got us tickets.

We then started the walk in – the sun was high up. We were at about 35 degrees or thereabout. Our melanin skins glistening under the burning orb.

This sapped Dad's energies. He was really exhausted as I recall.

Chemo was weighing in on him and he was out of it.

His excitement was tempered by ill health.

We walked slowly until we got in.

From the gate you will see the marvel of the Taj Mahal and why it's a wonder of the world, Un chef d 'ouvre.

There were thousands of tourist walking towards the main building along the gardens with the long pool. People taking photos all over.

We were probably the only Africans in there and the crowds really stared at us.

Some were distracted that they started asking for photos with us. Dad was irritated. Joju was elated.

One of the things that amused me is one Indian went to Joju and said he had seen him on TV. That Joju was a soccer player; more specifically he called him Kolo Toure.

Joju did not make any effort to correct this excited football fan.

"I don't want to break his heart," he confided in me empathetically.

So Joju nodded and this Indian guy shouted the same information to all the Indians around and soon people were lining up to take photos with Joju.

I was seated on one of the pillars with Dad watching the stampede. If only Kolo Toure who was then playing for Liverpool FC knew he was being impersonated.

"This was built by a man grieving his wife?..All this?"

"Imagine that."

"I should have built your mother something."

"You built her a miserable little semi permanent that's now a kitchen remember? That's your Taj Mahal. Thats your level."

We laughed.

We took photos. He requested for various photos of him in different positions. Different angles.

Behind the Taj is the beautiful Yamuna River which I am disappointed to say, looked polluted.

We finished our business and set off the 4 hour drive back to Gurgaon.

Dad bought me a souvenir at Agra – he fished out his wallet and paid for it. A little imitation of the Taj Mahal in a glass bottle. He had some dollars in Kenya which he had exchanged into rupees but had not once used. The first time he fished his wallet was to buy me that particular souvenir.

He just handed it to me.

The van was driving out of Agra. As we were on the back seat with Dad, my neck was permanently turned looking behind at the narrow pavements, and the cabro roads and the crowds of Indians on the streets that we were leaving behind, and Dad asked;

"You forgot something?"

"I have been here before. But I am happy that I have walked out with you by my side."

I had been here in a dream.

SAYONARA

I left India on a humid December dawn. The street lights were on, illuminating the informal set ups as we walked out to the taxi guy who was waiting for me.

Joju was asleep and Dad accompanied me out with my suit case.

I gave him a long hug and when I let go, he did not look at me.

I looked at his shirt and the creases on it since we did not have an iron box in India. They looked like the creases of his life.

I got in the cab and looked out. Instead of going back in, he was standing outside below the street light pole. He cut a lonely figure.

The taxi guy did not start the vehicle immediately. He was trying to map out how to navigate to the airport.

I took my phone out and flicked a shot of him. I am really that kind of person. I capture moments. I wanted to remember this moment for the rest of our lives.

I arrived in Nairobi at midday. Our city in the sun was blazing with light reflecting on the airport glass panes.

For the first time, I felt really exhausted -I felt like I had just arrived from a World War.

I took the measure of everything, momentarily sobering up on it all. The future did not seem as bright as Nairobi was. I was behind in work, in all my schedules and there was still a lot to be done.

I left two Georges in India and money was running short.

I got in bed and I slept for 24 hours straight. I did not even announce to friends or family that I was back.

I had also missed my kids...took some time to just be with them.

I needed a moment of silence.

I reported to work next Monday and did the best I could, asked to have a discussion with my siblings on what we should do about the last chemos.

We all agreed to set up a second harambee.

We were all broke. We had thrown everything to the first fund raiser and speaking for myself, I had taken massive loans that even when my salary came, I was ending up with pocket change.

If Dad was going to get any money going forward, it would come from other sources and not from my salary or any institution. I had also exhausted my social capital.

I did not go back to my Facebook timeline. I felt embarrassed to do so.

A few friends offered to loan me, but I declined because I had no idea how I would pay back. Naturally, I fear debt.

And it's easy to understand why reading this book. Debts had messed up my Dad and I saw it with my eyes how it interferred with his relationships.

Debts strip you off your dignity; they enslave you, you can never be authentic if you owe people –not in thought, not in mannerism.

I floated the idea that we needed to sell Sibuor, Dad's car – That hit a snag, as he had pawned the logbook to a Shylock, to deal with the debt he owed during the tender scandal.

Dad had no asset whatsoever that we could convert into cash. Dad had either spent his money on his women or his children and had no savings.

The landlord at Olympic was also showing up a lot to harass our Mikayi for timely payments. We had been slacking because all the focus was in India. In fact, he had heard that Dad would never rise from the mat where he lay and did not want to have to collect rent from mourners.

When I switched on my Kenyan line, I had about 5 people on my phone demanding cash they claimed to have given Dad.

I called a few of my colleagues and contacts in my field of work and requested for extra jobs whether it was coaching their kids or writing projects on their behalf. I also did a lot of research for students in universities abroad, which was illegal but hey!

I happened to be the account manager of one of Kenya's largest sugar factories. I was meeting the MD who had problems with our services and was threatening to engage a different supplier.

I was seated in his boardroom when he turned up.

"Where have you been? I have been calling your office and was being told you were on leave. You can't have been on leave that long?"

"Oh Raju. I was in India."

"What! India? What were you doing in India?" He sat down intently.

"I have a patient in India."

I told him the story sketchily but bravely. Bravely because I knew Dad was going to heal.

"How is India?" He asked me as if I had just come from heaven.

I told him about his ancestral home and about Aggra.

"Show me photos!" He requested.

He pored over photos on my phone like Joseph in Cairo catching up on how his father and Esau were doing back in Israel.

We discussed business there after and while I was leaving, he asked to wait for him at the reception.

He disappeared to his office and when he came back he handed me a brown envelope and inside it, was money that could pay for a whole chemo session.

It was unexpected and it was really special. I will never forget this guy - Raju Chatthe of Kibos Sugar.

I went to the bank and deposited the money straight from the envelope into Joju's account.

The second fundraiser we held was mostly of colleagues and friends, and it was not well attended but we got a substantial amount that would help us push.

I talked to Dad every evening to check his temperature.

He missed Kenya terribly.

George completed his run and was coming back to work as he exhausted his leave days. And finally our first born sister was going to finish the last lap with Dad.

I saw our first born sister in Kisumu before she travelled.

Ours is a somewhat formal friendly relationship full of respect.

It is attributed to the fact that we did not spend a long time together as siblings. We also have a personality difference. While I am an extrovert, she is very introverted and very calm as well. We felt on the last leg we needed the family medic as things got more and more complicated.

I was meeting her to also discuss that the doctor had given Dad six months without treatment, a year with treatment and a slim chance of 1% for survival.

She took it in like a medic experienced in bad news but she said so far he had done well and so we would continue fighting because while working as a medic, she had also seen her share of miracles.

So far, three houses had been represented in India. I represented the house of Nyaugenya, George represented the house of Nyasamia and our big sister was going to represent the Mikayi.

She also travelled loaded with food from her mother and stuff Dad had requested to help make him comfortable. She also carried drugs which in her experience, felt would also help.

She was going to spend Christmas in India with Dad .

She sent us a photo, she had taken Dad to the mall nearby where they had watched Christmas tidings and enjoyed a meal in a fancy restaurant.

On the new year on 2016, I was in Malindi, a coastal city in Kenya.

I thanked God that we got to see a new year with Dad in it.

I called and wished him a happy new year Kenyan time and he said "You missed it. I crossed the year some three hours ago."

He really was that kind of man. Very particular on birthdays and anniversaries to the AM/PM.

"It's just new year right now in Kenya."

"But it was three hours ago in India. You did not take that into consideration. How are your kids?"

"They are good, Daddy."

"I would like to see them this Easter. In fact all of you should organize for your kids to see me this year Easter."

"It's done."

He now only had January to be in India then get back to Nairobi so we run more tests and see what next.

January passed in a blink and Monicah had to get back to work. Her ticket was a week before Dad's travel and that meant Dad had to live by himself for a week under Neeraj's watch before travelling back home. It indeed was one of the most scary things we have encountered as a family.

He argued that instead of the family spending money on a ticket to just pick him, he would pull through the week and the money be used for drugs he would have to carry home. I had signed a lease up to a specific date and extending even by a day meant we pay for the next month. Made perfect sense only that Dad was really really weak.

He had been on chemo back to back and was now looking like a chemo patient poster boy. I was not sure the airline would accept him to travel by himself or even handle the transfer in Qatar. In fact he was supposed to start palliative treatment and we needed that done in Kenya as we would be able to manage the logistics and bills unlike in India.

If he were to get admitted in India, even his air ticket would be affected.

Our Indian friends were with him throughout, giving us updates ensuring he was taking his drugs and trying to eat.

Dad could not even get on the phone to speak.

"Get me back home Mami," He texted constantly

I requested the hospital to write a letter that will allow him to travel by himself. They were adamant. I gave them an international call and explained our circumstance.

They objected.

The landlord started harassing our Indian friend because she noticed Dad was all alone in the nights and with no caregiver and shuddered for anything to happen to him.

She needed Dad taken to a hospital, the very situation we were avoiding.

They ran some tests on Dad, then wrote a letter saying that he had been through chemo, was cancer free, on observation and was fit enough to travel.

I called Dad and encouraged him to be strong especially at the immigration and check in - he only needed to be strong at those two points not to raise suspicions to be declared unfit to fly.

Neeraj took him step by step at the airport and stayed with him till he got cleared by immigration.

He texted me and said; "By God's grace, he has just got through immigration. Now lets pray for him on the transfer in Doha."

In Doha, Souleymane was waiting for him as soon as the plane landed, walked him to the Nairobi gate and waited till he boarded.

We all held our breath that night. My siblings headed to the airport the next morning expecting anything. I was unable to since I worked out of Nairobi but I was on phone with them following the proceedings from the moment the plane landed.

Dad walked slowly out of the arrivals door on February 1st 2016 blinded by the bare Nairobi sun.

I was relieved beyond belief. I broke into a creeping sweat that usually follows a narrowly avoided accident.

Joju took a photo of him and sent to me.

I posted him arriving on my Facebook page, for the sake of the thousands who had invested their emotions, time and money on this journey - there were celebrations and ululations all over. People wanted to see him. To visit him. To gift him.

But the doctor had said his immune system was low. He was prone to infections and nobody could visit him yet. They decided to wait patiently.

I was being invited on talk shows as a cancer caregiver and I was approaching everything with caution.

Chemo had taken a toll on my father.

He now looked like his slim brother Kasera. His hair was all gone. He was out of it. He had lost massive weight, and grown very light.

I recall telling Joju jokingly and part accusingly, "But this is not how I left this guy in India a few months ago."

"Your job was to initiate the process and set us up since you are the ops in the family. That's why we had to take our elder sister last because she is a nurse by profession and needed to be there when chemo really kicks in."

Our elder sister must have had quite a hard time with Dad – but we will never know, because she doesn't speak much.

Dad was back in Nairobi in his house under the care of Mikayi.

I felt sorry for the Mikayi too. All her life her job had been to pick the pieces which she did quite gracefully. In her lifetime she had lost our sister Lilly, was now baby sitting Lillian's kids, and was again up in the alley to nurse Dad .

We had asserted ourselves as his kids. We had flown him halfway across the world. We had given him chemo. We had scratched the surface. We had got him back home safely.

The next strategy was his diet and we got a juicer and an array of diets to get him strong from the effects of chemo which once he was done, would subside in time. The painkillers he needed were available. We bought lots of drugs from India.

Then he would need to go for more tests to see how he was fairing. As our Mikayi is a deeply religious woman, she even contacted prayer warriors from her church who would visit home every single evening for prayer. Dad's house would be filled every evening by perfectly harmonised Adventist hymns from **Nyagendia.**

It was all ironical because all his life, Dad had never been a religious man. And even when we grew up, he raised us independent of faith and spirit.

Despite that, step mothers came with different faiths for instance Mikayi was a deep Adventist and it was imperative that all her kids end up as Adventist. Lilly ended up a catholic.

Nyasamia was a catholic I recall. But her kids have all taken different paths.

I went to a Catholic Primary School, Anglican High School, was raised by an Adventist and have see sawed in churches depending on who had the most compelling message to finding my own spirituality in humanity.

Dad never quite cared if his kids went to church or not. It was really upto us.

I recall staying home with him many times when the Mikayi and her kids were preparing for Holy Sabbath and would spend all Saturday in church. We would be listening to Rumba.

But I will say this about religion, if not for anything, it provides hope and it grounds people especially in their down times.

OLD GUITARIST BY PICASSO

A month of home nursing and Dad had a chest issue that could not subside. He kept complaining of pain in his chest and difficulty in breathing.

We took him to hospital and tests revealed the chemo he went through had got his immunity very low and his chest caught an infection. Drugs were prescribed.

He once again lost his appetite and the little weight he had started gaining declined.

He was now taking drugs and not eating well and the drugs were also taking a toll on his strength. You could see from his eyes he was dizzy and preferred to just close his eyes as he spoke.

One evening he complained his whole body was painful and he was running short of breath and Joju had to rush him to hospital. He was found to be dehydrated and was admitted immediately.

While in hospital, our relatives from Sori travelled to visit him.

Word had spread in the village like gun powder that he was back from India and they had not seen Dad since the burial of Uncle Kasera the previous year. They had only heard he was ill, and had been taken to India for treatment and was now back and was hospitalised.

When they reached Dad's bed and saw him, they started wailing and crying.

Dad was a bag of bones.

His hair had started growing back and he was this white man with a wisp of straight hair tagging on his skull. His skin was taut and his skull pressed and jutted out.

People hardly know just how sick they are until they see our reactions.

I could say for us, we had gone through the motions with him and our lens kept adjusting. But the people who saw him a year or before would either mask their shock or retreat privately to cry.

"Why are people crying like I am already dead?"

The question filled up with its own bucket of pain.

I took my husband to see him and Dad being the person to give his best side always, struggled to sit up.

He was swept by a tide of dizziness. He focused his eyes on the sheets covering him momentarily then slowly looked at my husband.

"I can see you are very strong. You can even sit up!"

While holding his bony hand webbed in a network of veins, in the Amandla fashion he said 'Aluta continua! '

Mama Mpenzi travelled to see her long time nemesis.

"George, can you get out of that bed fast as we have unfinished business."

'We can take our war outside even now if you wish.'

Trying to punch out like Ali from his lying position.

And he laughed a hollow laugh. A laugh from the belly. A laugh you look for in your intestines because your chest cannot. A laugh without a facial expression. He laughed while not looking at Mama Mpenzi as he could not turn his head. It was a herculean effort to do so.

And Mama Mpenzi laughed while blinking back tears rapidly.

Would you believe, if I told you, that even at this point, dad would ask for his various toothbrushes and would insist to go to the toilet by himself without a wheel chair.

He would be back. It was just a matter of time.

I was dealing with that, and mentally I was also dealing with his bill which was rising like the stock exchange. A week into his hospitalization we were at a staggering Kshs.700,000 even after trying as his kids to reduce it by about Kshs.300, 000 the previous week.

We were running on fumes as all of us were financially exhausted. Neck deep in loans and debts, everyone was stressed out. Tempers were running short severally in our Whatsap group, as we pondered the daily challenges.

He kept asking for the daily bill to see if we were being over charged and kept poring over what he did not think he was given.

Anytime I visited and I would do so, twice in a day he would ask, "How will this bill be paid Mami?"

"This coming from the guy who asked. How will we go to India? How will we pay for all these chemos? Your job is to get better. That's all we need you to do."

The cancerous cells had not been seated somewhere reading the Bible or singing Kumbaya. When Dad's immunity went low, the remission cancer cells sprung back like weeds, attacked with a vengeance. They took over all parts of his body and now spill into his liver - he deteriorated real fast you could actually watch it happen.

Our joy had been short lived. The foe that seemed defeated was only but recuperating lying in wait.

His eyes suddenly turned yellow and was on a terminal decline and they reminded me of Lilly.

And on this day when I visited him and he was unable to take himself to the toilet, I realised he was down.

He could not talk and was struggling to breathe. The nurses put an oxygen mask to aid him breath.

I sat there with him and I held his frail hand in mine and he looked at me in the eye.

Time was growing short like shadows in the noon.

In a flash, our whole life played in my eyes.

"I love you."

He moved his eyebrows

"You can hear me, Dad?"

He moved his eye brows again.

"I love you"

He moved his eyebrows again and squeezed my hand and let it go and slumped it on the bed. My husband who was behind me the whole time, drew me out as my siblings were all gathered waiting to see him, all of them in several stages of deep sobbing, especially the younger ones.

There it was, strokes of pain splashed all over the room from cancer's sinister mural. Brush marks like Picasso's old guitarist.

When everyone had seen him, the doctor gathered all of us and told us that Dad's vital organs were now failing and they had the option of taking him to the ICU where he would be under machines and see if he would stabilise, or keep him in the oxygen mask as he was now struggling to breath.

They needed us to make that call.

"It's not our call - mum is here and should make that call." I offered.

Everyone's eyes turned to the Mikayi.

For the very first time, she had a decision to make.

Mikayi carefully asked, "If we put him on the ICU will he live? Like if you unplug will he be ok?"

The doctor said, "Not in his condition. His organs have all been destroyed."

"Then don't."

And so it came to be, that the first woman Dad married, who he never saw all his life, who never had a voice all her life, when she made her voice heard, it was the final call.

Dad battled in the oxygen mask all night not willing to give up. His belly rising and falling with his breathing, and finally his whole body heaved up and when it rested, he did not breath again.

George Auko died in the night of 23rd March 2016.

***

Our father's death was sad because he was not ready to die.

Well, nobody ever is, but I have seen people who have battled disease to the point they get done, the kind of people who request for Euthanasia. The kind of people who were my mother.

But Dad still had that glow even in the yellowness of his eye. Still had that squeeze in his hand to show I am here. Was still interested to raise his eyebrow in his last hour.

I guess my father was in the category of 'battled disease bravely borne.' And that was sad.

***

As the world took colour in the morning after I lost my Dad, a mental fence stood before me.

On this side was me, my father's daughter. On the other side of the fence was the eerie world of a daughter without her father.

I did not want to enter that new world.

But I also knew in a very detached form that there was a bill of about Kshs.450,000 that had accrued in the hospital. And his body was being held until it was offset.

I knew that we needed to organise his funeral. I also knew that I had no money at all – none of us had any money at all. We had given this fight our all emotionally, physically and fiscally.

Anyone who holds any stakes in the life of the person who has died be it a parent, or a first born or spouse will tell you that you will need to organise everything from the bill that's pending, moving the body to the morgue, and Africans must be buried where their ancestors lie, so transport of the body upcountry, the church service, the funeral event which involves the outside caterers, the food, the drinks, the tents, the PA system, the chairs, the church, the programs and weeks before the main event you need to organize nightly meetings where people also take tea or just eat full meals.

I decided not to cross the fence. I stayed on this side.

I packed my grief in a box calmly, locked the box and put the keys away so I could figure out how we go from a world where Dad's body is being held in hospital, to a world where he rests with his ancestors. This was my last assignment and I was going to power through it all.

We had a meeting as siblings. Philip had to travel upcountry as the eldest boy since he did not have a simba and needed to build it fast. Outside that, he needed to sit with the elders in the community and agree on dates, what was required of us and also see if he could get any resources from Dad's clan.

We got dates, what was required traditionally but no resources –he was told from the worl go that nobody had any money to deal with the issue. Understandably, Dad was last alive in the house of Nyongalo and his step brothers could only do so much.

Dad's funeral was squarely on us, his children and we had two weeks to deal with it.

We agreed as his children to reach out to our contacts once again and invite them for a major fundraiser a week to Dad's funeral. We worked as a team, it did not matter who came from what house. We worked as Dad had raised us with one common denominator - the Auko name.

These weeks passed in a whirl wind of organising the funeral.

My siblings agreed unanimously that I should write Dad's eulogy.

The day I sat to write his eulogy, I wrote about him like a friend I once knew. I wrote the basics about his schooling, siblings, work – I was done in just an hour. I wrote matter of factly as if he lived his life clean cut like a monk.

Life is such a paradox. All the life I spent with him, he did not know that I was like a biographer stalking him and I would be the one to put words that people would finally read at his funeral.

I recall my husband reading the eulogy and saying; "I expected more from this eulogy. This is quite short. You have not put soul in this."

"I am not sure I have soul - but a time will come when I will put soul. I will one day write about this guy."

A week to Dad's funeral we all gathered up for his fundraiser at the All Saints Cathedral which once again was given to us free of charge due to Joju and Philip's contacts.

The fundraiser was full to the point, as his daughter, I did not have a place to sit.

It brought about people who I saw in the various stages of his life people he lived with in Umoja, in Eastleigh, in the slums, in Olympic, who he worked with, who he partied with, from the SDA churches, to his neighbours at Olympic, colleagues and friends of my siblings – two ladies from our days at Glory guest House also showed up.

We had a budget of about 1Million shillings so we offset the 450, 000 pending and utilise 300, 000 for the funeral.

Unbelievably, without letting me know the moment word got out that I had lost my father, my Facebook friends started their own private fundraiser and on this day, they handed me 500,000 shillings.

Not only did they do that, they hired buses and travelled home as a group. They also funded their own tent, cooked and did not burden us as a family in any way.

To this day I owe my Facebook timeline a lot.

Relatives kept asking me, are you an influencer? And I said Hell no! Infact I have less than 5,000 friends on Facebook but I do vet my followers and probably have the best Facebook can offer in Kenya (Pun intended).

In total as a family, we raised 1 million shillings.

I travelled to Sori two days before the funeral to ensure everything on the ground was in place, was met there by my sister the teacher who resides in Sori while the rest of my siblings were in Nairobi and would travel with Dad's body. We ensured all the suppliers we had contracted were on the ground getting ready from the outside catering, PA, chairs, enough and safe parking, food, drinks, program, water, temporary washrooms.

I also visited our then Member of Parliament who also handed me some police officers for extra security. It was the year before an election and so he needed some airtime to sell his manifesto as his competitor had also requested for airtime.

I made both of them pay for this favour.

Sori is a small rural market situated on the shores of Lake Victoria. A day before the funeral, local folks started witnessing masses of people pouring into the usually quiet centre save for the guy who sells radio cassettes and blasts them on his bass speaker by the bus stage.

We waited for Dad's funeral motorcade to arrive as they had left Nairobi earlier in the day and Philip kept updating me on their current location.

Livestock were released from all homesteads and driven down to the road towards Sori to meet the motorcade from Nairobi.

At 5pm or thereabout the hooting of vehicles could be heard approaching from Nairobi. It was the short rainy season and the vehicles were encrusted in brown dust. You would see most drivers through two fan shaped holes. They were joined by the motorcades that had arrived the day before and slowly we all snaked our way down the road towards our village. Women were hollering and men were crying with their bare chests.

Cows were stumbling on each other while being whipped by my little cousins as some ducked the whips into maize plantations by the roadside. Dogs were barking in unison indicating their anxiety with what was going on around their locality. The sky was orange from the ensuing sunset reflecting on the lake. Dust was rising and cars hooting incessantly. And masses of humanity with hands on their head were crying in exasperation.

This was all so familiar.

Philip was driving *Sibuor*, Dad's car ahead of the hearse as the motorcade followed.

I remembered so many years ago the two of us being in this same state and me telling him; "You are such a brave boy."

Now he was just a brave man.

We reached the *Otho* where little boys were hanging from the branches watching the motorcade and we took a right turn off the main road to enter the homestead. As the gate was narrow, it was slow and we stopped there a while before we entered the compound to the climax of the mourning.

Dad's casket was lowered from the hearse and placed under a set up tent.

I got out of my car and my friends accompanied me to view his body.

You will not believe that from the moment I said bye to him at the hospital to this moment, I had not visited the morgue to view his body and this is because I needed to really concentrate on organising the funeral. I was also on this side of the fence.

In his coffin he looked settled. At peace. My brothers had done him justice and dressed him in a very expensive agbada imported from Nigeria complete with its head gear. He looked so handsome.

In the still of the morning dawn, before the cock crowed thrice on 6th April 2016 when it was still dark and all you could hear were the sounds of hippos bleating further down at the shores, the air was cut by dirges and cries from a woman who had spent the night sleeping seated on a chair next to Dad's coffin with our Mikayi and many other women.

The many suppliers were asleep yet to wake and start preparations for the business of the day.

It was Mama Mpenzi. And she was joined by my aunties from my maternal side and they cried desperately as this marked the last day of Dad on this earth.

It was show time. Everyone woke up in that darkness and started taking care of whatever role they had for this day and needed to be done in just four hours as the funeral programme was starting at 10am.

Guests were arriving fast, and I was up and down to receive them, usher them to have a meal, ensure they were comfortable.

I did not attend my father's funeral. I did not sit down at that arena and I did not listen to a single account of what people had to say about him.

I was on the flanks as a quarterback serving, ushering, welcoming, bidding bye, giving lost guests direction, sending rescue to guests who had incidents on their way. I had so many guests that people came and went without even seeing me.

But I appreciated the invaluable support as a family we got from everyone who showed up to help us send our father. All my friends in the private tent who made it their job to take care of my workmates, my in laws, Facebook friends, my family from Ugenya.

I was also meeting most of my Facebook friends for the very first time in my life – not an ideal place for meetings but I am grateful.

Dad was laid to rest at around 3pm and once they laid him in his grave, I got a chance to walk to his grave and with friends picked shovels and put dust to dust. It was a beautiful casket and the soil hit it and it made cruel reverberating thuds. Dust swallowed the casket inch by inch until it disappeared and all we could see was the soil we were pouring in.

We were done with the funeral service.

At around 4pm, a carnival mood took over the compound and the SDA choir that had been infecting our souls with perfectly harmonised songs from '*Nyagendia*' was ushered away politely as an eager DJ took over and started playing Okatch Biggy's Luo benga.

I was still bidding the last of my guests goodbye while now concerned about the ones who would sleep over for the disco matanga.

A disco matanga is the celebration of life that happens on the night after a person is buried and it's a big deal in my community.

As the evening matured, everywhere I could look, people were walking around with whisky bottles in their hands. All manner of people. My brothers, friends. My friends. Relatives. Car boots were being opened revealing six packs of beer and bottles of Whisky, Gin, Vodka, Beer, every type of alcohol.

They did not come to play.

At some point I was standing with Philip and George and we were looking at our friends who by now had made themselves comfortable, sitting in different parts of our homestead, having a drink and storying.

Philip always the person rich in the magic component of insight and foresight or what they call perspicace asked me;

"What do you think?"

And I told him, "This is perfect. This is exactly how he would have wanted it."

The truth is our father's journey from the moment he was diagnosed with cancer to this moment had been funded by these people, very young people. And so yes, let them have their way. This was as much their funeral as it was ours.

I am my father's daughter. I had hired a whole band of Luo traditional percussion commonly known as Ajawa or Ohangla to take over from the DJ in the night. The band took over at about 1830hrs.

Mourners danced themselves limb. They ate and drunk to their fill.

At some point exhaustion set in and I retreated into my car, adjusted the seat and blacked out.

274

GRIEF, THE SEQUEL

I woke up from the adjusted seat of my car where I had retreated and momentarily had no idea why I was waking up from a car seat.

I peered outside my car window curiously.

I saw that I was in the village in our compound. No signs of anybody - only empty bottles of Jack Daniels, cans of beer and paper plates. Water and soda bottles were on the ground.

And it started to come to me.

Sleeping dogs lay exhausted from the previous day's feast and night mayhem.

Adjacent to me was Sibuor, Dad's car where I could see Philip's legs on the windscreen from the inside, where he also probably retired to.

I turned my head slowly to the right and my eyes caught it, behind Mikayi's house; the oval mound of fresh soil rising up cruelly from the ground.

And my mouth was suddenly dry with fear.

I rested my head back to the car seat and closed my eyes. Tears ran from my eyes into my ears. There was salt in my gums, and acid in my stomach. My whole body was swollen in a sob.

I was witnessing my own death.

Grief stood up from the chair in which it had been sitting silently observing proceedings for the last two weeks and ushered me across the fence where I followed dutifully...

(A sequel by Deborah Auko Tendo)

Dad and the Visiting Dove that often perched at his hospital window

EPILOGUE

Dad

My father was a human being.

He was perfect and he was imperfect. I consider myself really favoured to have spent the amount of life I did with him because he has proved to be a manual on how to live or not live my life. I picked more lessons from him than any school could ever provide.

This is a book about my father and not me. I feature a lot as a consequence to his actions/inactions.

There are a lot of biographies on bookshelves about politicians, corporate leaders, famous people but none about ordinary people who, I might add, own just as remarkable stories but with no one to tell them, and so I have dared to put the face of an ordinary man forward because all this happened for a reason.

My mother

I couldn't be more proud of her in spite of everything.

It took me growing up, getting married, having kids, and doing life to understand that women have choices.

They can walk.

It took courage for a woman to do that in her early 20s in the 80s.

Scores of women have died in abusive marriages and she chose to live. I know that it was not an easy decision for her. I know that because I am a human being and a mother. And that move will not be easy for any human being or mother.

It will come with a lot of judgement, resentment and self-questioning. But, she chose herself and that was beautiful.

I watched subsequent marriages to my Dad. I would never have wanted her to be in that position.

In as far as her denying me, I can come from a point of understanding. Mother carried the shame of teenage pregnancy all her life and had to conceal my existence to the very end. She could not explain me and her age without the issue of a teenage pregnancy showing up. These are all societal constructs, expectations and stigma that made both of us victims.

When the sun sets, we have a very clear destiny which beckons us, and is ultimately up to us, entirely.

There will be people in our lives to assist us or to derail us from getting there.

As far as my mother is concerned, it ended at being born. And that she did. She birthed me.

The world conspires, brings people to our paths, or takes people from our paths to help us in our journey and we can never really turn back and say, we did not achieve our full potential because someone came or left.

We have to be self-conscious about how people, our environment and circumstance have affected us either by aiding or derailing us, then we have to make the necessary adjustments.

Life balances things out. There are kids born in privilege who never achieved their full potential due to that fact. There are kids born in poverty who have achieved their potential due to that fact.

The key is to know who you are and what you are up against, and once you are not up against yourself, then you are set to go.

Every derailment is a lesson and the more the derailments, the more the lessons and the wiser and more equipped we are to deal with pitfalls.

There are no true wiser people out here who have not had major pitfalls.

Mikayi

The Mikayi of our home found a voice right after Dad's death. She maintained living in Olympic and operated for some years from the city.

I did have a problem with that as I had expected her to relocate to Sori.

I questioned why she would live in the city yet she was raised in the village and why she had left Dad by himself until I realised it was my grief speaking and selfishly so. I was so used to seeing her shrunk that it was foreign to see her make such a decision to live far away from Dad. Here, I was projecting the man who raised me, expecting her to still gatekeep a dead man.

I acknowledged this, accepted and supported her decision.

She recently moved permanently back home.

Nyasamia

Nyasamia moved to Australia with my step sister and recently re-married in December 2022. She is reaping from all the goodness she banked in her hey reign.

Nyaseme

Nyaseme re-appeared during Dad's funeral. She lives in Kisumu where she eventually settled and we do have a cordial relationship.

Raila Odinga

Anytime I grieve for my father, I am consoled that he did not live long enough to witness the elections of 2017 or 2022 both of which Raila Odinga contested for Presidency, because if cancer did not kill him, these two elections would have.

AUTHOR'S NOTE.

As early as my 12th year, my English compositions were pinned on our class board. When I sat KCPE, my teacher of English, one Mr. Ram sternly reminded me that he did not expect anything less than a straight A from me. Suffice to say, I did get an A. As I left Moi Girls High School in Eldoret at the end of my High School stint, my class teacher Mr. Bett said to me;

"Deborah Auko, you have a story. Ensure you tell it."

Anytime I write bits and pieces about life with my Dad on my social media platforms, the comment section is always filled with 'You should write a book.' It is because of everyone and anyone who ever said to me 'You should tell your story' or 'You should write a book' that this book is finally written.

I was raised by an ordinary man, a man you could not pick out from the next man in a public bus, but whose life was incredible like many ordinary people whose incredible stories are trapped within them for lack of a witness with the courage to tell their story to the world.

I was privileged to get a front seat in my father's life. He happened to me and he also happened for me.

The timely period to write this book was always on my Dad's first death anniversary in 2017.

But my insides were red with grief.

So the second, third, fourth, fifth anniversaries also went by as I healed.

'Write a book' has been a permanent entry on my personal Vision Board for the past six years.

On his sixth anniversary in 2022, my husband Walter told me "Just start and let's see how it goes."

I started and grief broke me. I stopped and did not look at the draft for months.

I had to get therapy from the foundational pain I experienced.

As I progressed my healing journey, I gathered courage, continued and unraveled, stopped and stayed off the draft again for more months.

I continued writing and soon, just like the landscape of our lives I found hilarious episodes that had me laughing till my stomach ached. I found beautiful episodes that had me smiling amidst tears. I crawled through the dark tunnels that had me sit down and weep. I found episodes that made me look back in wonderment at the sheer courage and resilience of the story.

Writing this book became therapy; allowing me to really introspect his life not as a participant but as a spectator, had me sitting back and questioning how I felt about certain things that I never took a pause to really reflect on, because life was happening.

I completed this book seated in the tropical beaches of Bali in December 2022.

I did not look at it for a while thereafter. It had been heavy lifting putting thoughts to words and dealing with rivers and avalanches of emotions.

Until finally, A BOOK.

The aim of this book is to journey the different generations back as it's a very wide timeline and everyone will find something in it they relate to. To dare someone to write their story even if they are not famous, and hopefully to make someone derive lessons from his life.

It is also proof of life and a testament to future generations that I was here, George Auko was here, and this was the story of his life.

ACKNOWLEDGEMENT

From the deepest chamber of my heart I would like to thank everyone who played a role to see this book through.

Walter S. Odhiambo, my husband; every year, you have tirelessly driven me 407kms down to Sori where Dad's body lies. Always on the steering on the murram road that has been gruesome for such a long time. So arid that everything; leaves, trees, stones get encrusted in fine brown dust. All the while silent, all the while playing TP OK Jazz as I weep silently.

I find it good karma that I married a man whose career and passion is children from broken homes, children without homes and children in difficult home environments. Every day I am in silent wonderment of your dedication to the children of SOS Children's Villages, your connection to the children, young people and the honourable role of being a father to many as the organisation's Country Director. These children, the young people, and their communities are lucky to have you.

Here is the book, finally!

Thanks for pushing me to write this book for five years straight. And thanks for the patience of understanding my grief process.

Thanks for owning this project fully and for funding it. I am lucky because for this project, all I had to do is sit and write and never have to worry about the financial aspect.

I would like to thank all my siblings, everyone with the mighty name Auko; Moni, Jackie, Liz, Em, Cyni, Philo, Joju, Claush, Toro, Jeff, Beaty for the understanding that I had to tell Dad's story through my eyes, and it relates in one way or another to you. This is not a picture perfect story. Picture perfect stories do not exist. We carry our imperfect story with courage and I hope so many years from today when none of us will be here, our generations will be able to hold this book and talk about their roots with pride. Our father impacted each of us in so many different ways and while we share some common stories, there are some that are completely different. I hope you derived and keep deriving lessons from how he lived his life.

Thanking my stepmum, the Mikayi for her resourcefulness with the family album and for being the common ever present denominator, for putting up with us despite our wayward ways growing up.

Gratitude to my uncle, Steven Osieyo, for his invaluable knowledge and recollection of all three of my parents, for his contribution in the writing of this book on my maternal side; I was named after his mother and he remains my only remaining 'son'. I loved you as a child and today I feel the exact same way.

My forever hero, Mama Mpenzi who when I told that I was writing a book and she was going to feature heavily in it was so amused; gave me her whole album and when I told her I was going to write everything about her, she defiantly said, 'Don't hold back!"

In the same beat, recognising my maternal cousin Lorna who we call the 'family photo heist' for she was in their time. If you gave her your album, rest assured she had plucked off some photos. Everyone hated her for this until this book had to come out and she turned out as the most resourceful historical gallery.

Uncle Agwarro, Dad's step brother for all the information on the Suba history tracing back the footsteps of Jo Wasaki who today live in Sori - Ero Kamano wuon Pope.

My appreciation to my Ugandan family spread all over the world from the UK to the US, Sweden to Uganda for their invaluable support through the years since we discovered each other, in sharing themselves and moments they had with

Alex Tendo Minge, and for always opening their doors to me whenever I visit the countries they are in, whether for work or on social travel.

Uncle Godfrey Kisuule, Auntie Vali, Auntie Robina, Auntie Getrude, Auntie Evelyn.

The Tamales; Jennie, Anne, Norman,Fiona,Rita and my in-law, Professor Sylvia, I will never forget how you made me feel on my first visit to Uganda.

My sisters Valentine, Jackie and Melissa - we should take that trip!

Auntie Sarah Nabirye and Uncle Mike Kintu you have such a special place in my heart.

Teachers worldwide are close to my heart. My teachers held my hand all my life, always passing the baton to the next like conspirators.

Mrs. Macharia, Miss Nyamu of St. Anne's Girls Primary Jogoo Road, the school where I first showed up without ever going to nursery and they gave me a chance despite being underage.

I am partly a child of the Sisters of Mary Mukumu community and convent especially Mrs. Joyceline Mukolwe – Thank you.

Mr. Ram, Mr. Lusinde, Mr. Mugasia, Mr.Amboso(RIP) all formerly of Mukumu Girls Primary Boarding School – Thank you.

I acknowledge Mr.and Mrs. Bett for their role in not only mentoring but being my therapists in my teens without billing. They saw my value beyond my struggle (if I ever make it in life, you can invoice me). If it were up to me, I would give you both Lifetime Teachers Award.

The immortal former Principal Mrs. Cheramboss (RIP) of Moi Girls High School, Eldoret - Thank you

The college lecturers that most made an impact are Onyango Ayieko and Tony Mwicigi. I am so sorry I never made it to a courtroom and chose a different path. That was my father's dream and not mine.

I carry infinite love for my bosom friends Cecilia Hellene, Vivian Orwa, Team Zanzi, Salline Handa, Verah Makosewe, Christine Otieno, Damaris Muga, Achieng Njoga ,for the great push when I would take long breaks from writing dealing with myself and they would softly tell me to slow down.

And after burying my head in the sand for long they would all shout, 'Get on with it!'

Sammy Mwangi of Heartstings Ensemble - I will be back in retirement haha! My times on stage rank as some of the best in my life.

Mrs Gai Cullen and Gray Cullen, I thank you for the great opportunity in earning my daily bread from when I stepped into the organisation fresh from college to now over 15 years later as the longest serving staff.

My colleagues Nemwel Gichana, Kassim Were,Harrison Chege, James Gachanga and Raphael Kaveva–Thanks for your roles throughout my Dad's journey with cancer.

My Indian friends Neeraj Yadav and your beautiful wife – words go bankrupt trying to express my Indian experience with both of you.

My social media community - Thank you for your followership and for sometimes patiently reading astonishingly long posts from me.

To the Gor Mahia community and Tony Anelka for the period on 2015/2016 when you stood resolutely for me, Ero uru Kamano

Writers at times go through a phase when they ask themselves if the content they are writing is worth it,and so the raw manuscript has to be read by other parties who can give an honest unbiased review. The raw manuscript was only counterread by Tryphosa Adhiambo Otieno Bennet(AO) of Severn Vale School in England, and who at different times in my life with her dear husband Brian Bennet fully sponsored my visit to the Shakespeare Museum at Stratford-upon-Avon, and to watch Romeo and Juliet at the Barbican, and from whom my library is full of books - I love and honor you AO. Thanks for making some of my dreams come true.

For investing in me, I felt to honour you with this baby when it was raw.

Peter N Wanyonyi, thanks for your invaluable input, putting to perspective the facts in history.

My editor, Scholar V Akinyi , thank you for saving the day in the quest to put jumbled up pieces together.

To everyone who ever said 'You should write a book' to me – your words carry power.

I would like to thank my ancestors, wherever they lie for conspiring to bring George Auko for this moment where their conspiracy is told to the world.

Dad and I on the first day at Dharamshilla Cancer Center in India

Dad and I at Hamad International airport with Souleymane

Dad as a Student in Homabay High School

Dad as a Soccer Student in Homabay High School

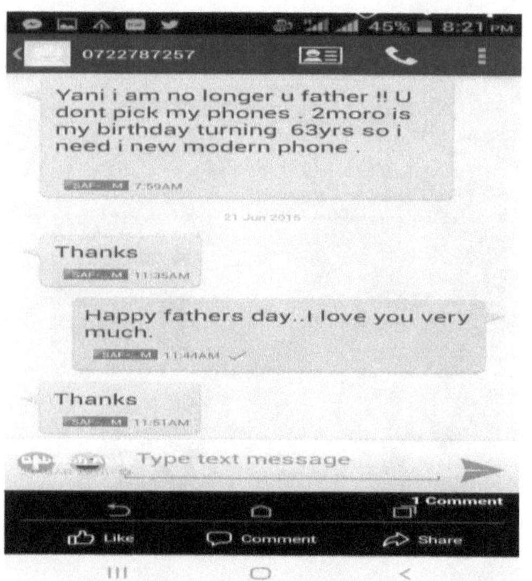

Dad behaving as if he is Jesus Christ

Dad and the then Kenyan Ambassador to India Amb. Bella Omino at the Embassy in India.

Dad cutting a lone figure as I leave India back to Kenya

Dad getting his Chemo in. He is asleep as I read from one of my Icons

Dad on the 4th Chemo.

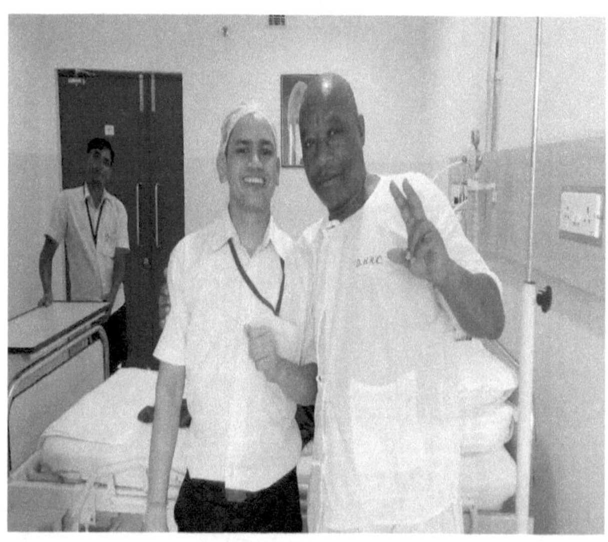

Dad getting admitted at the Dharamshilla Hospital in India.

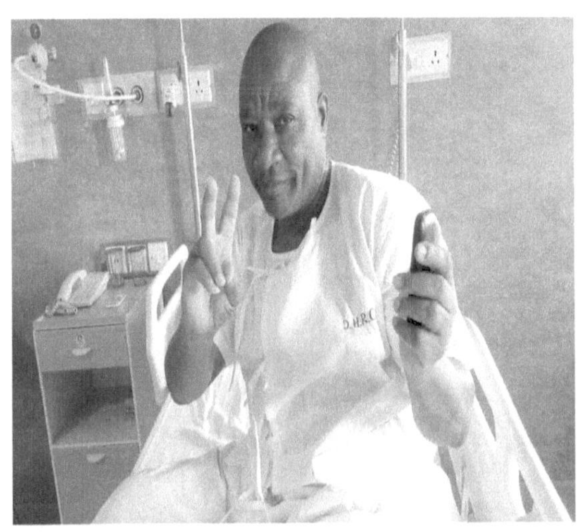

Dad going through Chemo as a Superstar showing the 'Peace Sign'.

Dad on Christmass Day of 2015 in India

*Dad on his usual seat watching Raila Odinga
in the morning and I interrupting him after
coming downstairs*

Dad Posing at the Taj Mahal in India.

Mummy at our house in Umoja 1,next to her is Uncle Philip's Mustang in the 80s.

Mummy receiving awards at work where she rose steadily to the very top

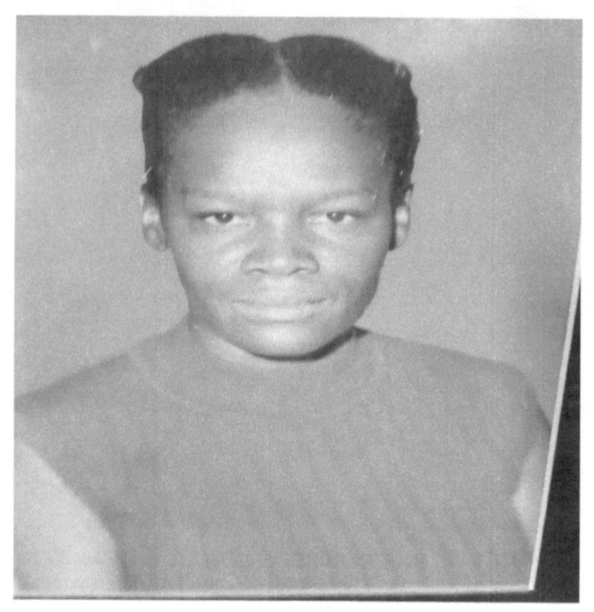

Auntie Anna

Dad Posing inside our compound at Olympic Estate with 'Sibuor Marach' His Premio car

Dad Posing with his 'Jaluo Oksechi' Tee shirt at Our first residence and Posh Palace in India. This T shirt about Luo Pride.

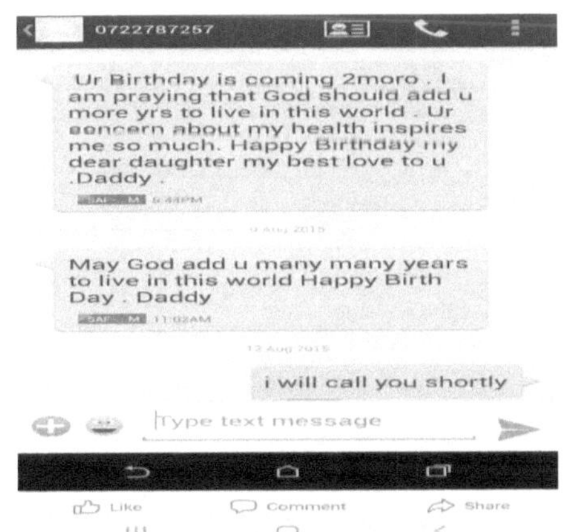

Dad wishing me a happy birthday a day before so he is the first one to do so.

Mum working at Care Kenya Kisumu Branch

*Mummy and her big Sister on her bridal
shower in the 80s*

Mama Mpenzi at her salon in Umoja Market in the 80s

Mama Mpenzi's daughter Sweetie and I,She took after her mother and is in the beauty industry.

*Alex Tendo Minge in
Imported Linen back
in the 80s*

*Alex Tendo Minge in matched
up Versace casuals in the 80s*

Myself in the stadium with a Green whistle patronizing part of my heritage Gor Mahia Fc

Nakaiza and I. The striking resemblance makes us pass for twins.

My little brother Philip(Not little anymore) .

My little brother Philip in Cape Town where he was working .

My Sister on the Ugandan Side Jackie, Nakaiza who passes as my Twin. Here we were in Stockholm.

My Maternal Grandma Deborah Nyananda. Seated with her is my mother. On the left is Mama Mpenzi and on the right Aunty Anna.

AFS student from Kenya to speak at Pomona High

Juniors and seniors attending Pomona's three public high schools interested in participating in foreign and domestic exchange programs are invited to attend a meeting tonight at 7:30 p.m. in Room 4 at Pomona High School.

They are requested to bring their parents.

Members of the Pomona Chapter of the American Field Service (AFS) will discuss the exchange program and provide information and application forms.

Stephen Osieyo, an AFS student from Kenya now attending Pomona High School, will attend, along with friends and faculty members who have participated in foreign and domestic exchanges.

Chapter members, as a fund-raising activity, will be selling tickets to a Gala Import Celebration to be held Oct. 11 at Broadway Plaza in Los Angeles. All proceeds will benefit AFS.

Teacher Gerald Algozer is president of Pomona Chapter of AFS. Roger Rusler is host parent.

STEPHEN OSIEYO

Uncle Steven as a Student in the US

My loving father and I at the Taj Mahal in India.

Mum and Dad on their Wedding Day next to her is her mother,Uncle Steve(partly covered,Auntie Anna, Unce Philp behind her)

Mama Mpenzi and her Tanzanian best friend twinning.

Joju(aka Kolo Toure) Myself,Neeraj's wife and Neeraj at the Taj Mahal.jpg

At London Bridge in Daughters of Raila regalia as the Head of Strategy for Diasporan Fundraising and Mobilizing the female vote

Uncle Steve and I headed to watch a live Arsenal match at the Emirates Stadium in England

Volunteering in a reusable Pads mini factory in Nairobi,the company is Huru and they are doing a commendable job dealing with the sanitary Pads dilemma in Kenya

Uncle Philip and his Mother Deborah Nyananda trying out Traditional liquor from Ugenya

Picketing in the build up to the 2017 election

Mum and Dad dating at Uncle Philip's

My Ugandan Paternal Uncle Godfrey Kisuule who is Alex's big brother. Here we were in Uganda for a funeral

Uncle Steven and I out for dinner

This is Jajja Tamalie, My biological Paternal Grandma, Mother of Alex Minge Tendo